SMITHERS'

MAMMALS

OF SOUTHERN AFRICA

A Field Guide

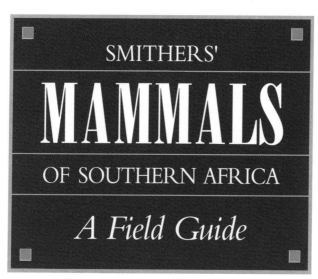

SMITHERS'
MAMMALS
OF SOUTHERN AFRICA
A Field Guide

Edited by Peter Apps

*Illustrations by Clare Abbott
and Penny Meakin*

Struik Publishers
(a division of New Holland Publishing
(South Africa) (Pty) Ltd)
Cornelis Struik House
80 McKenzie Street
Cape Town 8001, South Africa

New Holland Publishing is a member of the
Johnnic Publishing Group
www.struik.co.za
Log on to our photographic website **www.imagesofafrica.co.za**
for an African experience.

First published by Southern Book Publishers 1986
Revised edition (Southern Publishers) 1996
This edition published by Struik Publishers 2000

3 5 7 9 10 8 6 4

Cover design by Alix Gracie
Concept design by Alix Gracie
Illustrations by Clare Abbott, Penny Meakin and Noel Ashton
Set in 8.5 on 13 AT Symbol

Typesetting by Gerhardt van Rooyen
Printed and bound by Paarl Print, Oosterland Street,
Paarl, South Africa

ISBN: 1 86872 550 2

PREFACE

Despite the change in title, this is the third edition of *Land Mammals of Southern Africa. A Field Guide*, and its aims are those of the first and second editions: 'to assist anyone interested in the mammalian fauna of the southern part of Africa to identify the species that occur', and to provide information about them 'that may make their observation the more interesting'.

In 1986 Reay Smithers' *Land Mammals of Southern Africa. A Field Guide* broke new ground by providing a field guide to the subregion's mammals that included the small insectivores, rodents and bats as well as the carnivores, antelope and other 'game'. The 'Small Smithers' also set the standard for southern African mammal field guides over the subsequent decade, and there are now seven of them, providing similar information in slightly different ways. Thus, in the *Land Mammals'* tenth anniversary year the need for a standard field guide was already more than adequately catered for — but, with rising interest in wildlife, the interests of amateur wildlife enthusiasts and wildlife professionals had grown beyond the information that these standard guides provided.

Therefore, rather than simply updating the *Land Mammals* it was decided to extend it substantially, and to incorporate a good deal more information than was included in the previous editions. This required a complete revision and rewriting of the text, and design changes to make the extra information more readily accessible. The order in which the taxonomic groups appear has been changed from the previous edition in an attempt to have animals of roughly similar appearance, and thus likely to be confused with one another, appearing closer together than they did previously. The colour illustration of each animal now appears with its text, and some new colour illustrations and a series of new black and white line drawings have been expertly prepared by Penny Meakin and Noel Ashton. Hazel Smithers has provided additional spoor drawings, and has re-drawn some of the others.

I have tapped the expertise of biologists with special knowledge of southern African mammals, who provided summaries and updates of recent literature, and checked and corrected the text on their species. The contributors are listed overleaf.

Because most of the book's readers will be lay people, and a large number of them will not be native English speakers, I have avoided technical terms when there is a close enough equivalent in ordinary language. Some specialists might feel that the precision of language to which they are accustomed has been sacrificed, but specialists in any field too often forget that their technical terms are bafflingly unfamiliar to lay readers, and even to specialists in other disciplines. Readers who encounter terms that are unfamiliar to them, in this book or in others, can refer to the glossary on p 342.

Any book is the product of a team effort, and I would like to thank Penny Meakin, Hazel Smithers, Louise Grantham, Frances Perryer, Alix Gracie, and the contributors for their various inputs.

CONTRIBUTORS

Dr C.M. Baker, Zoology Department, University of Durban-Westville. Genets and mongooses.

Dr Simon Bearder, School of Social Sciences, Oxford Brookes University, Oxford. Bushbabies.

Dr Gary Bronner, Curator of Mammals, Transvaal Museum, Pretoria. Golden moles.

Nico Dippenaar, Isteg Scientific Publications and Transvaal Museum, Pretoria. Shrews and hedgehog.

Dr Johan T. du Toit, Department of Biological Sciences, University of Zimbabwe. Giraffe, kudu, and impala.

Dr Neil Fairall, Kleinmond. Hyraxes.

Ken Findlay, Oceanography Department, University of Cape Town. Marine mammals

Dr Tim Jackson, Department of Zoology, University of Cape Town. Springbok.

Rhidian Harrington, Centre for African Ecology, Zoology Department, University of the Witwatersrand. Roan antelope.

Professor Peter Henzi, Department of Psychology, University of Natal, Durban. Baboon, vervet monkey and samango monkey.

Professor Jenny U. M. Jarvis, Department of Zoology, University of Cape Town. Mole-rats.

Dr Graham Kerley, Terrestrial Ecology Research Unit, Department of Zoology, University of Port Elizabeth. Subfamily Otomyinae.

Dr M. H. Knight, Scientific Services, South African National Parks Board, Kimberley. Black rhino, blue wildebeest, red hartebeest, gemsbok, steenbok, grey duiker, eland, giant rat.

Dr Gus Mills, Specialist Scientist, South African National Parks Board, Skukuza, Kruger National Park. Lion, leopard, cheetah, wild dog and hyaenas.

Professor Mike Perrin, Department of Zoology and Entomology, University of Natal, Pietermaritzburg. Elephant shrews and gerbils.

Professor Anne Rasa, Abteilung Ethologie, Zoologisches Institut, Universitat Bonn. Suricate, banded mongoose, yellow mongoose, dwarf mongoose.

Dr P. Richardson. Aardwolf.

Professor Terry Robinson, Department of Zoology and Entomology, University of Pretoria. Rabbits and hares.

Dave Rowe-Rowe, formerly of Natal Parks Board. Mustelids.

Dr A. Sliva, Department of Zoology and Entomology, University of Pretoria. Small spotted cat.

Peter Taylor, Durban Natural Science Museum. Large-eared free-tailed bat, Subfamily Otomyinae, yellow mongoose.

Savvas Vrahimis, Free State Department of Agriculture and Environmental Affairs. Black wildebeest.

Hanlie Winterbach, Free State Department of Agriculture and Environmental Affairs. African buffalo

CONTENTS

INTRODUCTION

This edition is substantially longer than its predecessors, but it can still offer only the barest summary of the information that is available. As in the previous editions some rare species have been omitted, or are mentioned only by name, in order to allow more detailed attention to be given to the more common, more accessible and better studied species. More detailed information is available in more specialised works (see Further Reading, p 345) but these sources lack the general accessibility and portability that a field guide needs.

Awareness of the value of natural areas, with their wildlife and other products, is growing. Wildlife tourism is projected to become Africa's biggest earner of foreign exchange, and with proper management Africa's indigenous mammals would be able to provide a sustainable source of animal protein without the enormous inputs to disease and parasite control on which conventional livestock depends, and without the environmental destruction that livestock causes. At the same time the pressures on land caused by the increase in human population continue to threaten the limited areas on which sustainable use of natural resources is being practised. The challenge for the beginning of the next millennium will be to reconcile immediate demands for resources with their conservation for the use of future generations.

Effective conservation, which includes not wasting resources on conserving inefficiently, demands detailed information about mammals and their environments. The source of that information is research, the continual assimilation and integration of new knowledge. Knowledge of southern African mammals has expanded thanks to the efforts of researchers on a variety of fronts, but there are still perplexing gaps in our knowledge: while the reproductive physiology of the pouched mouse has been investigated in minute detail, we are still unsure how long gestation lasts in the grey duiker, which is Africa's most common and widespread antelope.

USING THE BOOK

Each species' account is headed by its common and scientific names and its 'Smithers' number', which is a cross-reference to its number in the massive *The Mammals of the Southern African Subregion* (1983), by RHN Smithers. When alter native common names are given the first is the preferred one. If more than one sci entific name is given these are species which have been separated on the basis of genetic characters, or features of skulls, but which have not yet acquired common names. If there are any external features by which these species can be differentiat ed in the field they are noted, and where their distributions differ they are shown separately on the distribution map.

A symbol is used to show the animal's main activity periods. A symbol for South African Red Data Book classifications is given for those species that are endangered, rare or vulnerable. In some species, such as the roan antelope, the South African population is in a far more precarious condition than other populations further north in Africa. In others, particularly the elephant and rhinoceroses, the South African and southern African populations are the most secure on the continent. Other species such as the puku are very rare within the subregion but are not listed in the Red Data Book because they do not occur at all in South Africa. An additional symbol is given for species which are endemic to the subregion.

SYMBOLS

E	endemic to the subregion
I	introduced
S100	Smithers' number
R	Rare
V	Vulnerable — South African Red Data Book Classification
E	Endangered
☼	diurnal: active during the day
☾	crepuscular: active at dawn and dusk
☾	nocturnal: active at night

The spoor drawings show the full track of the right fore- and hind feet, such as would be produced by an animal walking over soft, moist ground. Spoor varies with the speed of an animal's movements and the sort of surface that it is moving over, and it will be by no means unusual to find spoor which does not look exactly like the drawings.

As far as possible, the distribution maps have been updated. The distributions of nearly all large mammals are constrained by human influence, since on the one hand their habitat has been taken over for agriculture and other development, and their movements are restricted by fences, and on the other hand large herbivores a nivores have been widely translocated to areas both inside and outside their nat al distributions. Not all of these translocations are adequately documented, an nearly all of them are to areas which are small islands in a sea of agriculture, which cannot be accurately shown on maps of this scale. A general area over which translocated populations occur is shown, although it gives an impression that the species' distribution covered a much larger area than it does. With these restrictions, distributions can be given only as guides as to where species can be expected to occur, as an aid to deciding on identification when appearance alone leaves more than one possibility. The staff of parks, reserves and game ranches should also be able to provide information on which species have been brought into the area. Perhaps the time is ripe for mammals to follow birds and frogs into an atlas of distribution, preferably one that covers the whole of the subregion.

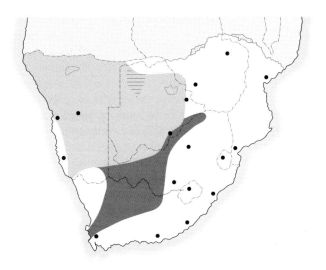

░ naturally occurring populations

■ general area in which translocated populations occur

With a few exceptions species descriptions are based on what can be observed in a live animal: for example, features such as grooved incisors are noted, but skull measurements are not. When identifying mammals, colour has to be used with caution. For example, it is a common feature of some species of bats that they occur in a number of colour phases; in bats that are commonly brown or greyish brown, some colonies contain a high percentage of golden yellow individuals. Among species that are widely distributed animals from the drier, western regions tend to be paler in colour than those from the wetter east. In some cases the gradation in colour is gradual, in others discontinuous. The illustrations show only one colour form; any variations are noted in the text. Mammals that wallow or dust-bathe are very often coloured by the soil that sticks to their skins. With the growing popularity of game viewing at night it is as well to note that colours and markings often appear less distinct by spotlight than in daylight.

Measurements and weights are given as averages, usually followed by ranges in parentheses, and in some cases with exceptional maximums. They are intended as aids to identification, and to give a clearer impression of the animal. The new line drawings relate the animals' sizes to each other and to a human figure 1,8 m tall or a hand 20 cm long, by illustrating the species on each page to a common scale.

Measurements used in the text

1 Total length is measured from the tip of the snout to the end of the vertebrae of the tail (A–B) .
2 The length of the tail is measured from its junction with the body to the end of the vertebrae (C–D).

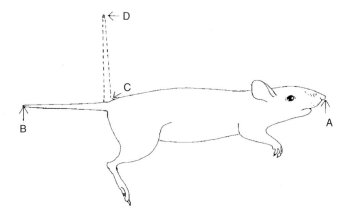

3 The length of the forearm (E–F) is an important measurement in bats.
4 Wingspan is the total length, tip to tip, of the fully outstretched wings of a bat.
5 Shoulder height is measured from the base of the hoof or pad to the top of the shoulder.

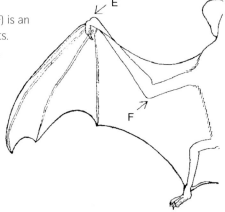

Diets are given in general terms, because they can be expected to change markedly with food availability, which varies with season and locality, and from year to year. Where the percentage occurrence of various items in droppings and stomachs is given, the percentages nearly always add up to more than 100 because a stomach or dropping can contain the remnants of more than one sort of food.

All figures given are, of necessity, approximate, because biological material is intrinsically variable.

Conservation is used as a section heading in its broadest sense to include sustainable use and the management of problem animals, as well as the protection of imperilled populations.

THE SUBREGION:
CLIMATE, VEGETATION AND HABITATS

The Southern African Subregion is the part of the continent south of the Zambezi and Cunene rivers, its offshore islands, and Prince Edward Island and Marion Island in the sub-Antarctic, which are not included in this book because they are accessible only on official business.

Visitors from the northern hemisphere should remember that the seasons are reversed in the south: summer is from September to March, and winter from April to August.

The subregion can be divided into a number of bio-climatic zones with different climates and vegetation, and within each zone there are a number of habitats, with their associated mammals. If the necessary habitat occurs in small patches, such as isolated rocky outcrops for example, then the mammals will also occur in small patches within their overall distributional areas.

Bio-climatic zones are not static: for example, the South West Arid zone is encroaching eastward into the Southern Savanna Grasslands. In addition, large areas have been drastically modified by agriculture, forestry and other human development, which has rendered them unsuitable for some of their original mammal inhabitants, and in some cases has improved the habitat for other species — for example, greater cane rats prosper in sugar cane and maize fields.

Southern savanna woodland

This zone covers most of northern Namibia, northern and eastern Botswana, nearly the whole of Zimbabwe and Mozambique, and in South Africa the Northern Province and the east of Mpumalanga Province, and narrowly along the coast as far west as Port Elizabeth. Rainfall varies from about 900 mm in the east to 375 mm in the west; throughout most of the zone it is about 500 mm, nearly all of which falls in the summer. At low altitudes the zone has a cover of open mopane (*Colophospermum mopane*) woodland, with baobabs (*Adansonia digitata*) in warmer areas, a sparse

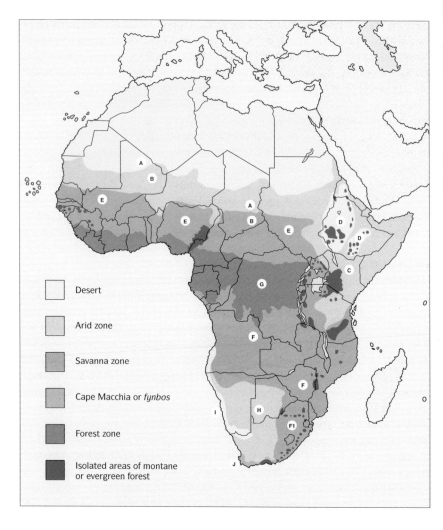

The main biotic zones of Africa south of the Sahara

Zones

A	Sahelian	**F**	Southern Savanna Woodland
B	Sudan	**F1**	Southern Savanna Grassland
C	Somali Arid	**G**	Forest
D	Ethiopian Highlands	**H**	South West Arid
E	Northern Savanna Woodland	**I**	Namib Desert
		J	Cape Macchia or *fynbos*

grass cover and little undergrowth. At higher altitudes the drier western areas carry open woodland or scrub thornbush, and the eastern higher rainfall areas carry well-developed woodlands with a ground cover of grass, sometimes in a mosaic with open grasslands or vleis. This zone supports a rich variety of browsing and grazing mammals, including many species of antelope.

Southern savanna grassland

This zone occurs in South Africa south of approximately 25°S and east of approximately 26°E as far east as the southern savanna woodland, from which it is separated by a narrow, broken band of forest. It includes the montane grasslands of the Drakensberg. This zone has suffered widespread modification by human development. The vegetation is not pure grassland; bushes and trees grow along streams and rivers, in narrow valleys and on rocky areas. Rainfall is about 500 mm per year, nearly all of it falling in the summer.

South west arid

Except for narrow strips on the northern, southern and western boundaries this zone covers almost the whole of the subregion west of approximately 26°E. Rainfall decreases towards the west and south from about 500 mm per year to less than 200 mm per year, nearly all of it falling in the summer. In the northern parts there is an open cover of thornbush or low scrub, with scattered patches of camelthorn trees (*Acacia erioloba*) and a good grass cover on soils of Kalahari sand. The southern parts support Karoo scrub towards the east, or succulent Karoo vegetation towards the west.

Cape macchia or fynbos

This zone occupies a strip along the south coast of South Africa as far east as Port Elizabeth, and up the west coast as far north as St Helena Bay. It supports an enormously diverse array of plants, with 8 600 species in the Cape Floral Kingdom, but is a rather poor habitat for mammals. The climate is Mediterranean, rainfall varies widely from 200 mm per year in inland valleys to more than 3 000 mm per year on the coastal mountains. This is the zone that has suffered the most from human impact.

Desert

The desert zone occupies a narrow strip up the coast of Namibia, and extends inland along the Orange River to about 21°E. The so-called Kalahari Desert is, in fact, part of the South West Arid zone. Mean annual rainfall is less than 125 mm per year, and in the coastal strip of the Namib Desert fog blowing inland is the main source of moisture. The vegetation is very sparse scrub, grass and succulents, except along rivers and drainage lines which support denser growth, including trees. In the Namib there are large areas of bare, shifting sands and gravel plains.

Forest

Natural forest occurs in a chain of rather small patches from the Tsitsikamma forest in the coastal Eastern Province of South Africa, eastward and northeastward into KwaZulu-Natal, northward along the Drakensberg escarpment and then westward in the Soutpansberg, and in Eastern Zimbabwe. Large areas of the southern savanna grasslands have been turned into commercial forestry plantations of alien pines and eucalypts. Rather few species of mammals penetrate into forest, but forest edges are an important habitat.

WATCHING MAMMALS

Many mammals can be identified from field sightings but, with a few exceptions, bats, rodents and shrews can only be reliably identified in the hand, and even then some species need examination of skulls, or even chromosomes. Specimens must usually be trapped, an undertaking that should be left to zoologists, but occasionally small mammals are brought home by house cats, or found drowned in swimming pools.

The animals in most established protected areas are so used to vehicles that they ignore them, and far better observations are possible from a vehicle than on foot. Foot trails provide an opportunity to study field signs, but are not the best way to get good sightings of the animals themselves.

While they are not indispensable, a pair of binoculars makes mammal watching far more rewarding. Magnifications of 7 to 10 times with a high twilight factor are appropriate, and will allow identification of the larger species at distances of several hundred metres, and detailed observation of behaviour.

Some mammals, such as springhares and genets, only become active after dark. Night drives with spotlights have become popular, and a range of nocturnal species that would otherwise not be seen are becoming familiar to wildlife enthusiasts. After an animal has been lit up with a spotlight it takes 30–40 minutes for its eyes to re-adapt to the dark, so do not keep the spotlight on an animal's eyes and do not shine more than one light onto an animal.

While wildlife tourism's 'big seven' — lion, leopard, cheetah, wild dog, elephant, rhinoceros and buffalo — are spectacular in their own right, the behaviour of many of the smaller and commoner species offers just as much interest as sightings of these larger mammals.

O R D E R
CHIROPTERA
B A T S

Bats are the only mammals that are capable of sustained, powered flight. Their fore-limbs are modified into wings, with membranes of soft, flexible, largely naked skin supported by the enormously elongated bones of the hands. They are all strictly noc-turnal. Bats fall into two suborders: the MEGACHIROPTERA, fruit bats, and the MICROCHIROPTERA, insect-eating bats.

SUBORDER MEGACHIROPTERA

FAMILY PTEROPODIDAE

FRUIT BATS

Seven species in the subregion. They are larger than nearly all of the insect-eating bats, with long-muzzled dog-like faces, and two claws on each wing, one on the thumb and the other on the second digit, which corresponds to the index finger. The lower margin of their ears forms a complete circle, with no tragus; the tail is small or absent, and there is only a narrow strip of membrane running along the inside of each hind leg. Their teeth are simple, with no well-developed cusp pattern. They have large eyes and very acute vision, and they find their way around by sight. In addition, *Rousettus* species use echolocation when it is too dark to see.

PETERS' EPAULETTED FRUIT BAT   S43 ℂ
Peters se witkolvrugtevlermuis
Epomophorus crypturus

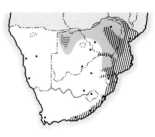

■ Peters' epauletted fruit bat
/// Wahlberg's epauletted fruit bat

Description Brown, buffy or nearly white, with the under- and upper parts of the body the same colour, and the head slightly darker than the body. Both sexes have white patches at the base of the ears, but only the males have the white epaulette patches on their shoulders, which cover a scent gland. Total length males 15 cm (13–17 cm), females 12 cm (11–12,5 cm); forearm males 8,3 cm (8–8,6 cm), females 7,9 cm (7,6–8,2 cm); wingspan males about 50 cm, females about 45 cm; weight males 105 g (up to 140 g),

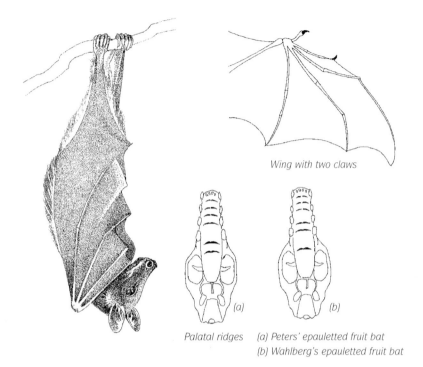

Wing with two claws

(a) (b)

Palatal ridges   *(a) Peters' epauletted fruit bat*
(b) Wahlberg's epauletted fruit bat

females 76 g (up to 88 g). *See scale drawing on p. 5.*
Habitat Occurs in riverine or evergreen forest, or moist woodland, where there are fruit-bearing trees.
Diet Fruit.
Life history Single young, rarely twins, are born in early summer, with a marked September peak in Zimbabwe.
Behaviour Colonies of up to a few hundred rest during the day hanging from the thinner branches of trees with dense foliage. Each bat hangs separately from the others. The colonies are very noisy, with much bickering as they settle for the day. They hang in the same trees as Wahlberg's epauletted fruit bats.

Forages at night. Soft fruit is eaten on site, harder fruit is plucked from the tree and manipulated with the claws on the wings as the bat hangs at an established feeding site. Unpalatable debris is dropped to the ground. Males give a repeated musical 'tink' call while hanging up.
Field sign Food remains under feeding sites, droppings under roosts.

Wahlberg's epauletted fruit bat (*Epomophorus wahlbergi*), S40, cannot be distinguished from Peters' in the field, except that it is usually darker. In specimens, Wahlberg's is distinguished by having only one palatal ridge behind the last cheek-teeth where Peters' has two. The two species frequently roost together.

STRAW-COLOURED FRUIT BAT

S45　**C**

Geel vrugtevlermuis
Eidolon helvum

Description   Pale yellow to yellowish brown, with bright yellow underparts, and an orange collar around the neck. The rump and legs are brown; the ears and wing membranes are dark brown. The fur extends onto the forearms, legs, and interfemoral membrane but not onto the wing membranes. The wings are long, narrow and pointed; straw-coloured fruit bats are the only fruit bats in the subregion with this wing shape. The largest bat in the subregion; total length 19 cm (16,5–20,7 cm); tail 1,5 cm; forearm 11,5 (10,2–12,2 cm); wingspan up to 75 cm; weight 240–280 g. *See scale drawing on p. 5.*

Habitat   Found as a non-breeding migrant throughout the subregion; most often seen in the east and south.

Diet   Mainly fruit, also eats flowers and freshly sprouted leaves.

Life history   Does not breed in the subregion. In East Africa single young are born in the summer, usually in November.

Behaviour   Flies slowly with strong, regular wing beats interrupted by gliding. Covers enormous distances in sustained flight and has been found resting on ships 240 km out to sea. In the subregion occurs singly or in small groups of up to 30; in East Africa forms huge colonies of up to 200 000. Females carry their young clinging to their fur. Food is manipulated with both feet while the bat hangs from the claws on its wings.

EGYPTIAN FRUIT BAT

S46　**C**

Egiptiese vrugtevlermuis
Rousettus aegyptiacus

Description   Dark brown with a light-coloured yoke on the neck, pale greyish buff underparts, and a brown-tinged throat. The wing membranes are dark brown, with fur on the inner edges. The tips of the wings are rounded. Total length 15 cm (14–16 cm); tail 2 cm; forearm 9 cm (8,3–9,6 cm); wingspan about 60 cm; weight 130 g (88–166 g).

Habitat   Requires caves in which to rest within a flying distance of up to 24 km from fruiting trees.

Diet   Fruit; can be a pest in orchards.

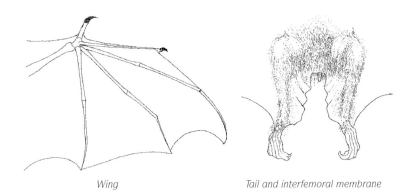

Wing   *Tail and interfemoral membrane*

Life history Mates from June to mid-September in the Cape, July and August in Kruger NP. Gestation 105–107 days. Single young are born September–November in the northern parts of the subregion, November and December in Kruger NP, October–June with a peak in December in Tsitsikamma, South Africa. Young are carried by the mother until they wean at 6–8 weeks; she then brings food back to them. Young first fly at 9–10 weeks.

Behaviour The only fruit bats in the subregion that roost in dark caves, where they form colonies of thousands, tightly packed into clusters. They navigate in darkness by echolocation, producing clicks with the tongue and listening for the echoes. Fruit is eaten on site or carried to a nearby roost where the bat hangs by one foot and holds the fruit with the other, or hangs by the claws on its wings and holds the fruit with both feet.

Field sign Discarded fruit peels, seeds and chewed pulp beneath feeding sites.

Angolan epauletted fruit bats (*Epomophorus angolensis*), S41, only occur marginally in extreme northwest Namibia. **Dobson's fruit bat** (*Epomops dobsonii*), S44, occurs in northeastern Botswana. **Bocage's fruit bat** (*Rousettus angolensis*), S47, occurs in eastern Zimbabwe and across the border in Mozambique.

common slit-faced bat (p. 20)

banana bat (p. 15)

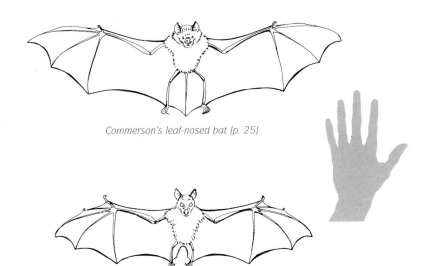

Commerson's leaf-nosed bat (p. 25)

Peters' epauletted fruit bat (p. 1)

straw-coloured fruit bat (p. 3)

INSECT-EATING BATS

Six families in the subregion. Nearly all insect-eating bats are smaller than fruit bats, and they have a single claw on each wing, on the thumb. The lower edges of their ears do not form a complete circle; depending on the family there are flaps of skin rising from them called the tragus and antitragus. The tail and the flight membrane between the legs are well developed. The teeth have sharp cusps, usually in a W pattern, for chopping insect prey. Microchiropteran bats find their way around by echolocation: bursts of ultrasound are emitted through the mouth or the nostrils, and the bat detects obstacles and prey from the echoes that reflect back from them.

FAMILY EMBALLONURIDAE

SHEATH-TAILED AND TOMB BATS

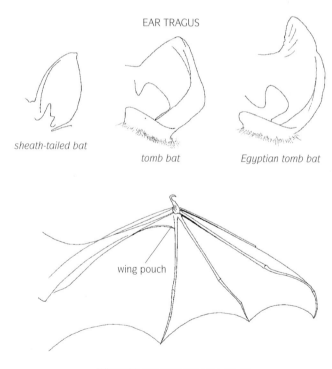

EAR TRAGUS

sheath-tailed bat

tomb bat

Egyptian tomb bat

wing pouch

Wing with one claw and wing pouch

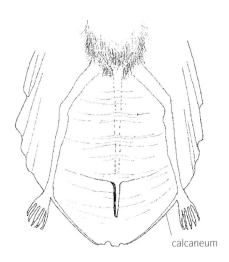

Tail to show characteristic formation with calcaneum which supports the interfemoral membrane.

Three species in the subregion, readily identified as belonging to this family by the unique structure of their tails, which lie half inside the interfemoral flight membrane and half projecting from it. The eyes are larger than in most bats, while the ears are triangular with rounded tips and are widely separated on the head. There are no noseleaves on the muzzle. Each species can be identified by the shape of its ears. They rest with their undersides against the wall of their shelter, and scurry away sideways if disturbed.

SHEATH-TAILED BAT
S48 ℂ
Skedestertvlermuis
Coleura afra

Description Brown with pale underparts and translucent pale brown flight membranes. Six lower incisor teeth (*Taphozous* have four). The smallest species in the family: total length 7 cm, forearm 5 cm, wingspan 25 cm.
Habitat Woodland; roosts in caves.
Behaviour Roosts in colonies of hundreds in caves in half light. They space themselves apart.

TOMB BAT
Witlyfvlermuis
Taphozous mauritianus

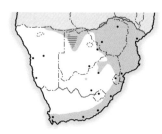

Description The upper parts of the body are grey; white tips to the hairs produce a grizzled appearance. The underparts are white, with white fur extending onto the translucent white membranes. The inside upper parts of the ears are covered by white hair, and the outside margins are fringed with white. The eyes are larger than in other bats of similar size. Four lower incisor teeth (the sheath-tailed bat has six). Total length 11 cm; forearm 6–6,4 cm; wingspan 34 cm; weight 27,5 g (20–36 g).

Habitat Woodland and forest edges and clearings.

Life history Single young are born in summer.

Behaviour Lives in pairs; two or three pairs may share a resting place on the vertical surfaces of tree trunks, rock faces or walls where there is overhead shelter from sun and rain. If disturbed, clambers away around corners or into secluded places. Remains alert during the day and may take off to catch butterflies flying nearby. Food is eaten while hanging up away from the daytime roost.

Field sign Established resting sites become stained brown with urine.

EGYPTIAN TOMB BAT
Egiptiese witlyfvlermuis
Taphozous perforatus

Description Dark brown with light brown underparts washed with grey, brown throat and neck, and whitish belly. The ears are more pointed than in tomb bats and have a series of small bumps on their inner edges. Four lower incisor teeth (the sheath-tailed bat has six). Total length 10 cm; forearm 6,2–6,7 cm; wingspan 34 cm; weight 30 g.

Habitat Woodland, roosting concealed in crevices in rocks, stonework or masonry.

Life history Single young are born in summer.

Behaviour Huddles in groups of 6–8, hidden in crevices in rocks or stonework.

FREE-TAILED BATS

Fourteen species in the subregion. Their characteristic features are mastiff-like faces, and tails with the end two thirds extending behind the interfemoral flight membrane. The ears are exceptionally large, roughly as broad as they are high, with the pinnae folded back along their inner edges. In some species the bases of the inner margins of the ears are connected across the top of the head by a broad flap of skin. The wings are long, narrow and pointed and their third, fourth and fifth digits have three joints, a feature shared only with the vesper bats. The outer toes on the feet are heavily built, with fringes of flattened hairs on the sides, and long hairs towards the tips. All species are agile climbers, and they crawl around freely on the ground.

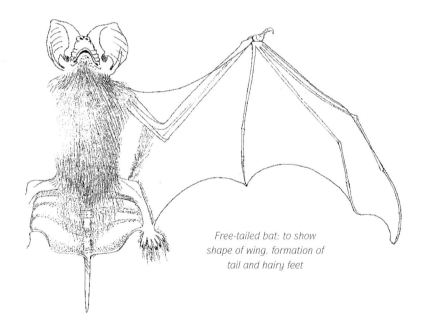

Free-tailed bat: to show shape of wing. formation of tail and hairy feet

LARGE-EARED FREE-TAILED BAT

Bakoor-losstertvlermuis
Otomops martiensseni

Description Blackish brown with a paler band across the top of the shoulders, and a distinct white band where the hair of the back meets the wing membranes. The ears are very large, with a row of small spines along their front edges, and a semicircular flap of skin near the base, which can close off the ear opening. The snout is long and pig-like. Total length 13–14 cm; tail 3–5 cm; wingspan 35 cm; forearm males 6,6 cm, females 6,3 cm; weight 28–43 g.

Habitat In the greater Durban area they roost high up in the roofs of large double-storey houses with access to the roosts between 8 and 15 m above ground.

Life history In Durban, single young are born in December.

Behaviour Roosts in small colonies of up to about a dozen, which may be harems of females with a single adult male. They hang separately. They need a free-drop to become airborne, and cannot take off from a flat surface. The population in northern Zimbabwe leaves the area from November to February.

Conservation There are fewer than 10 known colonies in the Durban area, which depend for survival on the goodwill of the owners of the houses that they roost in. Red Data Book: Indeterminate, but needs to be upgraded to Vulnerable.

FLAT-HEADED FREE-TAILED BAT

Platkop-losstertvlermuis
Sauromys petrophilus

Description Colour varies with locality: in northeastern South Africa tawny olive, in Namibia brownish grey and in the south, dark seal brown. The underparts are lighter than the upper. The flat head allows these bats to creep into narrow crevices. Total length 11 cm (10,3–12,7 cm); forearm 4,3 cm (3,8–4,8 cm); wingspan 26 cm; weight 13 g (9–16 g).

Habitat Roosts in narrow rock crevices. Scattered distribution reflects a preference for rocky areas.
Behaviour Groups of up to four roost packed together in narrow rock crevices. If disturbed they crawl into the deepest cracks that they can fit into.

MIDAS FREE-TAILED BAT

S54 ◖

Midas se losstertvlermuis
Tadarida midas

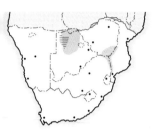

Description Dark chocolate brown, often sparsely flecked with white. A band of sparsely haired skin on the upper neck gives the appearance of a light-coloured yoke. The throat is dark fawn, the hair on the chest and belly is white-tipped. The flight membranes are dark brown with bands of white hair between the forearm and thigh. The large, rounded ears are connected by a band of skin across the top of the head, and have large antitragi. Largest of the free-tailed bats, and third largest of the Microchiroptera in the subregion; total length 14,3 cm (12,6–16 cm), tail 4,8 cm (4–5,8 cm); forearm 6 cm; wingspan about 38 cm; weight males 48,5 g (42–52 g), females 44,5 g (41–48 g).
Habitat Savanna woodland near large rivers or swamps. Roosts in roofs in total darkness, and in the crevices of masonry.
Life history Single young are born in late summer (February and March).
Behaviour A high fast flier. Roosts contain hundreds of bats packed tightly together with much squeaking and jostling for position.

Angolan free-tailed bats (*Tadarida condylura*), S55, occur in the northern and eastern parts of the subregion. **Nigerian free-tailed bats** (*T. nigeriae*), S56, have pale wing membranes with conspicuous bands of white hair close to the body. They occur only in northern Botswana and parts of Zimbabwe.

LITTLE FREE-TAILED BAT

S59 ◖

Klein losstertvlermuis
Tadarida pumila

Description Very variable in colour, most commonly dark brown to blackish brown; some individuals are lighter or tinged with grey. The throat is brown, the rest of the

---

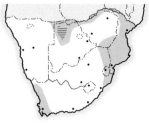

underparts are fawn grey; there is a pale yoke on the back of the neck and there may be a crest of long hair between the ears, which are connected by a band of skin across the top of the head. There is a band of white hair on the wing membranes between the upper arms and the thighs. Smallest of the free-tailed bats; total length 9 cm (7–10 cm), tail 3,5 cm (3–4 cm);· forearm 3,7 cm; wingspan 24 cm; weight 11,5 g (10–16 g).

Habitat Occurs at low altitudes, usually under 1 000 m. Roosts in crevices in rocks or masonry, or cracks in trees.

Life history Gestation 60 days. Single young are born in summer (November–April in the lowveld, October–March in Botswana).

Behaviour A fast, erratic flier. Small colonies, exceptionally a few hundred, roost huddled together in cracks and crevices.

EGYPTIAN FREE-TAILED BAT

S63 C

Egiptiese losstertvlermuis
Tadarida aegyptiaca

Description Dark sooty brown all over, with a darker head. There is no pale neck yoke as in other free-tailed bats. The hair on the underside extends a little way onto the translucent light brown wing membranes. The ears are not connected by a band of skin. Total length 11 cm; forearm 4,8 cm (4,6–5,4 cm); wingspan 30 cm; weight 15 g (14–18 g).

Habitat Occurs in all sorts of habitats. In arid areas, depends on access to open water for drinking. Roosts in caves, rock crevices, tree holes and cracks in masonry.

Life history Single young are born in summer. Maternity caves with all-female colonies are known.

Behaviour Roosts in small colonies of up to a dozen, which have a very strong smell.

Tadarida acetabulosa (S53), *T. bivittata* (S57), *T. chapini* (S58), *T. lobata* (S60), *T. ventralis* (S61), *T. fulminans* (S62), and *T. ansorgie* (S64) are also recorded from the subregion.

VESPER BATS

The subregion's largest family of bats, with 10 genera and 29 species. They have no noseleaves. Their ears are moderately large and widely separated, with well-developed tragi whose shapes are distinctive to each species. The tail is long and completely enclosed by the interfemoral flight membrane. The third, fourth and fifth digits in the wings have three joints, a feature shared only with the free-tailed bats.

SCHREIBERS' LONG-FINGERED BAT

`S67` `(`

Schreibers se grotvlermuis

Miniopterus schreibersii

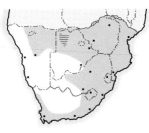

Description Deep chocolate brown with slightly lighter underparts. The wings are long and pointed with nearly black membranes. Total length 11 cm (9,3–12,8 cm); forearm 4,5 cm (4,2–4,8 cm); wingspan 28 cm; weight 10 g (6–13 g).

Habitat Avoids the drier western parts of the subregion. Roosts in caves, mines, hollow trees or rock crevices.

Life history Mates in late summer and autumn (March–April) just before hibernating. Gestation eight months. Single young, rarely (1 in 150) twins, are born in summer (November and December). Lifespan 13 years.

Behaviour Flies fast and high, like a swallow. Forms huge colonies in caves and

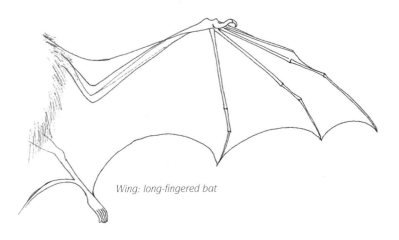

Wing: long-fingered bat

mines, with hundreds of thousands of bats hanging in tightly packed clusters in total darkness. Migrates up to 300 km; in late winter and spring females and some males migrate from hibernation caves in the southern highveld to maternity caves in the northern bushveld, where young are born. They return in late summer. Babies cling to their mothers for the first few hours and are then left hanging in clusters in secluded parts of the maternity cave while the females forage.

TEMMINCK'S HAIRY BAT

S71 (

Temminck se langhaarvlermuis
Myotis tricolor

Description Upper parts coppery red, underparts whitish washed with pale coppery red. The wing membranes and ears are reddish brown, the ears are long with rounded tips. The fur is soft and woolly and extends onto the bases of the interfemoral membrane. Total length 11 cm; tail 5 cm; forearm 5 cm; wingspan 28 cm.

Habitat Mostly in savanna woodland, but also in more open areas. Roosts in caves and mine adits.

Life history Gestation 63 days. Single young are born in early summer (late October to mid-November in the Cape, mid-November to mid-December in KwaZulu-Natal).

Behaviour Forms colonies of dozens hanging from both roof and walls. May move long distances; 90 km has been recorded.

BANANA BAT

S75 (

Piesangvlermuis
Pipistrellus nanus

Description   Colour varies from reddish to dark brown, with lighter underparts which are often tinged grey. The wing membranes are dark brown. The ears are triangular with pointed tips, and the mouth is large. The first digits of the wings and feet have sucker pads to grip the smooth leaf surfaces on which these bats roost. Total length 8 cm; forearm 3,2 cm; wingspan 19 cm; weight 3–4 g. *See scale drawing on p. 5.*

Habitat   Wetter areas to the east and north, especially where there are banana, plantain or strelitzia trees.

Life history   Single young, or twins, are born in early summer.

Behaviour   Flight is erratic and fluttering. Roosts in small colonies of up to seven in roofs or, characteristically, in the rolled-up terminal leaves of banana, plantain or strelitzia trees.

BUTTERFLY BAT

S77 (

Vlindervlermuis
Chalinolobis variegatus

Description   Upper parts yellow tinged with brown, underparts pale yellow. The wings and interfemoral membrane are pale yellow with a unique network of dark brown lines over the blood vessels. The ears are pale yellowish with brown margins and rounded tips. Total length 11 cm; forearm 4,4 cm; wingspan 28 cm; weight 12–14 g.

Habitat   Open savanna woodland and riverine woodland. Not found in forest. Roosts in thatched roofs.

Behaviour   Flight is high, slow and fluttering, with fast swoops after prey. In flight it gives squeaks that are audible to humans. Forms colonies of up to about 10, huddled close together.

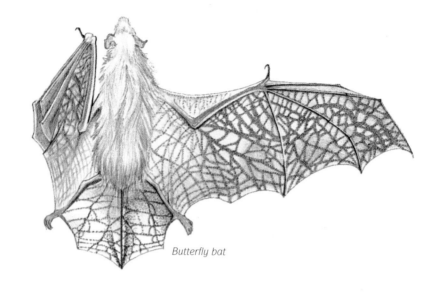

Butterfly bat

CAPE SEROTINE BAT

S86

Kaapse dakvlermuis
Eptisecus capensis

Description Very variable in colour from dark to light greyish brown, underparts white or light buff, wing membranes blackish brown. The ears have rounded tips. Total length males 8 cm (7–10 cm), females 9 cm (7–11,5 cm); forearm males 3,2 cm (2,9–3,5 cm), females 3,4 cm (3,1–3,9 cm); wingspan 24 cm; weight males 6 g (4–10 g), females 7,3 g (4–10 g).

Habitat Widespread; avoids desert. Roosts under the bark of trees, at the base of aloe leaves, or in crevices in the roofs of houses.

Life history Single young or quite commonly twins or triplets, one record of four foetuses, in summer.

Behaviour Flies slowly and erratically; when foraging tends to follow a fixed, circular route. Hunts insects that have been attracted to lights, and readily enters houses. Roosts in small groups of two or three huddled closely together.

tragus

antitragus

YELLOW HOUSE BAT

Geel dakvlermuis
Scotophilus dinganii

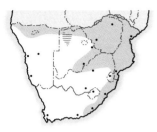

Description   Upper parts olive brown or greyish olive, sometimes with a distinct sheen. Underparts usually yellow but may be very pale cream. Wing membranes brown, with fur extending onto their undersides between the elbow and thigh. The ears are small and rounded. Total length 13 cm (11–14 cm); forearm 5,5 cm (5,2–5,7 cm); wingspan 30 cm; weight 27 g (21–38 g).

Habitat   Savanna woodland; roosts in crevices in roofs, or in hollow trees.

Life history   Two or three young are born in early summer (October and November).

Behaviour   Roosts in colonies of up to a dozen. One shelter may house more than one colony. Often enters houses at night to catch insects attracted by lights. Flies fast and sometimes close to the ground. Newborn young are carried by their mothers as they forage.

SCHLIEFFEN'S BAT

Schlieffen se vlermuis
Nycticeius schlieffenii

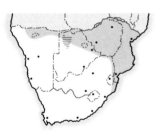

Description   Varies in colour from dark to pale reddish brown; the underparts are paler than the upper parts, the membranes are dark brown. The ears are large, strongly convex on their inner edges, and concave on the outer, with rounded tips. Tiny; total length 7 cm; tail 3 cm; forearm 3 cm; wingspan 18 cm; weight less than 5 g.

Habitat   Woodland, usually at altitudes of less than 1 200 m. Roosts in roofs or crevices and hollows in trees.

Life history   Up to three young are born in summer, with a peak in November.

Behaviour   A slow, erratic flier; forages in groups. Roosts singly.

DAMARA WOOLLY BAT

Damara-wolhaarvlermuis
Kerivoula argentata

Description Upper parts rich brown, grizzled silve
underparts greyish brown or whitish, membranes red
dish brown. The ears are large and have rounded tips
There is a fringe of hair on the hind edge of the inter
femoral membrane, which is distinctive to the woolly
bats. Total length 9,3 cm (8,3–10 cm); tail 4,7 cm
(4,2–5 cm); forearm 3,7 cm (3,6–4,1 cm); wingspar
25 cm; weight 7,6 g (6–9 g).

Habitat Woodland; roosts in clumps of leaves, under the eaves of thatched roofs
and in disused weaver bird nests.

Behaviour Flight is slow and fluttering; forages within a few metres of the ground
Usually roosts singly, but may form colonies of up to six.

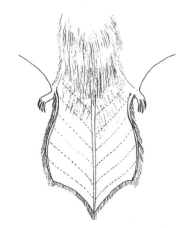

*Interfemoral membrane, woolly bats: to show the
characteristic hairy fringe*

Greater long-fingered bats (*Miniopterus inflatus*), S65, occur in eastern Zimbabwe
and **lesser long-fingered bats** (*M. fraterculus*), S66, in the southeastern and east
ern parts of the subregion.

Lesser woolly bats (*Kerivoula lanosa*), S93, are smaller than Damara woolly bats,
and are found only in the eastern parts of the subregion. Of the 18 other species of
vesper bats, 8 are known from only a few records, and the others cannot reliably be
identified without examining their teeth and skulls.

SLIT-FACED BATS

Six species in the subregion. They get their name from a slit in the skin on the front of the face that opens into a cavity in the head holding a pair of noseleaves, which are only visible when the slit is opened. The ultrasound used for echolocation is emitted through the nostrils, and the noseleaves probably serve to direct the beam of sound. Slit-faced bats are easily recognised because they all have long, roughly parallel-sided ears, the tail is completely enclosed by the interfemoral membrane and it has a unique forked last vertebra. The wings are broad, and slit-faced bats are very agile fliers. After catching their prey they fly to a feeding site where they hang while eating, littering the ground below with discarded scraps.

HAIRY SLIT-FACED BAT
Harige spleetneusvlermuis
Nycteris hispida

S94 **(**

Description Not especially hairy. Sepia brown with paler, usually greyer, underparts and dark brown wings and ears. The ears are shorter than in other slit-faced bats. The upper incisor teeth have three lobes (also in large slit-faced bat; two lobes in common slit-faced bat and greater slit-faced bat). Total length 9 cm; ear length up to 2,5 cm; forearm 3,6–4,5 cm; wingspan 28 cm.
Habitat Woodland; roosts in rock fissures, thick bushes and thatched roofs.
Behaviour Roosts singly or in small colonies. A slow but very agile flier. Comes to lights and into houses to hunt flying insects.

LARGE SLIT-FACED BAT
Groot spleetneusvlermuis
Nycteris grandis

S95 **(**

Description Light reddish brown, with paler, grey-washed underparts. Upper incisor teeth have three lobes (also in hairy slit-faced bat). Largest of the slit-faced bats; total length 16 cm; ear length 3,1 cm; forearm 6,4 cm; wingspan 35 cm; weight 36–43 g.
Habitat Evergreen riverine forest. Roosts in tree-holes, hollow fallen logs, culverts and holes in rocks.

Diet Mostly insects but also takes fish, frogs and bats.
Life history Single young are born in summer.
Behaviour Forms small colonies. Hunts from perches in trees, and eats while hanging up.
Field sign Prey remains below feeding sites.

GREATER SLIT-FACED BAT
Groter spleetneusvlermuis
Nycteris macrotis

Description Warm reddish sepia with grey underparts. Upper incisor teeth have two lobes (also in common slit-faced bat; three lobes in large slit-faced bat and hairy slit-faced bat). Total length 12 cm; forearm 4,5–5 cm; ear length up to 3 cm.
Habitat Riverine forest in the Zambezi valley, Zimbabwe. Roosts in caves, culverts and holes in the ground.
Behaviour Roosts singly.

COMMON SLIT-FACED BAT
Gewone-spleetneusvlermuis
Nycteris thebaica

Description Buffy or greyish brown; some individuals are rufous. The underparts are paler, the long ears and wing membranes are light brown. Paler in the drier western areas than in the east. The fur is long and soft. The upper incisor teeth have two lobes (also in greater slit-faced bat; three lobes in large slit-faced bat and hairy slit-faced bat). Total length 10 cm; ear length up to 3,7 cm; wingspan 24 cm; weight males 10,5 g, females 11,4 g. *See scale drawing on p. 5.*
Habitat Occurs in all sorts of habitats including deserts but is most common in savanna woodland. Roosts in half or total darkness in caves, mines, wells, hollow trees, holes in the ground and roofs.

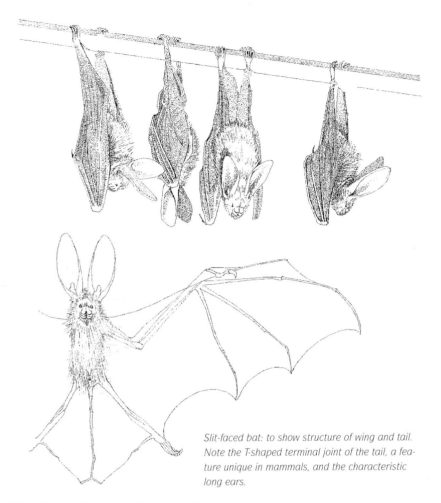

Slit-faced bat: to show structure of wing and tail. Note the T-shaped terminal joint of the tail, a feature unique in mammals, and the characteristic long ears.

Diet Solipugids and scorpions as well as insects.

Life history Gestation five months. Single young are born in early summer, and are weaned at eight weeks.

Behaviour Roosts in colonies of up to hundreds in loosely scattered groups. A slow but very agile flier. Prey is carried to feeding sites to be eaten. Spiders and solipugids are taken from the ground, and grasshoppers from vegetation. Mates in flight. Young are carried by their mothers.

Field sign Prey remains below feeding sites.

Wood's slit-faced bat (*Nycteris woodi*), S96, occurs in southeastern Zimbabwe and northern and northeastern Northern Province. **Vinson's slit-faced bat** (*Nycteris vinsoni*), S99, is recorded only from the Save River in Mozambique.

HORSESHOE BATS

Ten species in the subregion. While it is easy to recognise, from the structure of its noseleaves, that a bat belongs in this family, it is very difficult to identify species without examining noseleaves, teeth and other details.

The shape of the noseleaves varies between species, but the basic pattern is the same in all horseshoe bats: there is a horseshoe-shaped structure enclosing the nostrils, and a series of folded, roughly triangular flaps above them (no triangular leaves in leaf-nosed and trident bats). These noseleaves serve to focus the bats' echolocation clicks, which are emitted through the nostrils. The ears are large and widely separated, with a large antitragus, but no tragus. The wings are short and rounded, the flight weak and fluttering. The length of the forearm is a useful feature for identifying species.

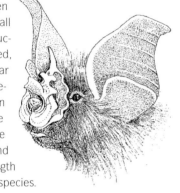

HILDEBRANDT'S HORSESHOE BAT

Hildebrandt se saalneusvlermuis
Rhinolophus hildebrandtii

S100 C

Description   Greyish brown, usually with slightly paler underparts. The wing membranes are translucent dark brown. The ears are large, convex on their inner margins, concave on the outer, with pointed tips. Females have a pair of functionless false nipples near the anus in addition to a functioning pair on the chest. The largest horseshoe bat in Africa; total length 12 cm; forearm 6,2–6,7 cm (Rüppell's horseshoe bat 5–6 cm); wingspan 39 cm; weight males 27 g (23–32 g), females 31 g (26–34 g); width of horseshoe more than 9 mm.

Habitat   Woodland; roosts in caves, mines, cavities in rocks, or large hollow trees, in total darkness.

Diet   Moths and beetles.

Life history   Gestation three months. Single young are born in early summer (October–December). Barn owls are the chief predator.

Behaviour   Forms colonies of up to a few hundred, hanging in loose clusters of up

50 individuals. Forages in zig-zagging, low-level flight; also hangs on twigs and ases insects that pass by. Frequently enters houses when foraging.

Rüppell's horseshoe bat (*Rhinolophus fumigatus*), S101, has a horseshoe more an 9 mm wide, but its forearm measurement is only 5–6 cm (Hildebrandt's horse- oe bat 6,2–6,7 cm).

GEOFFROY'S HORSESHOE BAT

eoffroy se saalneusvlermuis
hinolophus clivosus

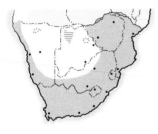

Description Light brown on the upper parts of the body, with the paler bases of the hairs showing through, pale buffy grey on the underparts. The ears are large and pointed, convex on their inner margins, concave on the outer. Females have a pair of func- tionless false nipples near the anus in addition to a functioning pair on the chest. Second largest horse- shoe bat in the subregion; total length 9,6 cm; fore- rm 5,3 cm (5,1–5,7 cm); wingspan 32 cm; weight 16 g (12–25 g).

Habitat Found in a wide range of habitats from desert to woodland. Roosts in caves, nines and rock cavities.

Life history Single young are born in summer (December).

Behaviour May form enormous colonies; those in caves in the coastal Western Cape Province contain up to 10 000 bats, hanging in loose clusters. Shares caves with ape horseshoe bats, but the two species form separate clusters. Forages singly, and iangs up to eat what it catches. The ground below feeding sites becomes littered vith scraps.

CAPE HORSESHOE BAT

Kaapse saalneusvlermuis
Rhinolophus capensis

Description Dark brown with the paler cream bases of the hairs showing through, inderparts buffy grey, wing membranes dark brown. The ears are exceptionally broad, and not as sharply pointed as in Hildebrandt's and Geoffroy's horseshoe bats. Females have a pair of functionless false nipples near the anus in addition to a func- ioning pair on the chest. Total length 8,8 cm (8,4–9 cm); forearm 4,9 cm (4,8–5,2

cm); wingspan 30 cm.

Habitat Coastal Western and Eastern Cape Provinces. Roosts in caves.

Life history Mates in August and September at the end of winter hibernation. Gestation 3–4 months. Single young are born in November–December.

Behaviour Roosts in colonies of thousands. Shares caves with Geoffroy's horseshoe bats, but the two species form separate clusters.

DENT'S HORSESHOE BAT
Dent se saalneusvlermuis
Rhinolophus denti

S108 **(**

Description White or pale cream, washed with brown or grey on the mid- and lower back. Some individuals are golden. The membranes are pale translucent brown with white edges. The ears are broad at the base, with pointed tips. Females have a pair of functionless false nipples near the anus in addition to a functioning pair on the chest. Total length 7 cm; forearm 4,2 cm; wingspan 20 cm; weight 6 g.

Habitat Drier areas, but not desert. Roosts in caves, rock crevices and thatched roofs in semi-darkness.

Behaviour Roosts in colonies of up to a dozen, or sometimes hundreds.

FAMILY HIPPOSIDERIDAE

LEAF-NOSED AND TRIDENT BATS

Four species in the subregion. Like horseshoe bats, they have a set of elaborate nose-leaves with a horseshoe-shaped structure around the nostrils, but they do not have the triangular leaves above the nostrils that are found in horseshoe bats. All except the first toes have two joints, instead of three as in horseshoe bats, and there is one less premolar tooth on each side of the jaw. Leaf-nosed bats have large, broad ears set far apart on the head. The upward fold at the base of the ear, the antitragus, is smaller than in horseshoe bats, and there is a minute tragus inside the ear. The wings are short and rounded, and the flight is rather slow and fluttering.

COMMERSON'S LEAF-NOSED BAT

S110 〔

Commerson se bladneusvlermuis

Hipposideros commersoni

Description Pale fawn, with the head and underparts lighter than the rest. Males have a patch of white hair on the sides of the shoulders. The hair is very short and sleek. The wings are pale brown, tending to be darker towards the tips. The lower legs and feet are black. The ears are sharply pointed. The largest insect-eating bat in the subregion;

total length males 15 cm (14–17 cm), females 13 cm; tail 3–4,5 cm; forearm males 10 cm (9,3–10,5 cm), females 9,5 cm (9,3–10,2 cm); wingspan up to 60 cm; weight 115–132 g. *See scale drawing on p. 5.*

Habitat Woodland. Roosts in pitch darkness in caves and roofs.

Behaviour Roosts in colonies of hundreds, spaced apart. Hangs for short periods in trees when foraging.

SUNDEVALL'S LEAF-NOSED BAT

S111 〔

Sundervall se bladneusvlermuis

Hipposideros caffer

Description Very variable in colour from grey-brown to bright yellowish golden. The best criterion for identification is that it is the only small bat in the subregion with hipposideros nose leaves. Females have a pair of non-functional false nipples near the anus in addition to a functional pair on the chest, a feature also found in horseshoe bats. Total length 8,5 cm (7,8–9,2 cm); forearm 4,8 cm (4,2–5 cm); wingspan 20 cm; weight 7,7 g (6,5–9 g).

Habitat Woodland, probably dependent on open water for drinking. Roosts in caves, mines, culverts, wells or roofs.

Reproduction Gestation 220 days in KwaZulu-Natal. Single young are born in summer (October–December).

Behaviour A very agile flier. Roosts singly, in small groups, or in colonies of hundreds, hanging separately.

SHORT-EARED TRIDENT BAT

S112 C

Drietand-bladneusvlermuis
Cloeotis percivali

Description Colour varies from slate grey to buffy brown; the head is usually tinged yellowish and the underparts are grey. The hair is soft and silky. The ears are tiny, rounded on their outer edges, and nearly hidden by hair. The characteristic feature of this bat is the three-pronged, trident-shaped process at the top of the noseleaves. The only other bat with a similar structure is the Persian leaf-nosed bat, which is twice as big. The smallest member of the family; total length 6,8 cm (6,3–7,6 cm); forearm 3,5 cm (3,4–3,8 cm); wingspan 15 cm; weight 4 g (3,4–4,8 g).

Habitat Roosts in caves and mines in total darkness.

Life history Single young are born in early summer (October–December).

Behaviour Roosts in colonies of hundreds, hanging in tight clusters.

PERSIAN LEAF-NOSED BAT

S113 C

Persiese-bladneusvlermuis
Triaenops persicus

Description Colour varies from fawny brown to bright cinnamon, but is usually yellowish brown. The underparts are lighter. The ears are small with a deep notch in their outer edge, and pointed tips. Total length 14 cm; forearm males 5,2 cm, females 5 cm; wingspan 35 cm.

Habitat Roosts in caves and mines in total darkness.

Life history Single young are born in summer.

Behaviour Roosts in colonies of hundreds.

ORDER
INSECTIVORA
INSECTIVORES

Three families in the subregion: the SORICIDAE, shrews; the ERINACEIDAE, hedge-hog, and the CHRYSOCHLORIDAE, golden moles. They live mainly on insects and other arthropods, and their teeth are adapted to this diet. Golden moles live underground; the others are terrestrial.

FAMILY SORICIDAE
SHREWS

Sixteen species in four genera in the subregion, all in the subfamily Crocidurinae, the white-toothed shrews. Shrews are superficially similar to mice but have long, narrow, pointed snouts, small eyes, small, rounded ears, five toes on each foot, and lateral scent glands on their flanks between the front and hind legs. They have rapid metab-olisms, and correspondingly high food intakes of one to two thirds of body weight per day. Their main food is invertebrates, especially insects, but some of them also take seed and small vertebrates. They can dig short burrows, but are more likely to make use of existing cover under rocks or fallen logs, where they excavate and construct nests of soft vegetable debris.

Some species can be identified in the field, others require examination of skulls.

LONG-TAILED FOREST SHREW **E** | S1 | **(**
Langstertbosskeerbek
Myosorex longicaudatus

Description Dark grey-brown, with slightly lighter underparts. The long tail is characteristic: dark on top, and paler underneath. Total length 15 cm; head and body 8,4 cm; tail 6,6 cm; weight 13 g.
Habitat Very restricted distribution from near the coast at Nature's Valley to the Outeniqua Mountains northeast of Mossel Bay, and in an isolated popula-tion in the Langeberg Mountains northeast of Heidelberg. Within these areas it occurs from sea level to mountain peaks in forest, forest edges, fynbos and boggy grassland, always in moist microhabitats.

Diet Invertebrates and occasionally seeds.
Behaviour The long, prehensile tail is used when climbing.
Conservation Endemic to South Africa; its restricted distribution makes it vulnerable to habitat loss. Red Data Book: Indeterminate; the Langeberg Mountains population may be Vulnerable.

The **dark-footed forest shrew** (*Myosorex cafer*), S2, is very similar in appearance to the forest shrew.

FOREST SHREW
Bosskeerbek
Myosorex varius

E | S3 | **(**

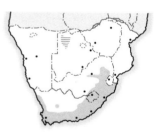

Description Grey-brown to dark grey-brown on the upper parts, unevenly grizzled with fawn or yellow; the hair on the underparts is grey with whitish tips. The feet are off-white; the tail is dark brown on top, paler below. Total length 12,6 cm; tail 4,3 cm; weight 12 g.
Habitat Moist, densely vegetated areas ranging from primary forest and montane grassland to waterside vegetation on the highveld. Locally very common, the most widely distributed of southern African forest shrews. In the Drakensberg it is the first small mammal to reappear after fires. Endemic to southern Africa.

Diet Feeds on a wide range of invertebrates, including earthworms and spiders. Obtains extra nutrients by licking its everted rectum (refection).

Life history Breeds from September to March. Litters of 2–5 (usually 3) are weaned at 20–25 days. Lifespan 12–16 months. Often taken by barn owls (*Tyto alba*); also by water mongooses, striped weasels and striped polecats.

Behaviour Nocturnal; shelters in nests of soft vegetable debris under rocks and in rodent burrows. Scent marks with chin and lateral glands, and leaves piles of strongly scented faeces.

Young cling to their mother's nipples for the first 5–6 days, then grip her fur in their teeth, first in a cluster, and by the tenth to thirteenth day in a chain, with each youngster gripping the fur of the one in front.

Field sign Strongly scented piles of faeces.

GREATER DWARF SHREW   S4   ☾
Groter dwergskeerbek
Suncus lixus

Description The upper parts of the body are grey-brown, the underparts slightly paler. The feet are off-white; the tail is brown on top and paler underneath. Total length 11,5 cm; head and body 7 cm; tail 4,5 cm; weight 5 g.

Habitat Ranges from riverine forest to woodland, semi-arid scrub and grassland.

Life history Litters of three are born in summer. The greater dwarf shrew is preyed on by barn owls (*Tyto alba*).

Behaviour Often found in termite mounds.

LEAST DWARF SHREW

Kleinste dwergskeerbek
Suncus infinitesimus

Description Grey-brown on the upper parts, grey on the underparts. The feet are paler than the body; the tail is dark brownish grey on top, paler underneath. The smallest shrew in southern Africa: total length 7 cm; head and body 4,5 cm; tail 2,5 cm; weight 3 g. *See scale drawing on p. 40.*

Habitat Forest, savanna, bushveld and grasslands.

Life history Nothing is known about reproduction. Preyed on by owls.

Behaviour Often found in termite mounds.

SWAMP MUSK SHREW

Vleiskeerbek
Crocidura mariquensis

Description Dark brown to blackish brown above, slightly paler underneath; feet and tail the same colour as the body. The blackish colour and wet habitat are good identification features. Total length 13,6 cm, head and body 8 cm, tail 5,6 cm; weight 11 g.

Habitat Wet areas on river banks and the fringes of swamps, which makes its distribution very patchy.

Diet Feeds on insects; reported to be carnivorous.

Life history Breeds from August to April; litters of 2–5 (usually 3 or 4), with a recorded maximum of 7. Preyed on by fiscal shrikes (*Lanius collaris*) and owls.

Behaviour Predominantly nocturnal. Walks with the tail often slightly curved

upwards and the toes of the hind feet widely splayed, probably in response to wet, soft surfaces. Shelters on patches of dry ground, usually at the base of grass tussocks. Particularly active and agile, and tolerant of conspecifics. Both the shrew and its faeces are strongly scented.

The **giant musk shrew** (*Crocidura occidentalis*) is brown to dark brown above, slightly paler underneath. The largest shrew in the subregion, occurring only north of the Limpopo; total length 20,4 cm; tail 7,9 cm. Mainly nocturnal; inhabits dense cover in wet areas near streams and swamps, and in wet reedbeds. Feeds on invertebrates; probably also some small vertebrates. Litters of four are born in early to mid-summer.

GREATER RED MUSK SHREW

Groter rooiskeerbek
Crocidura flavescens

Description Brown to fawn with paler underparts. The largest shrew south of the Limpopo; total length 15,6 cm; tail 5,1 cm; weight 24 g. The only bigger shrew in the subregion is the giant musk shrew, which occurs only north of the Limpopo.

Habitat Occurs in a wide range of vegetation types in areas receiving more than 500 mm of rain per year. Often found in houses and gardens.

Diet Invertebrates, including earthworms; also takes small rodents, and is recorded as having killed and eaten a captive puff adder (*Bitis arietans*). Sometimes scavenges. May become cannibalistic in captivity. Excess food may be hoarded. As a source of extra nutrients it licks its everted rectum (refection), and eats faeces direct from its rectum or from faecal piles (coprophagy).

Life history Breeds from August to April. Gestation 28–36 days. Litters of 1–7 young (usually 4) are weaned at 18–22 days. Sexually mature at 2–3 months. Lifespan 18 months. Preyed on by owls, mustelids and mongooses. Domestic cats

catch them but usually do not eat them, probably because of the odour of the lateral glands.

Behaviour Predominantly nocturnal, with peaks of activity at dusk and dawn. Solitary except when mating. Territorial, probably with male and female territories overlapping. Lateral, chin and ano-genital glands are used for scent marking, and the faeces are strongly scented. An agile climber, but not arboreal. Rarely burrows. An exceptionally aggressive predator; prey is not always killed before being eaten.

Young are born in saucer-shaped or spherical nests in grass tussocks or rock crevices above the damp soil. For their first week the mother moves her young by carrying them in her mouth, from day 6 they begin caravanning, gripping the fur of the mother or their litter-mates to form a chain or a cluster.

LESSER RED MUSK SHREW
S14

Klein rooiskeerbek
Crocidura hirta

Description Colour varies with locality: cinnamon brown with pale silvery grey underparts in the east, attractive pale fawn faintly washed with reddish brown and with off-white underparts in the drier west, especially Botswana. The feet are usually paler than the body. The tail is short and thick. Total length 14 cm; tail 5 cm; weight 16 g. *See scale drawing on p. 40.*

Habitat Occupies a wide range of habitats, including gardens, but is not found in highveld grassland. Requires some cover in piles of debris or under logs and rocks; prefers damp areas but also occurs in the dry Kalahari where it must be seasonally independent of water.

Diet Mainly insects; also has carnivorous tendencies. Licks its everted rectum (refection) to obtain extra nutrients.

Life history Breeds from September to May. Gestation at least 22 days; 2–5 (usually 3 or 4) per litter, weaned at 17–19 days. Females can produce two litters per

season, and can breed in the season in which they were born. Preyed on by owls and black-necked spitting cobras (*Naja nigricollis*).

Behaviour   Mostly nocturnal, but also commonly active at dawn and dusk. Terrestrial, and relatively tolerant of conspecifics. It does not dig its own burrows, but constructs cup-shaped nests under cover. It uses its lateral glands for scent marking, and its faecal piles have a strong odour. For their first 8–9 days the mother moves her young by carrying them in her mouth, then they begin caravanning, gripping the fur of the mother or their litter-mates.

CLIMBING SHREW

Klimskeerbek
Sylvisorex megalura

Description   Dark brownish grey with grey underparts. The tail is dark brownish grey on top and pale underneath and is distinctively long; this is the only species of southern African shrew in which the tail is longer than the head and body; total length 16,4 cm; tail 8,4 cm; weight 6 g.

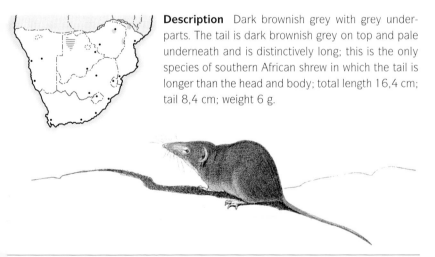

Habitat Thick scrub and tall grass. Distribution restricted to the Mashonaland Plateau in eastern Zimbabwe, the Zimbabwe escarpment, and adjacent areas of Mozambique where rainfall is 800–1 200 mm per year.

Six other species of shrew occur in the subregion: the **lesser dwarf shrew** (*Suncus varilla*), S5; the **tiny musk shrew** (*Crocidura fuscomurina*), S8, formerly *C. bicolor*; the **Makwassie musk shrew** (*Crocidura maquassiensis*), S9; the **reddish-grey musk shrew** (*Crocidura silacea*), S11, formerly *C. gracilipes*; and the **greater grey-brown musk shrew** (*Crocidura luna*), S13.

FAMILY ERINACEIDAE
HEDGEHOGS

One species in the subregion.

SOUTHERN AFRICAN HEDGEHOG

S16 R ℂ ⚹

Suid-Afrikaanse krimpvarkie
Atelerix frontalis

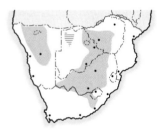

Description Unmistakable; the only African mammal with short spines covering the whole of the back and flanks (porcupines have long quills and are very much larger: see p. 123). Each spine is a thick, stiff hair, white at the base, black or dark brown in the middle, and white or buff at the tip. Some spines are white, and these may lie in broad bands along the back. The face, legs, tail and underside are covered with hair, dark or greyish brown on the face, legs and tail; black, white or a mixture of the two on the underside. There is a conspicuous white band across the forehead, the snout is pointed, the ears are small and the tail is short. Five toes on each foot. Females have two pairs of nipples on the chest and one pair, occasionally more, on the belly. Head and body length 18 cm; tail 2 cm; weight 240–400 g. *See scale drawing on p. 40.*

Habitat Semi-arid and sub-temperate areas with 300–800 mm rain per year. Occurs in a wide variety of vegetation types but not in wet areas.

Diet Mostly invertebrates, but also takes frogs and lizards, mice, birds' eggs and chicks, carrion and fungi.

Life history Breeds October–April. Gestation 5–6 weeks. Up to 9, usually 4, in a litter. Newborn young are blind and naked; spines emerge through the skin 1–3 hours after birth. Infant spines are replaced at 4–6 weeks, at the same time as the young begin to forage with their mother. Weaned at 5 weeks, independent at 6–7 weeks. Giant eagle owls (*Bubo lacteus*) eat hedgehogs in large numbers, despite the spines which provide protection against mammalian carnivores.

Behaviour Solitary. Meetings are noisy with much snuffling and snorting and head butting. Mostly nocturnal but also quite commonly active at dawn and dusk, and occasionally during the day in cool weather. Shelters during the day under vegetable debris in thickets, under logs, and in similar protected spots.

Moves slowly when foraging but can run at 6–7 km/h. Prey is detected mainly by smell, and is rooted out from litter and under rocks and logs. Noisy, relying on its spines rather than concealment for protection against predators. When disturbed, rolls up and pulls the spiny skin on its back down over its head and legs to present a uniform ball of interlocked springy spines to its attacker, a defence that is effective even against lions. The alarm call is a high-pitched screech.

Courtship is noisy and prolonged; male and female circle each other with much sniffing and snorting. While mating the female flattens the spines on her rump, and the male, who has a particularly long penis, holds himself in position by biting the spines on her shoulders.

In response to cold (15 °C), short day length (10 hours' light), and low food availability, hedgehogs become torpid, with reduced oxygen consumption, slower breathing, relaxed posture and reduced coordination. Cold weather and shortage of food lead to extended periods of torpor, and hedgehogs are rarely seen in winter. In the eastern Free State they are inactive from June to August, and lose up to 19% of body weight, but true hibernation has not been confirmed. Hedgehogs that weigh less than 200 g do not have enough reserves to survive through winter.

Field sign Faeces are cylinders with rounded ends, about 1 cm thick and up to 5 cm long. They nearly always contain fragments of insects.

Conservation Hedgehogs are killed by people for their meat and for the spines, which are used in traditional medicine. Large numbers are killed on roads. Like most wildlife, they suffer from habitat loss due to urban development and agriculture. Red Data Book: Rare.

FAMILY CHRYSOCHLORIDAE

GOLDEN MOLES

Eighteen species in the subregion, some of which were last collected 40 years ago. Their taxonomy has recently been re-examined, and some names have changed. Identification of some species requires examination of skulls or chromosomes. All golden moles are highly specialised for living underground: they have compact, streamlined bodies, snouts protected by pads of hard skin for burrowing, eyes covered by skin, short, strong front limbs armed with heavy claws for digging, short hind limbs with small claws and webbed feet for shovelling soil, and no external tail. Most species are brownish or blackish rather than golden but in all of them the fur has distinct sheens of various colours. Giant golden moles and rough-haired golden moles have long, coarse fur, in the others it is short and dense.

GIANT GOLDEN MOLE

Reuse gouemol / reuse kruipmol
Chrysospalax trevelyani

Description Fur long and coarse. Dark brown on the back with a silver sheen, paler on the underparts, dull yellow on the throat and the underside of the forelimbs. Sometimes there are yellowish patches where the eyes would be. The forefeet have four toes: the claws on the first and fourth are small, on the second and third large and robust (13–15 mm long on the second, 17–21 mm long on the third, both 6 mm wide at the base). The largest species of golden mole; total length 17–24 cm, weight 265–470 g.

Habitat Restricted to patches of flat or gently sloping ground with deep soil and leaf litter and a high density of shrubs in indigenous mist forests.

Diet Invertebrates, especially giant earthworms (*Microchaetes* sp.) and millipedes; probably also small vertebrates.

Life history One or two young are born in summer. Predation by feral dogs is a serious threat.

Behaviour Forages above ground in leaf litter, mainly in the evening and the middle of the night, but may also be active in daylight in cool, cloudy weather. Excavates burrows up to 13,6 m long among tree roots. Burrow entrances are connected by surface runways. The only golden mole to show even slight sociality in that several individuals may overwinter in a shared burrow.

Field sign Patches of leaf litter disturbed by foraging, runways between burrows.

Conservation Habitat destruction for fuel, building wood and bark has fragmented the distribution range. Near human settlement, predation by feral dogs has caused populations to shrink. Red Data Book: Vulnerable

Rough-haired golden moles *(Chrysospalax villosus)*, S18, also have long, coarse hair. They are smaller than giant golden moles (13,8–17,5 cm; 93–142 g) and live in grassland with dry sandy soils near marshes and streams. Their burrow entrances have a bowl-shaped latrine just outside. Only two specimens have been collected in the past 15 years. Red Data Book: Vulnerable. Endemic.

CAPE GOLDEN MOLE
Kaapse gouemol / Kaapse kruipmol
Chrysochloris asiatica

ⓔ | S21 | **☾**

Description Fur soft and silky, variable in colour; blackish, slate-grey, dark brown or pale fawn, always with a bronze, violet or green sheen. The underparts are duller; the chin, throat and forelimbs are light buffy brown. There are light buffy bands from where the eyes would be onto the cheeks and sometimes the muzzle. Individuals

from moist fynbos habitats are larger and darker than those from the drier succulent Karoo and Namaqualand. The first and fourth claws of the forefeet are small, the second and third are long and slender; the third 11–14 mm long and 3,5–4,5 mm wide at the base. Total length 10,4 cm (9–13 cm), weight 40,3 g (29–50 g).

Habitat Sandy soils in fynbos, grassland and succulent Karoo; thrives in gardens and cultivated fields.

Diet Earthworms, millipedes and insects; eats up to 70 times its body weight a year, providing a valuable pest destruction service to gardeners.

Life history Young are born April–August, usually 2 in a litter, and weaned at 2–3 months when almost fully grown.

Behaviour Forages in tunnels just below the surface, raising ridges as it goes. Rests and nests in deeper tunnels about 30 cm down. Sometimes enters houses.

Field sign Ridges above foraging tunnels, mounds of soil thrown out of deeper tunnels.

Conservation Flourishes in gardens, nurseries and cultivated fields, especially if irrigation ensures a year-round food supply. Should be welcomed in gardens for eating invertebrate pests.

Visagie's golden mole (*Chrysochloris visagiei*), S22, resembles the Cape golden mole except for the shape of one of its ear bones. Only one specimen has ever been collected, and it may simply be an aberrant Cape golden mole.

GRANT'S GOLDEN MOLE AND NAMIB GOLDEN MOLE

Grant se gouemol en Namib gouemol
Eremitalpa granti

Description Body short and stout rather than long and tubular as in other golden moles. The fur is soft and long. Greyish yellow on the back, more intense yellow on

the flanks and underparts. Claws broad and hollowed out; first 6–7 mm, second 7–8,6 mm, third 9–11 mm, fourth modified to form a broad scraper. Grant's golden mole (*Eremitalpa granti granti*) occurs south of the Orange River, and is slightly larger and drabber in colour, with longer fur. The Namib golden mole (*E. g. namibensis*) occurs north of the Orange River, and is smaller, with shorter, yellower fur. The two may be separate species. Smallest of the golden moles; length 6,4–8,6 cm; weight 16–30 g.

Habitat Loose sands and succulent karoo of the Namaqualand coastal plain, Namib desert in dry riverbeds and dunes with clumps of grass.

Diet A wide range of invertebrates, some reptiles. In the Namib termites make up 95% of the diet.

Life history Poorly known. Females with one or two foetuses have been collected in October. Where young are born is a mystery because nesting chambers cannot be built in loose sand.

Behaviour Most active at night when the sand cools. 'Swims' through the sand just below the surface, or moves about on the surface. Typically covers 60–600 m a night, in one exceptional case 5,8 km. Detects prey by vibrations and smell. Rests in cooler sand about 50 cm down, allowing its body temperature to fall to reduce oxygen requirements. Solitary and aggressive.

Field sign Foraging trails are twin parallel ridges or closely spaced alternating diagonal marks of the forefeet, interrupted by signs of digging.

Conservation Namib golden moles occur in protected areas, but Grant's golden mole's habitat is unprotected, and degraded by surface mining. Red Data Book: Rare.

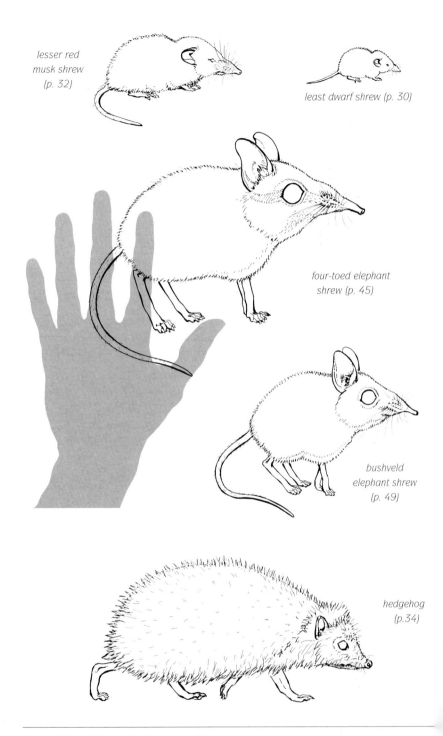

lesser red
musk shrew
(p. 32)

least dwarf shrew (p. 30)

four-toed elephant
shrew (p. 45)

bushveld
elephant shrew
(p. 49)

hedgehog
(p.34)

De Winton's golden mole (*Cryptochloris wintonii*), S19, and **Van Zyl's golden mole** (*Cryptochloris zyli*), S20, were last collected over 40 years ago. De Winton's is pale fawn, tinged yellow with a silver sheen, Van Zyl's is dark lead grey with a violet sheen. Both are pale, buffy yellow on the sides of the face and sometimes there are lighter spots where the eyes would be. The fourth foreclaws are less than 2 mm long compared to more than 2,5 mm long in Grant's, and they have a broad foot pad at the base of the first foreclaw which is absent in Grant's. Red Data Book: Indeterminate. Both are endemic.

Arend's golden mole (*Carpitalpa arendsi*), S24, has a total length of 11,5–14,1 cm, and weighs 34–70 g, with males slightly larger than females. It is brownish black on the back and greyish brown underneath, with a distinct violet or silver sheen. There are faint whitish bands on the face to where the eyes would be. Occurs in loamy soil in grassland and forest fringes on the eastern escarpment of Zimbabwe. Easily distinguished from the yellow golden mole, which occurs in the same area, by its larger size and grey underfur. Rare. Endemic.

Duthie's golden mole (*Chlorotalpa duthieae*), S25, has a total length of 9,5–13 cm, and weighs 20–41 g. Males are slightly bigger than females. Uniform reddish black or brownish black. Occurs in alluvial sand and sandy loams, mostly in coastal forest. Eats mainly earthworms. Breeds in summer. Habitat is well protected and the species can be classified as Out of Danger. Endemic.

Sclater's golden mole (*Chlorotalpa sclateri*), S26, has a total length of 9,5–13 cm, and weighs 22–54 g. Males are slightly larger than females. Reddish brown on the back, dull grey tinged reddish underneath, buffy yellow on the sides of the head and muzzle. Lives in montane grassland, scrub and forested kloofs. Breeds in summer; one or two young in a litter, females can have more than one litter in a season. Endemic.

YELLOW GOLDEN MOLE

Ⓔ S27 R ☾

Geel gouemol
Calcochloris obtusirostris

Description Colour varies from light yellowish orange, through orange, bright reddish brown and dull brown to dark brown on the back, and yellow-orange, orange, bright brown and reddish brown on the underparts. The yellow-orange underfur distinguishes this species from all other golden moles, which have grey underfur. Small: length 8,2–11 cm; weight 15–37 g. Males are slightly larger than females.
Habitat Sandy soils of the Mozambique coastal plain supporting coastal forest,

thornveld, or acacia, miombo and mopani savanna.
Diet Feeds on a wide range of invertebrates.
Life history One or two young in summer, as far as
is known.
Behaviour Most active at night, and much more
active after rain. Forages in subsurface runs. Detects
prey by vibrations and drags it below the surface.
Field sign Ridges above subsurface runs.

Conservation Habitat is adequately protected in conservation areas. Classified as
Rare in the Red Data Book but can be considered Out of Danger.

Gunning's golden mole (*Neamblysomus gunningi*), S28, is a relatively large species
with a total length of 11,1–13,2 cm and a weight of 39–70 g. Males are slightly larger than females. Colour varies: dark brown, dark reddish brown or very dark reddish
brown on the back; dull orange underneath. Lighter and tinged yellow on the cheeks
and chin. Inhabits montane forests and adjacent grassland, thrives in cultivated lands
and young plantations. Breeds in late summer. Needs to be classified as Rare due to
its restricted distribution. Endemic.

Juliana's golden mole (*Neamblysomus julianae*), S31, is 9,2–11,1 cm long and
weighs 21–46 g. Males are slightly larger than females. Animals from Pretoria and
the Nyl floodplain, Northern Province, are reddish brown or brown on the back and
orange or orange-yellow underneath; from the Kruger NP they are dark reddish
brown on the back, and dull reddish brown underneath. Distinguished from
Hottentot golden moles by smaller size and paler fur. Distribution is widely discontinuous; confined to sandy soils in savanna. Forages in subsurface runs. Litters of one
or two young are born at any time of year. The Pretoria population is suffering from
habitat degradation due to urbanisation and the species needs to be classified as
Rare. Endemic.

HOTTENTOT GOLDEN MOLE

Hottentot gouemol
Amblysomus hottentotus
Amblysomus septentrionalis
Amblysomus sp.

■ *A hottentotus*
III *A. septentrionalis*
■ *A. sp*

Description   Variable in colour: usually brownish black to reddish brown in the middle of the back, shading to reddish brown on the flanks and bright brown to dull orange underneath. There are sometimes light orange-yellow patches on the sides of the muzzle, which may extend above the position of the eyes. Total length 10–14 cm; weight 40–70 g.

The old *Amblysomus hottentotus* has been shown to be made up of four species. Three of these are cryptic species recognised by chromosome number: *A. hottentotus* 2n = 30, *A. septentrionalis* 2n = 34, and *Amblysomus* sp. (which still awaits a formal name) 2n = 36. The fourth is Marley's golden mole, described below.

Habitat   Occurs in a wide range of habitats including coastal forest, temperate grassland, montane vleis and tree savanna, but not in dry bushveld.

Diet   Takes a wide range of invertebrates and sometimes eats bulbs, including garlic.

Life history   One to three young per litter; females breed repeatedly at any time of the year as long as conditions are favourable. Young are suckled until almost fully grown, and evicted from the mother's burrow when they weigh 35–45 g. Taken by barn owls (*Tyto alba*) when moving above ground.

Behaviour   Active intermittently with peaks at sunrise, sunset and midnight. Solitary and aggressive to other golden moles, but shares its burrow peacefully with mole rats. Forages in subsurface tunnels which connect to deeper burrows. One burrow system may have up to 200 m of tunnels with nest chambers, latrines, blind side-tunnels and spiralling bolt holes. Four to 12 m of tunnel are dug per day; loose soil from the deeper workings is pushed up into mounds. The forelimbs are immensely strong:

a Hottentot golden mole is reported to have shifted a railway sleeper weighing 150 times its own body weight.

Field sign Ridges above subsurface tunnels.

Conservation Widespread and common, its tunnelling makes it a nuisance in gardens, but it does good by eating invertebrate pests.

The **Zulu golden mole** (*Amblysomus iris*), S29, has now been recognised to be a subspecies of *Amblysomus hottentotus*.

Marley's golden mole (*Amblysomus marleyi*), which used to be considered as a subspecies of *Amblysomus hottentotus*, has been recognised as a full species because it is markedly smaller and has a differently shaped skull. Total length 9–12 cm; very dark to dark reddish brown on the back; orange, dull orange or dull brown underneath. 2n = 30. Occurs in moist habitats and forests on the eastern slopes of the Lebombo Mountains. Its conservation status is much more precarious than that of *A. hottentotus* because it has a small range where the habitat is being degraded by human impact. It should be classified as Vulnerable or Endangered. Endemic.

The **fynbos golden mole** (*Amblysomus corriae*) has a total length of 10,8–13 cm and weighs 41–64 g. Uniformly reddish black, or with a reddish brown tinge on flanks and belly. Inhabits forest and coastal renosterveld, as well as gardens and other cultivated areas where its mounds are a nuisance. Breeds at any time of year. Endemic.

O R D E R
MACROSCELIDEA

FAMILY MACROSCELIDIDAE
ELEPHANT SHREWS

Elephant shrews look superficially like mice or rats, but are easily recognisable by their long, mobile snouts, from which they get their name. They are not closely related to shrews. They have large eyes and ears, and long tails. Their hind legs are much longer than their forelegs, and they have large hind feet. There is a patch of naked, glandular skin at the base of the tail.

Baby elephant shrews are very precocious: they are born fully furred with their eyes open and are active from birth.

FOUR-TOED ELEPHANT SHREW
S32 R ☾ ☀

Bosklaasneus
Petrodromus tetradactylus

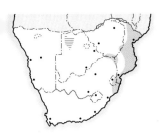

Description Reddish brown down the middle of the back, grey or buffy grey on the flanks, white underneath. There are narrow white rings around the eyes, and a dark reddish brown band on each side of the face, running from behind and below the eye to below the ear. This is the only species of elephant shrew in the subregion with only four toes, and with females having two pairs of mammae. Larger than other elephant shrews in the subregion; total length 35 cm (32–37 cm); tail 16–17,5 cm; weight 206 g (up to 280 g). *See scale drawing on p. 40.*

Habitat Dense underbrush in coastal and riverine forest with more than 700 mm of rain per year, in the extreme east of the subregion.

Diet Insects and other arthropods, especially ants and termites, exposed by scratching away leaf litter with the hind feet.

Life history Single young, rarely twins, are born at any time of year.

Behaviour Active during both day and night; shelters in holes under tree roots, fallen logs and similar refuges. Lives in pairs which defend territories criss-crossed by a network of pathways with patches cleared of litter approximately every 70 cm where the elephant shrews land as they hop along. The alarm call is a shrill squeak; the contact signal is produced by drumming the hind feet on the ground.

Field sign Paths with bare patches every 70 cm or so.

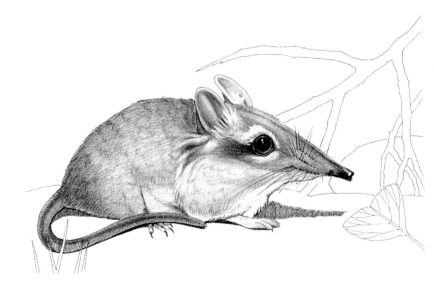

Conservation Very vulnerable to habitat destruction, but widely distributed and common further north in Africa. Red Data Book: Rare.

ROUND-EARED ELEPHANT SHREW

S33 ☾ ☼

Rondeoor-klaasneus
Macroscelides proboscideus

Description Colour varies with locality, grading from dark buffy grey in the southern Cape to pale buff in northern Namibia. The underparts are white, with the grey bases of the hairs showing through. The ears are short and almost circular; there are no white rings around the eyes, and no white patches at the base of the ears. Total length 23,5 cm (22–25 cm); tail 12 cm (11,5–13 cm); weight 40 g (31–55 g).

Habitat Arid areas, including the Namib, with sparse grass or scrub.

Diet Insects (in 77% of stomachs in summer, 43% in winter), spiders and other small invertebrates, green vegetation (40% in summer, 70% in winter), berries, fruit and occasionally reptile eggs and small lizards.

Life history Gestation about eight weeks. One or two fully furred, active young are born between September and February. Weaned and independent at 3–4 weeks, sexually mature at 5–6 weeks.

Behaviour Active by day or night. Shelters in a burrow with its entrance under a bush, which it digs itself or takes over from rodents, or in rock crevices. Searches actively for prey. Food is carried in cheek pouches and eaten under cover. Solitary, with territories of 0,1 to 1 km²; males and females associate for a few days for mating, and a mother may be accompanied by one or two young. Foot drumming is a contact and aggressive signal.

SHORT-SNOUTED ELEPHANT SHREW

Kortneus-klaasneus
Elephantulus brachyrhynchus

S35   ☾ ☼

Description Colour of the upper parts varies with locality: reddish yellow in the west, browner in the east. The flanks are buffy grey, the underparts and upper lip are white. There are white, buffy or off-white rings around the eyes, and rich, pale brownish yellow patches behind the ears. The soles of the feet are brown (black in rock elephant shrew). Females have three pairs of mammae. Total length 21 cm (20–23 cm); tail 10 cm (9–11 cm); weight 44 g (30–52 g).

Habitat Sandy ground with dense grass, scrub and scattered trees, woodland and savanna. Where distribution overlaps with that of the bushveld elephant shrew and rock elephant shrew they are separated by their habitat preferences.

Diet Mainly insects, especially ants and termites, but will also take seeds and fruit.

Life history One or two young are born at any time of year; females can have five or six litters a year.

Behaviour Active both day and night, sheltering in holes in the ground, in piles of debris and under fallen logs. Solitary or in pairs; males, and possibly females, are territorial. Dashes from cover to cover, and sits motionless in cover to avoid detection. The alarm call is shrill and penetrating. Foot drumming is probably a contact signal. There are large glands behind the ears whose secretion is deposited on the soil in sand baths.

Peters' short-snouted elephant shrew (*Elephantulus fuscus*), S34, occurs only in the extreme northeastern corner of the subregion. It is closely related to the short-snouted elephant shrew, and is similar in appearance, but darker and greyer, and with a small, swollen flap of skin growing from the inside surface of the ear.

Smith's rock elephant shrew (*Elephantulus rupestris*), S36, occurs in a narrow strip running approximately northwest from the Eastern Cape coast to northern Namibia. It is light grey, tinged with yellow on the flanks and the sides of the face, and greyish white on the underparts. There is a distinctive patch of reddish yellow at the base of each ear extending onto the nape of the neck. The end half of the tail is profusely covered with coarse, dark hair which forms a long brush at the end of the tail. Total length 27 cm; tail 15 cm, weight 65 g. Endemic.

BUSHVELD ELEPHANT SHREW

Bosveldklaasneus

Elephantulus intufi

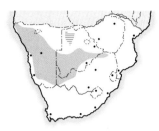

Description Paler than other elephant shrews, with longer, finer fur. The body is pale yellowish buff, lighter on the flanks, and white on the underparts and chin, with a naked patch on the belly. In northern Namibia the body colour is distinctly greyer. There are white rings around the eyes, conspicuous russet patches behind the ears, and conspicuous white hairs on the inside edges of the ears. The soles of the hind feet are naked and brown (brown in short-snouted elephant shrew, black in rock elephant shrew). Total length 23,5 cm (21–27 cm); tail 12 cm (10–14 cm); weight males 47 g (35–56 g), females 52 g (40–74 g).

Habitat Dry areas with less than 500 mm of rain a year, on sandy ground with sparse scrub or grass cover. Where the distribution overlaps with that of the short-snouted elephant shrew, the species live in different habitats.

Diet Insects, mainly ants but also larger prey such as grasshoppers which are carried into cover to be eaten. Possibly also eats some plant material.

Life history Usually two young, sometimes one, are born August–March.

Behaviour Active during the day except in hot weather. Shelters in burrows with entrances under bushes. Digs its own burrows or takes over rodent holes. Solitary, territorial and monogamous; male and female associate only for mating. Foot drumming is used as an alarm and contact signal. Develops runways between burrows and feeding sites; at high population densities different individuals' runways interconnect.

Field sign Runways. Small scatterings of insect wing cases at feeding sites.

ROCK ELEPHANT SHREW

Klipklaasneus

Elephantulus myurus

Description Upper parts greyish, washed with brown; the flanks buffy grey, underparts white. Overall the colour is greyer than in other elephant shrews. There is an indistinct white ring around the eyes, and yellowish brown patches behind the ears which contrast less with the body colour than they do in other elephant shrews. The soles of the hind feet are black (brown in bushveld elephant shrew). The tail is not as hairy as in Smith's rock elephant shrew. Total length 26 cm (20–29 cm); tail 14 cm (10–15,6 cm); weight 60 g (41–98 g).

Habitat Favoured habitat is rocky areas with crevices for shelter from predatory birds. Occurs at low densities on isolated rock outcrops or unbroken ground. Preference for rocky areas separates rock elephant shrews from short-snouted elephant shrews where their distributions overlap.

Diet Insects, especially ants and termites.

Life history Gestation eight weeks. Litters of two or, occasionally, one are born between September and March. Females are sexually mature at 5–6 weeks, and most of them produce 1–2 litters, only a few produce 3. Lifespan 13 months, exceptionally up to 19 months.

Behaviour Usually active during daylight, sometimes at dawn and dusk, occasionally at night. Shelters in rock crevices. Hunts from ambush, sitting in the shade and dashing out to capture passing insects. May become torpid in winter to save energy when food is scarce. Solitary or occasionally in pairs. Foot drumming signals alarm

and aggression. Gives a series of high-pitched squeaks with the mouth wide open and the nose curled back over the face.

The **Cape rock elephant shrew** (*Elephantulus edwardii*), S39, occurs in the Eastern Cape Province and the northwestern Western Cape Province. It is greyish brown with a yellow tinge and blackish brown pencilling. The flanks and the sides of the head are ash-grey, tinged with brown. The underparts are light grey. There are light grey rings around the eyes, and patches of reddish brown behind the ears. The end of the tail is black, with a small tuft of hair. Total length 25 cm; tail 13 cm; weight 50 g. Endemic.

ORDER
RODENTIA
R O D E N T S

Rodents have a pair of continuously growing, chisel-like incisor teeth at the front of both jaws, kept sharp by working against each other as the animal chews. Between the incisors and the cheek teeth, of which there are three, four or occasionally five on each side of each jaw, there is a space, called the diastema. The top lip can close this space to allow food to pass to the cheek teeth to be chewed, or open the diastema so that inedible fragments fall out through it. There are 9 families of rodents in the subregion, containing 80 species.

FAMILIES CRICETIDAE AND MURIDAE

RATS, MICE AND GERBILS

The Cricetidae and Muridae both have three cheek teeth on each side of the upper jaw, whose structure separates the families: the Muridae in the subregion have three cusps in the first row of cusps on the first upper molar. There are no external characteristics which consistently separate the two families, and it has become standard practice in field guides to deal with them together. The division of rats and mice is based roughly on size, rats being the larger species and mice the smaller ones, and this does not necessarily correspond to their zoological classification: one genus; *Aethomys*, contains both 'mice' and 'rats'.

SUBFAMILY OTOMYINAE

Stockily built with blunt faces, and tails less than half as long as the head and body. Reliable identification to species level requires examination of the skull and teeth; the third upper molar is the largest tooth, and the cheek teeth are laminate.

BRANTS' WHISTLING RAT
Brants se fluitrot
Parotomys brantsii

Description Colour varies with locality. The palest form, in the southern Kalahari, is slightly rusty yellow with paler flanks and white underparts. The darkest form, in the northern Western Cape province, is pale brownish yellow streaked blackish or dark brown, with greyish white underparts. In the field, against a background of red sand,

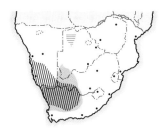

the colours appear greyer. The nose and the top of the first part of the tail are reddish orange, the rest of the tail reddish brown. The legs and tail are short, and the ears are large. There are grooves down the front of the upper incisors (no grooves in Littledale's whistling rat). Females have two pairs of mammae on the belly. Total length 24,5 cm (22–27,5 cm); tail 9,3 cm (8–11 cm); weight 130 g (90–165 g).

Habitat   Semi-arid areas with rainfall of less than 300 mm per year. Needs deep, sandy soil to burrow in and is not found where soils are shallow or stony.

Diet   Exclusively herbivorous on a wide range of plants (15 species in the Kalahari, 47 species in the southern Karoo). In the Karoo 60% of the diet is succulents, especially Mesembryanthemaceae. Gets all its water from its food.

Life history   Litters of 1–3, average 2, in spring or summer. Young cling to their mother's nipples for their first week and she drags them around with her even while she forages. Populations build up to high densities after good rains and crash during droughts. Preyed on by raptors, especially pale chanting goshawk (*Melierax canorus*), snakes, especially cobras, and mongooses.

Behaviour   Active during the day, especially early morning and late afternoon, and sometimes on moonlit nights. A pair of adults with their offspring shelter in warrens that they dig themselves. Warrens may be very large: up to 25 m² with 21 entrances in the Kalahari; 50 m² and an average of 46 entrances in the Karoo, with tunnels up to 1 m deep. Climbs into bushes to get at the edible parts. Pieces of plants are bitten off and carried back to the burrow entrance to be eaten in safety. Areas around occupied burrows are littered with twigs and other inedible debris.

The high-pitched, piercing whistle from which it gets its name is an alarm call, usually given while the rat sits upright at its burrow entrance before disappearing into it if further threatened.

Field sign Warrens with tunnels 8 cm in diameter. Twigs and other inedible debris around entrances show that a warren is occupied.

Littledale's whistling rat (*Parotomys littledalei*), S151, is similar to Brants' whistling rat but is slightly darker in colour and has a longer tail: 10,4 cm (9,2–12,2 cm), 70% of head and body length of 14,8 cm (13–17 cm) (compare 9,3 cm, 63% in Brants'). The only reliable distinguishing feature where the two species' distributions overlap in the Northern Cape is the absence of grooves on the upper incisors in Littledale's whistling rat. Endemic.

Laminate vlei rats (*Otomys laminatus*), S152, occur in coastal and submontane grassland. They are large and heavily built with short legs. The ears are hairless (covered with hair in vlei rats). The hair is shaggy, dark yellowish brown on the upper parts, dull yellowish on the belly and dull, pale yellow on the throat. The tail is thickly haired, dark on top and dull buff underneath. The upper surfaces of the feet are slate grey. The distinguishing feature is their having 9 or 10 laminae in the third upper molar. Head and body length males 20 cm (19–21,3 cm), females 18 cm (16–20 cm); tail 11 cm (10–11,5 cm); weight males 190 g, females 140 g. Endemic.

ANGONI VLEI RAT

S153

Angoni-vleirot
Otomys angoniensis

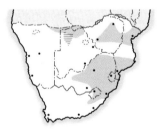

Description Pale to dark buff with dark grey underparts. There are sometimes buffy rings around the eyes (absent in the vlei rat), and a patch of the same colour on the throat. The nose is more pointed than in the vlei rat. The ears are large, and the very short tail is dark on top and buffy white underneath. The feet are purple-black; the first and fifth toes of the hind feet are short. The hair is long and soft. Head and body length males 14 cm, females 14,5 cm; tail 8 cm; weight males 90 g, females 97 g. Chromosome number 2n = 56.

The subspecies *O. a. maximus* in northern Botswana used to be considered as a separate species, *Otomys maximus* (S154). It is larger: total length 29 cm, head and body length 18 cm (15–21 cm); tail 11 cm (8 -13 cm); weight males 180 g (112 - 242 g), females 205 g (140–255 g).

Habitat Wet vleis, swamps and swampy ground near rivers, but may also be found in drier grassland and bushveld away from water, where vlei rats do not occur. Depends on dense cover for protection from predators.

Diet Stems and rhizomes of grass and fine reeds. Eats its own faeces to obtain nutrients from hind-gut fermentation.

Life history Gestation 37 days. Litters of 2–5 are born August–March. Young cling to their mother's nipples. Sexually mature at a minimum of five weeks in males, eight weeks in females. Preyed on by owls, small cats, and mongooses.

Behaviour Active mainly during the day and sometimes at night. Shelters in dome-shaped nests built in grass tussocks above the water level. Worn runways through the vegetation radiate out from the nest to feeding areas. Solitary, or in pairs or families. Does not make sounds audible to humans (vlei rats are more vocal).

Field sign Dome-shaped nests (saucer-shaped in vlei rat), runways, small piles of discarded grass stems.

Saunders' vlei rat (*Otomys karoensis*, formerly *Otomys saundersiae*), S155, occurs in mountainous habitats, especially in patches of rushes on high mountain slopes. The upper parts are light buff, the underparts greyish buff. The tail is pale buff on top and buffy grey underneath. The smallest of the vlei rats: total length 24,5 cm; tail 9,5 cm; weight 100 g; males are larger than females. Endemic.

VLEI RAT
S156 ☾ ☀
Vleirot
Otomys irroratus

Description Dark grey with irregular buff tingeing, lighter and greyer on the flanks and belly. The tail, which is noticeably short, is dark brown on top and buffy underneath. The body is stocky, the legs short and the head large. The ears are large, rounded and covered with hair. There are no buffy rings around the eyes, which dis-

Chromosomal races

\\\ A1   /// A2   ■ A3   ▨ A4

tinguishes this species from the Angoni vlei rat in live animals. The feet are dull, dark grey, and the first and fifth digits of the hind feet are short. Females have two pairs of mammae on the belly. Total length 26 cm (23–30,3 cm); tail 10 cm (8–12); weight 144 g (102–206 g). *See scale drawing on p. 94.*

There are four chromosomal races, with chromosome numbers of 2n = 23–32. Their distributions are related to climate and do not overlap.

Habitat Vleis and swamps, also grassland at some distance from water. Favours wetter habitats than the Angoni vlei rat.

Diet Stems and leaves of grasses and reeds; forbs and seeds, and bark from pine seedlings, which makes them a pest in plantations. They eat their own faeces to obtain nutrients from hind-gut fermentation. The young eat the faeces of adults to inoculate their guts with fermenting microorganisms.

Life history Up to 7 litters per season between August and May; gestation 40 days. One to four young per litter. They nipple-cling and are dragged around by the mother until weaned at two weeks. Some females are sexually mature at 4 weeks, others at 9–10 weeks; males at 8 weeks and 13 weeks. Reproduction is poor in crosses between races. Lifespan two years. Preyed on by servals and other small carnivores, barn owls (*Tyto alba*), grass owls (*Tyto capensis*), snakes. Also used as human food.

Behaviour Active in bouts throughout the day and night. Shelters in saucer-shaped nests built in grass tussocks above the water level; also uses other rodent burrows and tunnels in termite mounds. Worn runways through the vegetation radiate out from the nest to feeding areas. Grasses are bitten off near the ground, and cut into short sections to be eaten.

Occurs alone, in pairs or in families. Parts of home ranges are defended as territories. Males have dominance hierarchies. Gives a metallic 'chit' call as a threat to

other vlei rats (Angoni vlei rats are silent). Youngsters disperse over distances as short as 11–12 m.

Field sign Nests saucer-shaped (dome-shaped in Angoni vlei rat), runways, piles of grass stems at feeding sites.

SLOGGETT'S RAT / ICE RAT

Ⓔ S157 ☼

Slogget se rot
Otomys sloggetti

Description Dark reddish brown upper parts with lighter buffy flanks and belly. There are rusty yellow patches on the sides of the face and behind the ears. The body is stout and the head is blunt. The fur is soft, fine and thick. The tail is short, and the ears are small with dark fringes. Females have two pairs of mammae on the belly. Total length 17,5 cm (12–22 cm); tail 6 cm (4–8 cm); weight 83 g (38–150 g).

Habitat Occurs in the Drakensberg above 1 600 m; usually in alpine and sub-alpine zones above 2 000 m, up to the highest peaks. Typically found on flat or gently sloping ground that catches the sun all day, with surface or subsurface rocks; also in boggy soil where its burrowing raises hummocks. Does not occur on steep slopes or in valley bottoms. Reports of occurrence in the Karoo are, at best, doubtful.

Diet Exclusively herbivorous, eating the green parts and flowers of a wide range of plants, particularly alpine everlastings (*Helichrysum*).

Life history Breeds October–March. Gestation 38 days; 1–4 (average 2) young per litter. Babies nipple-cling for the first 2–3 days, first take solid food at 12 days, wean at 16 days and emerge from the burrow at 5 weeks. First mating at 18 weeks. Can breed up to densities of 100 or more per hectare. Preyed on by small grey mongoose, barn owls (*Tyto alba*), steppe buzzards (*Buteo buteo*) and jackal buzzards (*Buteo rufofuscus*).

Behaviour Active only at the warmest times of the day, sunbathing on rocks in the morning and afternoon, even when snow is lying on the ground. Shelters in burrows, and does not emerge during bad weather. Food is carried back to the burrows to be eaten, and is hoarded against times when foraging is impossible.

Lives in family groups in which only one pair breeds. For 2–3 days after giving birth mothers stay in the nest.

Field sign Hummocks raised in boggy areas; runways leading to burrows under rocks.

KAROO BUSHRAT

Boskaroorot

Otomys unisulcatus

Description Upper parts are ash-grey, interspersed with black hairs; the belly is creamy white, the feet pale buffy. Stoutly built with short legs and a short tail. Total length 24 cm; head and body 15 cm (13–16 cm); tail 9,6 cm (7,7–11,5 cm); weight males 139 g (125–156 g), females 110 g (101–135 g).

Habitat Karoo and west coast. In contrast to other species in the subfamily, prefers drier habitats and avoids wet areas. In the Karoo, prefers areas with more than 40% plant cover, such as dry watercourses.

Diet Exclusively herbivorous, taking over 60 plant species. About 40% of the diet is succulents, which provide all the rat's water requirements.

Life history Breeds throughout the year, with a peak of births in June and July on the west coast. Litters of 1–3 young nipple-cling for the first 9–10 days and first take solid food at 14 days. Preyed on by small carnivores, snakes, black eagles (*Aquila verreauxii*) and pale chanting goshawks (*Melierax canorus*).

Behaviour Active during the day. Builds large nests out of sticks. There are up to 155 nests per hectare in the bushier areas of the Karoo, especially along dry water-courses, and 380 per hectare on the west coast. Nests are up to 1 m high, usually about 0,5 m, and are usually built into the base of a spiny bush. One nest contained 13 329 sticks and weighed 8,3 kg. Besides sticks they may contain seaweed, dry dung, shells, bones and stones. They provide refuges from predators and harsh weather conditions. Each pair of rats uses more than one nest.

Karoo bush rats forage by biting off leafy twigs, and dragging them back to the nest where the edible parts are eaten and the remnants added to the nest.

Field sign Large stick nests, usually built into thorny shrubs (the debris piles of the Namaqua rock mouse are made of grass and thin twigs).

SUBFAMILY MURINAE

Twelve genera are indigenous to the subregion; one genus, *Rattus*, is introduced. The distinguishing characteristic of the subfamily is the presence of three cusps in the first cusp row of the first upper molar.

GROOVED-TOOTHED MOUSE
Groeftandmuis
Pelomys fallax

S159 ☾ ☁

Description Rusty brown to tawny yellow, grizzled with black and with a distinct greenish or bluish sheen and an indistinct dark line down the middle of the back (the single-striped mouse has a distinct line). The rump may be rustier in colour than the rest of the body. The underparts are off-white or light buffy brown, the sides of the face, throat, flanks and upper parts of the limbs are lighter than the rest of the body. The tail is black on top and buffy or white underneath. The fifth toe of each forefoot is short and carries a nail, not a claw. This is the only species in the subfamily with heavily grooved incisor teeth. Total length 29 cm (22–36,5 cm); tail 14,5 cm (11,4–18,3 cm); weight males 141 g (100–170 g), females 118 g (100–150 g).

Habitat Dry ground near wet areas.

Diet Young shoots of reeds and grasses, also seeds.

Life history Litters of up to four are born in summer.

Behaviour Mainly nocturnal but also active in the early morning. Shelters in self-made burrows.

SPINY MOUSE

S160 ☾

Stekelmuis
Acomys spinosissimus

■ Spiny mouse
/// Cape spiny mouse

Description Sepia grey, turning reddish during winter; pure white underparts. Identifiable by the coat of sharp bristles (also in Cape spiny mouse). Total length 17 cm (15–19 cm); tail 9 cm (8,5 to 9,7 cm); weight 27,5 g (20–36 g).
Habitat Typically found in rocky areas, also on alluvial sand along rivers, and in woodland and thickets.
Diet Seeds, insects, other invertebrates, and berries.
Life history Litters of up to five are born in summer.
Behaviour Nocturnal. Several may share a refuge in a rock crevice.
Field sign Piles of cylindrical, reddish droppings.

The **Cape spiny mouse** (*Acomys subspinosus*), S161, is similar to the spiny mouse. Dark greyish brown, lighter and tinged rusty on the flanks. Chin, chest and lower belly are white, upper parts of the belly light grey, feet white. The tail is dark on top and light underneath and has a black tip. As in the spiny mouse, the coat is sharp bristles rather than hair. Its distribution does not overlap with that of the spiny mouse. It is a similar size to the spiny mouse but not as heavy (weight 21 g, spiny mouse 27,5 g). Nocturnal and terrestrial in rocky habitat. Endemic.

SINGLE-STRIPED MOUSE
Eenstreepmuis
Lemniscomys rosalia S162

S162

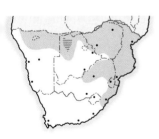

Description Colour varies with locality: pale reddish buff in drier areas to reddish orange in higher rainfall areas. The distinguishing feature is the definite dark stripe that runs from the top of the head, down the middle of the back and along the top of the tail (the grooved-toothed mouse has an indistinct line). The underparts of the body and the underside of the tail are rusty white or white. Total length 27 cm (24–30 cm); tail 15 cm (12,5–16,5 cm); weight 58 g (51–74 g).

Habitat Occupies areas of dense, tall grassland in a range of vegetation types from savanna woodland to dry open scrub.

Diet Seeds.

Life history Gestation 24–33 days; litters of up to 5 (average 4) are born in summer. First takes solid food at 14 days, weaned at 20 days.

Behaviour Active during the day. Digs burrows under the cover of tall or matted grass and lives singly, in pairs or in family groups.

STRIPED MOUSE
Streepmuis
Rhabdomys pumilio

S163 ☼

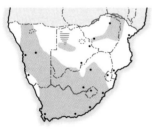

Description Varies in colour from pale reddish brown in the west to dark greyish buff in the east, but can always be identified by the four distinct stripes running down its back. The underparts are white, the backs of the ears are reddish or yellowish brown, the tail is darker on top than underneath. Size varies with locality: in the southwest Kalahari, total length 21 cm (20–22,5 cm); tail 10,5 cm (9,5–12 cm); weight 44 g (32–55 g); in eastern Zimbabwe, total length 18,5 cm (17–20 cm), tail 8,5 cm (8–9 cm); in southwestern South Africa, total length up to 26,4 cm. *See scale drawing on p. 94.*

Habitat Occurs in a wide variety of habitats with rainfall from 100 mm to over 1 200 mm per year, providing that grass is available, and preferably short and dense. Occurs in gardens and will enter buildings.

Diet Green vegetation, insects and seeds, according to seasonal changes in availability. Prefers seeds to greenstuff. Sometimes cannibalistic. In fynbos eats the fleshy flower bracts of proteas such as *Protea acaulos* and *P. subulifolia,* which bear their flowers near the ground or inside the bush, and is an important pollinating agent for these species.

Life history Breeds September–April in most areas, also in winter in the south-western Kalahari. Gestation 25 days; litters of up to 9, average 6. Sexual maturity is reached at two months.

Behaviour Active during the day, especially early in the morning and in the mid- and late afternoon. Digs burrows with their entrances hidden at the base of grass tufts, and builds round nests in clumps of grass near the ground. Forages under cover rather than in the open. Breeding females have small territories which are over-lapped by larger male territories.

Field sign Round nests 12 cm in diameter and 9 cm high made of grass stems cut 5–8 cm long, built low down in grass clumps.

WOOSNAM'S DESERT RAT

Ⓔ S164 R ☾

Woosnam se woestynrot

Zelotomys woosnami

Description Pale smoke grey pencilled with black, paler on the flanks, and creamy white on the under-parts. The tail and feet are white. Females have three pairs of mammae on the chest and two pairs on the belly. Total length 24 cm (21–26,4 cm); tail 11 cm (10–12 cm); weight 54 g (48–62 g).

Habitat Sparse scrub and bush on sandy soils in areas with a rainfall of 200–500 mm a year.

Diet Seeds (60%), insects (20%); may be carnivorous.

Life history Litters of up to 11, probably usually 5, are born between December and April.

Behaviour Nocturnal; solitary individuals, pairs or families shelter in burrows that they dig themselves or take over from gerbils. Lives mainly on the ground but can climb and jump well.

Conservation Red Data Book: Rare.

WATER RAT

S165 ⛄ ☀

Waterrot

Dasymys incomtus

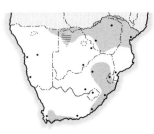

Description The hair is long and woolly; dark brown, grizzled buffy, paler on the underparts. The ears are large, rounded, almost naked on the back and covered with short hair inside. The feet are dark with whitish claws. The tail is heavily scaled and nearly as long as the head and body. (*Otomys* vlei rats and canerats which live in similar habitats are stockily built and have short tails.) Females have one pair of mammae on the chest and two on the belly. Total length 33 cm (30–35 cm); tail 16,4 cm (14,6–18 cm); weight 130 g (102–164 g).

Habitat Swamps and wet areas along rivers and streams.

Diet Stems and ripening seeds of grasses, reeds and other plants; insects.
Life history Up to nine per litter are born August–January.
Behaviour Active mainly at dawn and dusk but with some activity during the day. Semi-aquatic; swims well. Nests are built above water level on sloping ground or in grass tussocks, with burrows leading out below the nest.

The **Mozambique woodland mouse** *(Grammomys cometes)*, S166, is slightly larger than the woodland mouse, and very variable in colour. The only field identification feature is the white patches behind the ears, and even these are not present in all specimens. The taxonomy of the woodland mice is due for revision.

WOODLAND MOUSE
Woudmuis
Grammomys dolichurus

S167

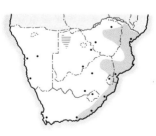

Description Very variable in colour: tawny-reddish with redder rump in Zimbabwe; dark slate grey with a tinge of red on the rump in the Northern Province; dull tawny in northern KwaZulu-Natal; dark reddish with yellowish flanks in the Eastern Cape Province. The underparts are always pure white. The feet are usually white but may be tinged with rusty or buff. The tail is very long and thin. Total length 26,6 cm (20,5–30 cm); tail 17 cm (14–20 cm); weight 29 g (24,5–35,5 g).
Habitat Forest, thickets in woodland, reedbeds.

Diet Mostly green bark; also fruit, seeds, wood.
Life history Gestation 24 days; litters of up to 4 are born at any time of year.
Behaviour Nocturnal; lives mainly in trees. Builds nests up to 20 cm in diameter, 0,5–2 m above the ground, in the densest parts of thickets, and also uses tree holes and weavers' nests. Nests are shared by family groups.
Field sign Nests.

HOUSE MOUSE ❶ S168 ☾
Huismuis
Mus domesticus

Description Greyish or buffy brown with slightly lighter underparts and light buffy brown feet. The tail is brown on top and lighter brown underneath. The ears are large and rounded. Total length 16 cm (15–18,5 cm); tail 8,6 cm (8–10 cm); weight 16 g (9–25 g).
Habitat Closely associated with human activity and lives almost exclusively in buildings.
Diet Omnivorous, can be a serious pest.
Life history A prolific breeder. Females mature at 3 weeks and give birth to litters of up to 13 after a gestation of 19 days.

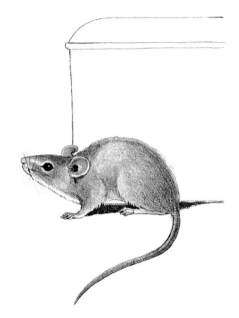

Behaviour Nocturnal. Social; a dominant male controls a group of females and their young. Groups are territorial.

Field sign Damaged goods, holes in woodwork. Infested buildings develop a typical mousey odour.

PYGMY MOUSE

S172 ℂ

Dwergmuis
Mus minutoides

Description Colour varies from brownish buff to reddish, with pure white underparts. The tail is relatively short, especially in animals from the northeast. (The chestnut climbing mouse is also very small but has a long tail and a dark stripe down its back.) The ears are rounded, less than 13 mm high (Setzer's pygmy mouse has ears more than 13 mm high). Females have two pairs of mammae on the chest and two pairs on the belly (same in Krebs' fat mouse). Total length 10 cm (8–16 cm); tail 4 cm (2–5 cm); weight 6 g (4–12 g). *See scale drawing on p. 94.*

Habitat A wide habitat choice including fynbos, savanna woodland, grassland, and forest fringes.

Diet Mainly seeds and insects, with some green vegetation.

Life history Gestation 19 days (or less). Litters of up to 8, usually 4, are born in summer and weaned by 17 days. Females are sexually mature at 42 days and first give birth at 62 days.

Behaviour Nocturnal, terrestrial and solitary except for mating pairs and families. Digs burrows in soft ground, but more commonly shelters under logs, in termite mounds or among rocks. Has the habit of nesting under sheets of corrugated iron left lying on the ground.

Setzer's pygmy mouse (*Mus setzeri*), S169, the **grey-bellied pygmy mouse** (*Mus triton*), S170, **Thomas' pygmy mouse** (*Mus sorella*), S170 A, and the **desert pygmy mouse** (*Mus indutus*), S171, also occur in the subregion. The systematics of the various pygmy mouse species need detailed investigation.

Rudd's mouse (*Uranomys ruddi*), S173, varies in colour from light brown to grey with a distinct sheen, paler on the flanks and underparts. The hair is long and springy in texture, each hair like a fine bristle. Total length 15 cm, tail 5 cm. It lives on flood-plain and grassland on alluvial soil near rivers, eats insects and seeds, and is nocturnal and terrestrial. It is rare in the subregion but very common further north in Africa.

MULTIMAMMATE MOUSE
S174 ☾

Vaal veldmuis
Mastomys natalensis
Mastomys coucha (S174A)

Description The two species cannot be separated on appearance alone. Light to dark grey-brown, often suffused with black; paler on the flanks, with a yellow or fawn

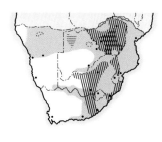

'lll   *M. natalensis*

lll   *M. coucha*

tinge. Dark grey on the underparts (a good identification feature), each hair having a narrow white tip. There is often a diffuse line of yellow or buff between the flanks and the underparts. The feet are white or off white. The tail is darker on top than underneath, finely scaled and with a sparse covering of very short bristly hairs. Females have up to 12 pairs of mammae in 2 rows on the underside, a unique feature among southern African mammals. Each is marked by a patch of whitish hair. Total length 24 cm (22–27,5 cm); tail 12 cm (10–14 cm); weight males 63,5 g (47–81 g), females 67,4 g (54–81 g). Chromosome number: *Mastomys natalensis* 2n = 32, *M. coucha* 2n = 36.

Habitat Occupies a wide range of habitats, except forest, as long as the rainfall is more than 400 mm per year. Penetrates into drier areas along river valleys. *M. natalensis* favours savanna woodland with more than 600 mm of rain per year, *M. coucha* favours grassland and arid areas with less than 700 mm of rain per year. Both species frequently enter outbuildings and houses, and can become pests.

Diet Omnivorous; typically seeds, fruits, grass and insects. Can be a pest in food stores and crops. During population explosions they become carnivorous: in the northern districts of South Africa in 1995 they could frequently be seen scavenging the remains of their road-killed conspecifics.

Life history A very prolific breeder under favourable conditions. Breeds throughout the year, with less reproductive activity in June and July. Gestation 23 days. Up to 22 (more than any other southern African mammal) in a litter, usually 6–12. Females have their first litter at 11 weeks; average interval between litters is 33 days. Numbers can build up very rapidly, and they are prone to population explosions which appear to be correlated with good rains after drought, such as in 1995 in northern South Africa. Being common, multimammate mice fall prey to all the small carnivores and raptors.

Behaviour Nocturnal. Shelters in nests of vegetation built in rock crevices, under tree roots, beneath fallen logs, or in burrows that it digs for itself or takes over from other species. The two species do not interbreed in the wild: mates of the appropriate species are recognised by ultrasonic calls and odour.

Note Multimammate mice are a reservoir for plague and, because they commonly live in buildings, they are important in its transmission to people. *M. coucha* is more susceptible to the disease than is *M. natalensis*.

Shortridge's mouse (*Mastomys shortridgei*), S175, resembles the multimammate mouse but is darker in colour and the females have only five pairs of mammae. Lives close to water and in damp areas. Nocturnal; does not enter buildings as readily as the multimammate mouse.

Verreaux's mouse (*Myomyscus verreauxi*), S176, is dark buffy grey to blackish grey with a dark stripe running forward from between the ears, and dark markings around and in front of the eyes. The flanks are paler and slightly more buffy than the back. The underparts and the sides of the muzzle are greyish white. The tail is brown on top and white underneath and is finely scaled. Head and body 10,6 cm (9–13,3 cm); tail 14,3 cm (12,4–15,7 cm); weight males 44 g (41–54 g), females 38 g (36–42 g). Lives in scrub, riverine forest and forest margins in the extreme southwest of South Africa. Nocturnal; eats protea seeds and insects. Endemic.

TREE MOUSE

S177 C

Boommuis
Thallomys paedulcus
Thallomys nigricauda (S177A)

Description Grey, tinged with yellow on the back, paler on the flanks. Pure white on the underparts, which show up clearly as the mouse climbs. The fur is long and thick. There are darker rings around the eyes and dark patches on the sides of the muzzle. The ears are broad and brown. The feet are white. The tail is slightly longer than the head and body. In *T. nigricauda* the tail is black, and the markings on the face are clear; in *T. paedulcus* the tail is brown and the markings on the face are faint. Total length 31 cm (28–36 cm); tail 16 cm (14–19 cm); weight 81 g (63–160 g), size is very variable with location.

The two species have different chromosome numbers: *T. paedulcus* 2n = 43–47, and *T. nigricauda* 2n = 47–50, and their skull shapes differ: *T. paedulcus* has a wider

brain case. On the basis of skull shape the distributions of the two species overlap completely, and intermediate forms which may be hybrids occur throughout the range of both species.

Habitat Woodland and tree savanna; needs large trees with holes in which to build nests.

Diet Fresh leaves, twig tips, pods and seeds of acacias, young leaves of shepherd's tree (*Boscia albitrunca)*, husks of buffalo thorn (*Ziziphus mucronata)* fruits, bark and gum. Twig tips are bitten off and carried back to the nest to be eaten; remnants are added to the nest. Possibly takes insects.

Life history Litters of 2–5 are born in summer.

Behaviour Nocturnal, emerging from nest holes at sunset or later. Nests are built from leafy twigs, in holes in large trees; with continual addition of new material the nests sometimes overflow the holes, building up in the forks of branches, and sometimes spilling onto the ground. The nests provide insulation from cold winter nights and may be shared by up to about eight mice, which may be a family group.

Tree mice can tolerate an exceptionally wide range of temperature. Their thick fur insulates them from cold while foraging, and to avoid overheating during the day in summer they reduce their metabolic rate by 40%, and lose heat by evaporative cooling.

Field sign Bite marks on bark. Twig tips trimmed off. Opened pods with teeth marks under feeding trees. Large nests in tree forks and holes.

NAMAQUA ROCK MOUSE
Namakwalandse klipmuis
Aethomys namaquensis

S179 | C

Description Generally reddish brown to yellowish brown, sometimes thickly sprinkled with black hairs, giving a darker shade. The underparts are pure white or slightly greyish. The tail is noticeably long and thin, especially in the north, and is finely scaled (the red veld rat has a shorter, thicker, more coarsely scaled tail). Reliable differentiation from the red veld rat depends on the presence of three cusps in the first

cusp row of the first lower molar teeth. Females have one pair of mammae on the chest and two pairs on the belly. Total length 26,5 cm (23–29 cm); tail 15–16 cm; ratio of tail length to head and body varies from 1,4 : 1 to 1,25 : 1 (1,15 : 1 in Grant's rock mouse; 1,25 : 1 in the red veld rat, tail shorter than head and body in the Nyika veld rat); weight 47,5 g (33–58 g).

Habitat Occurs in a wide range of habitats with a preference for rocky areas.

Diet Seeds of grasses and other plants. Large quantities of green vegetation may be eaten seasonally (90% of the diet in the Kalahari). Also eats insects. In fynbos, eats the fleshy bracts and nectar of proteas such as *Protea acaulos* and *P. subulifolia* which bear their flowers near the ground or inside the bush, and is an important pollinating agent for these species.

Life history Breeds from September to May. Up to seven per litter.

Behaviour Nocturnal; shelters in rock crevices, under fallen trees, in tree holes, in piles of debris or in burrows. Accumulates large piles of leaves, grass and fine twigs which cover the entrances to the nests. Small colonies share each nest. Forages under bushes rather than in the open.

Field sign Large piles of leaves, grass and fine twigs over nest entrances (karoo bushrat nests are built from sticks and twigs).

Grant's rock mouse (*Aethomys granti*), S180, is greyish brown with light grey underparts (underparts also light grey in red veld rat). The tail is covered with dark bristly hair and is 1,15 times as long as the head and body (1,4 : 1 to 1,25 : 1 in Namaqua rock mouse, 1.25 : 1 in red veld rat, tail shorter than head and body in Nyika veld rat); total length 21 cm. Endemic.

The **Silinda rat** (*Aethomys silindensis*), S178, is very rare. It resembles the red veld rat and the two species occur together near the Zimbabwe–Mozambique border. They differ in the structure of their teeth, and in microscopic features of their hair. Endemic.

RED VELD RAT

Afrikaanse bosrot
Aethomys chrysophilus

Description Variable in colour, usually reddish fawn; lighter on the flanks than on the back. The underparts are pale grey (also in Grant's rock mouse), each hair having a grey base and a white tip. Larger and more heavily built than the Namaqua rock mouse, and the tail is thicker and more heavily scaled. Reliable differentiation from the Namaqua rock mouse depends on the presence of two cusps in the first cusp row of the first lower molars. Females have one pair of mammae on the chest and two pairs on the belly. Total length 28 cm (21–34,5 cm); tail 15 cm (10–19 cm); weight males 77 g (38–112 g), females 68 g (26–125 g). There are two chromosomal species: 2n = 44 and 2n = 50. Externally they are indistinguishable, but their sperm has different shapes.

Habitat Grassland and savanna woodland, depending on some cover in the form of scrub, rock piles, holes or thick grass. Sometimes moves into outbuildings and houses.

Diet Grass seeds, berries, fruits, nuts and acacia pods. Sometimes raids crops. Discarded food scraps may be found near burrow entrances.

Life history Up to six per litter, at any time of year.

Behaviour Nocturnal. Digs burrows under cover. Solitary or in pairs or families.

Field sign Food scraps outside burrows.

The occurrence of the **Nyika veld rat** (*Aethomys nyikae*), S182, in the subregion is based on a single specimen from eastern Zimbabwe. It is the only *Aethomys* species with a tail shorter than the head and body.

HOUSE RAT / ROOF RAT / BLACK RAT
Huisrot
Rattus rattus

❶ S183 **☾**

Description From light to dark grey on the upper parts, either grey or white underneath. The hair is long and coarse, the feet are large and strong, the tail is long, thick, heavily scaled and sparsely haired. Total length 37 cm (34–40 cm); tail 20 cm (18–21,5 cm); weight males 124 g (105–180 g), females 163 g (150–184 g).

Habitat Typically in outbuildings, stores and houses. It has moved out into the field where there is heavy cover in areas receiving more than 500 mm of rain per year.

Diet Omnivorous, can become a serious pest.

Life history Gestation 21–30 days; litters of 5–10 are born at two-month intervals throughout the year.

Behaviour Nocturnal, although it is occasionally seen during the day. An agile climber. Eats and damages stored foods and animal feed, and damages buildings by gnawing holes.

Field sign Runs are marked by smears of dark, greasy secretion from their feet or fur.

Note Ships' rats and their fleas brought plague to southern Africa between 1898 and 1900; it infected indigenous rodent populations and has spread throughout the subregion.

The **brown rat** or **Norway rat** (*Rattus norvegicus*), S184, is confined to harbour cities and towns. It is larger than the roof rat and its tail is shorter in proportion to its head and body. It is omnivorous and a serious pest.

GERBILS

Mouse-sized, but their hind legs are much longer and stronger than their forelegs, making them look like miniature kangaroos. They have a groove down the front of their incisor teeth. Gerbils are a reservoir for plague.

SHORT-TAILED GERBIL

Kortstertnagmuis
Desmodillus auricularis

S185   **C**

Description Medium-sized and stocky with a distinctively short tail. Body colour varies from brownish or cinnamon-buff to grey- or red-brown. The underparts are white. The ears are small and oval with distinctive white patches at their bases (indistinct in bushveld gerbil). Females have two pairs of mammae on the chest and two pairs on the belly. Total length 18 cm; tail 9 cm (8–10 cm); weight 52 g (39–70 g).

Habitat Arid to semi-arid areas, on hard ground with sparse grass or small bushes. Occurs around dry pans in Botswana, elsewhere on fine soils, calcrete outcrops and river beds.

Diet Can survive without water on a diet of dry seeds from grasses, herbs, bushes, trees and wild melons. Seasonally eats large amounts of green herbage (85% of diet in the Kalahari). Also eats insects.

Life history Gestation 21 days; up to 7 per litter, average 4. Weaned at 21 days, independent at 45 days.

Behaviour Nocturnal, sheltering in complex burrow systems. Burrows are close together but their occupants are solitary. Forages under cover rather than in the open and carries food to the burrow to be eaten. Excess food is cached or hoarded. To save water the urine is 14 times as concentrated as the blood.

HAIRY-FOOTED GERBIL

S186　C

Haarpootnagmuis
Gerbillurus paeba

Description Body colour varies from reddish orange to greyish red, with pure white underparts. The tail is hairy, and dark on top with a small tuft at the end. Except for a narrow strip down the centre the soles of the feet are hairy for better grip on sand. The claws are long for digging. The upper incisors are narrow and grooved, the lower incisors ungrooved. The eyes are deep reddish brown, the outsides of the ears pale yellowish brown. Females have one or two pairs of mammae on the chest and two pairs on the belly. Small and lightly built: total length 21 cm (19–23 cm); head and body 8,6–9,7 cm; tail 11 cm (10–12,5 cm); weight 25,5 g (20–37 g).

Habitat Arid and semi-arid areas with sandy or alluvial soil and sparse grass, scrub or sometimes light woodland. Common on Kalahari sands. Does not penetrate deep into the Namib dunes. Females prefer more cover than males. In the Eastern Cape *G. p. exilis* moves onto beaches to feed.

Diet Can survive on dry seeds, but fresh vegetation, succulents and arthropods are much preferred. Arthropods are 53% of the diet in the Namib, 17% in the Karoo, and 15% in the Kalahari.

Life history Gestation 21 days; litters of 2–6 (average 3,7) are weaned at 15–30 days. Breeds throughout the year in Botswana, December–April in the eastern Namib Desert, September–April in the Karoo. Numbers increase quickly after rain. Preyed on by spotted eagle owls (*Bubo africanus*), black-backed jackals and genets.

Behaviour Active at night, during the day shelters in grass-lined nests in simple, single-entrance burrows. Aggressive and solitary, but somewhat social in *G. p. exilis*, with home ranges of 1–4 ha. Forages in the open rather than under bushes. Excess food is hoarded. To save water the urine is 12 times as concentrated as the blood.

Three gerbil species occur in the severe desert conditions of the dune fields or gravel plains of the Namib: the **dune hairy-footed gerbil** (*Gerbillurus tytonis*), S187, the **brush-tailed hairy-footed gerbil** (*Gerbillurus vallinus*), S188, and **Setzer's hairy-footed gerbil** (*Gerbillurus setzeri*), S189. All three are endemic.

BUSHVELD GERBIL

S190   C

Bosveldse nagmuis
Tatera leucogaster

Description Colour varies from orange-buff to reddish brown; animals from the west are lighter than those from the east. The feet, underparts and the sides of the muzzle are white, and there are indistinct white patches above and behind the ears (distinct in short-tailed gerbil). The hair is distinctively silky in texture. The tail is darker on top, and hairy, especially towards the tip, which is never white. Large; total length 27 cm (21–33 cm); tail 15 cm (12–17,5 cm); weight 70 g (52–114 g).

Habitat Light, sandy soils or sandy alluvium with a very wide range of vegetation from open grassland to woodland, with rainfall above 250 mm per year. Bushveld

gerbils do particularly well where vegetation and litter have been reduced by burning, and they are common in abandoned cultivated areas.

Diet Eats 30% green vegetation, 25% seeds, and 40% insects.

Life history Litters of up to 9, usually 4–5. Breeds throughout the year with a peak in summer.

Behaviour Nocturnal. Shelters during the day in burrows 4–4,5 cm in diameter with entrances under low bushes, in termite mounds, or under tree roots. Lines sleeping chambers with vegetable debris and throws up mounds of fresh soil at the entrance to the burrow every night. Burrows are shared by pairs, and adjacent burrows may interconnect to form warrens.

CAPE GERBIL
Kaapse nagmuis
Tatera afra

E S191 **C**

Description Colour varies from reddish orange to pale buff with a dark brown wash. The underparts are white and clearly demarcated. The ears are large (24 mm). The tail is the same colour throughout its length. Fur is distinctively long, soft and woolly. Females have two pairs of mammae on the chest and two pairs on the belly. Large; total length 30 cm; head and body 14 cm (13–15,7 cm); tail 15 cm (14–17,5 cm); weight 97 g (84–113 g).

Habitat Open grassland on well-drained, loose sandy soil in the Cape macchia zone of the extreme south west. Common in cultivated areas.
Diet Grass, bulbs, roots, seeds and green vegetation.
Life history Mates after the winter rains, and litters of up to six are born in summer.
Behaviour Nocturnal. Shelters in burrows floored with fragments of vegetation which is carried in to be eaten; excess food is stored in the burrow. Probably social; the burrows interconnect to form large warrens.

HIGHVELD GERBIL
S192　 ℃

Hoëveldse nagmuis
Tatera brantsii

Description Colour varies from light rufous brown to pale red washed with brown; animals from the east tend to be darker. The chin, throat and underparts are white or buffy grey. The tail is the same colour as the body at its base, but becomes paler about half way along, a useful feature for identification. The fur is long, soft and woolly, but not to the same extent as in the Cape gerbil. Females have one pair of mammae on the chest and two pairs on the belly. Total length 27–28 cm (20–35 cm); tail about 14 cm (10–18,6 cm); weight 80 g (up to 126 g).
Habitat Widely distributed and common in open grass or scrub on sandy soils, also in peaty areas near marshes. Lives alongside bushveld gerbils over wide areas.

Diet Seeds, grass, and insects, especially termites.

Life history Gestation 22–23 days; litters of up to 5 (usually 3–4) are born at any time of the year except very dry or very cold periods. May be numerous enough to become a pest.

Behaviour Nocturnal and social, sheltering in large, communal burrow systems. On the South African highveld males' home ranges are about 0,5 ha, females' less than 0,25 ha. Opens up its living areas by eating off ground cover and disturbing the soil by burrowing. Does not hoard food.

GORONGOZA GERBIL

S193 C

Gorongoza nagmuis

Tatera inclusa

Description Orange buff washed with black; underside and feet are white. Large; total length 32 cm; tail 16 cm; weight 120 g; females are larger than males.

Habitat Open grassland and savanna woodland on sandy, or sometimes harder, soils where rainfall is at least 800 mm per year. Sometimes common in cultivated areas.

Diet Seeds; also fresh vegetation and insects.

Behaviour Nocturnal; shelters in burrows. Not strongly social, but pairs may share a burrow.

WHITE-TAILED MOUSE

Ⓔ | S194 | V | ☾

Witstertmuis

Mystromys albicaudatus

Description Light grey or buffy grey, pencilled with black. The hairs on the underparts are grey at the base with pale grey or white tips (underparts pure white in pouched mouse). There is a diffuse dark band on top of the head from between the eyes to between the ears. The limbs and sides of the face are paler than the body. The tail is very short, thin and white all over (slightly darker on top in the pouched mouse). The feet are white. The fur is dense and soft. Stockily built with a large head. Females have two pairs of mammae on the belly. Total length 21–22 cm; head and body males 16,3 cm (14–18,4 cm), females 14,4 cm (10,5–14,7 cm); tail males 5,8 cm (5–8,2 cm), females 6,3 cm (5,3–9,7 cm); weight males 96 g (78–111 g), females 78 g (75–81 g).

Habitat Savanna grassland, karoo and Cape macchia.

Diet Feeds on insects, seeds and green vegetation.

Life history Gestation 37 days; 2–5 young per litter. Young nipple cling for 2 weeks continuously, then detach periodically until weaned at 30–38 days. Females first give birth at about five months old.

Behaviour Nocturnal; shelters in nests made of soft plant debris in burrows and cracks in the soil. May move into suricate burrows.

Conservation Red Data Book: Vulnerable.

GIANT RAT
S195 R C

Reuse rot
Cricetomys gambianus

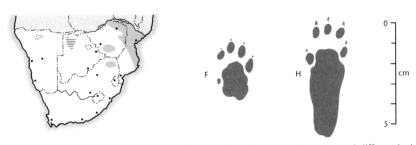

Description A huge rat. Grey to buffy grey with whitish underparts and diffuse dark rings around the eyes. Large ears. The tail is long and its end two fifths is white (tails are short in cane rats which are the only other rats with comparable body size). Total length 80 cm (67–84 cm); tail 42 cm (37–46 cm); weight males 1,3 kg (1–2,8 kg), females 1,2 kg (0,9–1,4 kg). *See scale drawing on p. 94.*

Habitat Cool evergreen forest or woodland receiving more than 800 mm of rain annually. Cannot tolerate temperatures above 34 °C.

Diet Eats fruits, seeds, bulbs and tubers; some insects, especially termites. Can be pests in crops, orchards and gardens: 8 kg of shelled macadamia nuts were found in one burrow.

Life history Gestation 28 days; litters of 2–4 are born in summer. The mother stays in the nest for a week after giving birth, presumably living off hoarded food. First takes solid food at 17 days, weaned at 18–28 days, first forages around 45 days and leaves the nest at 60–98 days.

Behaviour Nocturnal, but only leaves the burrow for a quarter of the night. Temporary holes may be dug close to food supplies. Food is carried back to the burrow to be eaten; small items in cheek pouches, larger items in the teeth, and inedible debris accumulates in the nest. Excess food is hoarded, allowing the giant rat to avoid being active in bad weather, and limiting the time that it is exposed to predators while foraging. Although it eats fruit it is not an agile climber. Solitary, in home ranges of about 5 ha in the Soutpansberg Mountains, Northern Province.

Conservation Red Data Book: Rare

POUCHED MOUSE
Wangsakmuis
Saccostomus campestris

S196   ℂ

Description Stockily built with a large head and short tail. Medium grey or grey tinged with brown; the underparts are pure white (light grey in white-tailed mouse) with a clear demarcation between the colours. The fur is thick, soft and silky. The tail is less than a third of the total length, slightly darker on top than underneath (uniform white in white-tailed mouse). The only mouse in southern Africa which has cheek pouches for carrying food. Females have three pairs of mammae on the chest and two pairs on the belly. Total length 15,5 cm (13,4–17,8 cm); tail 4,5 cm (3,4–5,5 cm); weight males 48,5 g (33–68 g), females 42 g (30–54 g). Maximum weight 110 g. There are 16 chromosomal variants, 2n = 28–50, which can interbreed.

Habitat Occupies a very wide range of habitats within a rainfall range of 100 to over 1 200 mm per year. Avoids hard ground and heavy clay soils, and prefers areas with scrub or woodland for cover.

Diet Eats larger seeds from trees, bushes and forbs; also a little grass seed.

Life history Breeds January–April in Botswana, February–April in Zimbabwe, October–February in KwaZulu-Natal. Gestation 20–21 days; up to 10 per litter (average about 7) are weaned at 21 days. Preyed on by most small carnivores, and recorded as a victim of ants that attack it in its burrows.

Behaviour Nocturnal and solitary. Digs burrows in soft soil, or shelters in holes dug by other species, under logs and rocks, and in the tunnels of termite mounds.

Forages up to 200 m from its burrow. Food is carried in the cheek pouches back to the burrow to be eaten. Inedible debris accumulates in the nest and at the burrow entrance; 700 ml of seeds and husks was found in one burrow. Food is also hoarded in the burrow. Becomes torpid in cold weather.

Field sign Food debris outside burrows.

SUBFAMILY DENDROMURINAE

Eight species in the subregion.

LARGE-EARED MOUSE
Bakoormuis
Malacothrix typica

S197 ℂ

Description Colour varies with locality from pale reddish brown to buffy. There is always a distinctive dark cape on top of the head, neck and shoulders, extending into a stripe down the middle of the lower back, and two elongated dark patches on the hips. The underparts, forelegs and sides of the muzzle are white or pale grey. The tail is short and the ears are very large. There are four toes on each hind foot. Total length 11 cm (10–12 cm); tail 3,5 cm (3,2–4 cm); weight males 16,4 g (12–20 g), females 10,4 g (7–13 g).

Habitat Short grass on hard ground in areas with 150–500 mm rain annually.

Diet Green vegetation and grass seed.

Life history Gestation 23–27 days; up to 6 per litter (average 4) are weaned at 32

days. Females can produce their first litter as early as 51 days old.

Behaviour Nocturnal; shelters in self-made burrows and forages over distances of at least 100 m. Freezes if it detects danger.

GREY CLIMBING MOUSE

S199 (

Grysklimmuis
Dendromus melanotis

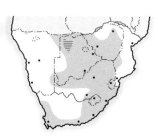

Description A small, attractive mouse. Ash-grey with a rufous tinge. There is a dark band running down the back from just in front of the shoulders to the base of the tail. Some have a dark spot on the forehead. The ears are darker than the back. The fifth toe of the forefeet is just a stub; the fifth toe of the hind feet has a tiny nail, not a claw. Females have two pairs of mammae on the chest and two pairs on the belly. The tail is long, thin and very mobile, twining around grass stems as the mouse climbs. Total length 15 cm (12,7–17 cm); tail 9 cm (8–10 cm); weight 6,7 g (6–8,2 g).

Habitat Widespread in stands of tall grass, especially if mixed with bushes.

Diet Mainly insectivorous, but will also eat seeds.

Life history Litters of up to four are born in summer.

Behaviour Nocturnal; uses the burrows of other rodents, and even holes dug by large

---

dung beetles. In summer, builds sturdy, spherical nests 4–6 cm in diameter with a single entrance, woven between several grass stems or twigs of bushes up to 1 m above the ground. Gives birth in these nests. Nests are abandoned in the winter.

Very agile climbers, the tail twines around twigs and stems but is not truly prehensile and the mouse cannot hang from it.

Field sign Spherical nests 4–6 cm in diameter are woven in grass or bushes up to 1 m above the ground.

The **Nyika climbing mouse** (*Dendromus nyikae*), S198, is rare. It resembles the grey climbing mouse but in the former Transvaal is brighter and redder in colour.

BRANTS' CLIMBING MOUSE

S200 R (

Brants se klimmuis
Dendromus mesomelas

Description A small, attractive mouse. The southern population is brownish pink, the northern population reddish brown. In both there is a blackish brown tinge on the back, and, usually but not invariably, a black band running down the middle of the back from just in front of the shoulders to the base of the tail. The ears are the same colour as the back. The flanks are lighter than the back, and the outside of the limbs is lighter than the flanks. The underside is off-white, the hairs usually having slate-

coloured bases. There is no fifth toe on the front feet and the fifth toe of the hind feet has a claw, not a nail. The tail is long, thin and mobile. Total length 17,5 cm; head and body 7,5 cm (6,7–8,5 cm); tail 10 cm (9–11 cm); weight males 12 g (11–13 g), females 10,6 g (9–14,5 g).

Habitat Tall grass and rank vegetation near water. Rare; distribution is discontinuous.

Diet Eats insects and seeds.

Life history Litters of up to four are born in summer.

Behaviour Nocturnal. An agile climber; the tail twines around stems and twigs but it is not truly prehensile and cannot support the mouse's weight. Builds spherical nests of woven grass.

CHESTNUT CLIMBING MOUSE

Roeskleurklimmuis
Dendromus mysticalis

Description A small, attractive mouse. Bright chestnut with a black band down the middle of the back from just in front of the shoulders to the base of the tail. White on the underparts. There is no fifth toe on the forefeet and the fifth toe on the hind feet carries a claw, not a nail. The tail is long, thin and mobile. Smallest of the climbing mice: of the rodents in the subregion only the pygmy mice are smaller: total length males 15 cm (13,6–15,6 cm), females 14 cm (13,8–15,7 cm); tail males 8,6 cm (7,9–9 cm), females 8 cm (7,7–8,5 cm); weight 7,7 g (5,5–11,8 g).

Habitat Grassland, especially in stands of tall, rank growth.

Diet Feeds mainly on insects; some seed.

Life history Litters of up to four are born in summer.

Behaviour Nocturnal. In winter shelters in other rodents' burrows and even in holes

dug by large dung beetles; in summer lives in spherical nests of woven grass up to 2 m above the ground, in which the young are born. An agile climber, the tail twines around grass stems and twigs but it is not truly prehensile and cannot support the weight of the body.

Field sign Woven, spherical nests.

FAT MOUSE

S202   ☾

Vetmuis
Steatomys pratensis

Description Colour ranges from dark to light rusty brown on the back, brown on the flanks and pure white on the underparts and feet. The hair has a definite sheen. The tail is less than half as long as the head and body. Females can be definitely identified by their large number of mammae, at least 8, usually 12 and sometimes 16 (the only other species with so many mammae are the multimammate mice, which have grey underparts and a long tail). Total length 13 cm (11–16 cm); tail 4,3 cm (3–5,5 cm); weight males 21 g (12–29 g), females 25 g (10–44 g).

Habitat Prefers sandy soils. In areas with low rainfall it occurs on the fringes of rivers and swamps. Especially common in cultivated areas.

Diet Feeds mostly on seeds, with some insects.

Life history Litters of up to 9, probably usually 3–4, are born between October and May. The fatty skin of this mouse makes it popular as human food.

Behaviour Nocturnal and solitary. Shelters in self-made burrows. During the summer when food is plentiful it lays down a thick layer of fat under the skin, which serves as a reserve during the cold dry months. This is reflected in the wide range of body weights. Only intermittently active during the winter; in cold weather it remains in burrows dug beneath grass clumps. Sometimes feigns death when handled.

The **tiny fat mouse** (*Steatomys parvus*), S203, is the smallest of the three southern African fat mouse species: total length 12 cm (11–16 cm); tail 4,3 cm (3,4–5 cm); weight 13 g (11–15 g). Colour varies with locality: in KwaZulu-Natal, buffy brown with tail brown on top and pale underneath; in northern Botswana and the Kalahari, much paler with a white tail. The hair has a definite sheen. Females have two pairs of mammae on the chest and two pairs on the belly (fat mouse females usually have at least six pairs). Lives on sandy soils, and is nocturnal and solitary, breeding in summer.

Krebs' fat mouse (*Steatomys krebsii*), S204, is similar to the fat mouse but is slightly larger: total length 13 cm (11,8–14,6 cm); tail 5 cm (4,4–6,1 cm); weight 24 g. Where the species' distributions overlap, Krebs' fat mouse is greyer than the fat mouse. The underparts and front feet are white, the hind feet are the same colour as the body (hind feet white in the fat mouse and tiny fat mouse). Females have two pairs of mammae on the chest and two pairs on the belly (same in pygmy mouse and tiny fat mouse; fat mouse females usually have at least six pairs).

SUBFAMILY PETROMYSCINAE

One genus in the subregion.

The **pygmy rock mouse** (*Petromyscus collinus*), S206, occurs in arid, rocky areas in the western subregion. It is buffy yellow with greyish white underparts and feet. The ears are large. The tail is heavily scaled and sparsely haired. Total length males 20 cm, females 17 cm; tail males 9,5 cm, females 8,6 cm; weight males 20 g, females 22 g. Litters of up to three are born in summer.

The **Brukkaros pygmy rock mouse** (*Petromyscus monticularis*), S205, is rare and has a very restricted distribution in southeastern Namibia. It is smaller than the pygmy rock mouse; its tail is shorter than the head and body, and the ears are less than 12 mm long. Endemic.

CANERATS

Two species in the subregion.

GREATER CANERAT

Groot rietrot
Thryonomys swinderianus

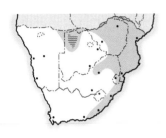  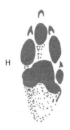

Description A rat as big as a rabbit, stockily built with coarse, spiny hair. Speckled dark brown on the upper parts, sometimes with a rusty tinge around the base of the tail; the underparts are white or light grey. The ears are small and rounded, and almost hidden by the hair. The muzzle is blunt and has a protruding pad in front of the nostrils. The incisor teeth have two grooves near their inside edges (the lesser cane rat has evenly spaced grooves). There are three fully developed toes on each foot, each with a slightly curved claw. The tail is short. Females have three pairs of mammae on the flanks. Total length males 72 cm (67–79 cm), females 66 cm (65–67 cm); tail males 19 cm, females 18 cm (16,5–19,5 cm); weight males 4,5 kg

(3,2–5,2 kg), females 3,6 kg (3,4–3,8 kg). Exceptionally males from the subregion reach over 7 kg, and they can be fattened up to 9 kg in captivity. *See scale drawing on p. 94.*

Habitat Reedbeds and thick, tall grass near water. Crops such as maize and sugar cane provide good habitat.

Diet Roots, shoots and stems of grass and reeds. It can become a pest by eating cereals and root crops such as potatoes and groundnuts.

Life history Gestation 137–172 days; up to 8 per litter (average 4) are born in August–December. Babies are born fully furred, active and with their eyes open, and can follow their mother after an hour. They are weaned at four weeks. Preyed on by leopards, baboons, pythons and servals. Canerat meat is very palatable, and large numbers are caught and eaten by people.

Behaviour Mostly nocturnal but may also be active at dawn and dusk. Shelters in the densest parts of reedbeds, in grass tussocks or in holes and under tree roots. Grass and reeds are bitten off near the base and the stems are cut into short lengths which are eaten one by one.

Small groups of up to about 10 live in patches of suitable habitat, but how social they are is uncertain. The alarm signal is a whistle, and when startled they thump the ground with their hind feet. If suspicious of danger they freeze, and if alarmed dash away and then stop suddenly. They swim well. Disputes involve butting with the pad at the front of the muzzle.

Field sign Runways through vegetation, piles of discarded stems and leaves and faeces at feeding sites. Droppings are compact flattened pellets about 2 x 1 cm, light coloured and rough surfaced with a distinctive groove up one side.

Conservation Canerats are agricultural pests, but they are also a valuable source of meat. Destruction of wetlands deprives them of habitat, but they thrive in cereal crops and sugar cane.

LESSER CANERAT S148   C
Klein rietrot
Thryonomys gregorianus

Description Similar in build and colour to the greater canerat, but considerably smaller. The grooves on the front of the incisor teeth are more or less evenly spaced (near the inside edge of the teeth in greater canerat). Total length 52 cm (41–58 cm); tail 14 cm (11–17,5 cm); weight 1,9 kg (1,4–2,4 kg). *See scale drawing on p. 94.*

Habitat Dense grass and reedbeds, but also inhab-

its drier areas, including rocky hillsides.

Dict Roots, shoots and stems of grass and reeds.

Life history Litters of up to three are born in late summer or early winter.

Behaviour Nocturnal, sheltering during the day under the cover of thick vegetation on in holes in the ground. Lives in family groups but forages singly. Grasses and reeds are bitten off near the base and eaten in short lengths, one by one.

Field sign Runways through vegetation, piles of cut stems, and scattered faeces.

FAMILY PETROMURIDAE

DASSIE RAT

This family contains only one species.

DASSIE RAT S149
Dassierot
Petromys typicus

Description Resembles a squirrel, but although the tail is long and hairy, it is not bushy. Colour varies from grizzled grey to dark chocolate or nearly black; the underparts vary from white to yellow. The head is wide and flat, enabling the dassie rat to fit into rock crevices. There are four digits on the forefeet and five on the hind, all with curved claws. Females have two pairs of mammae on the flanks, just behind the shoul-

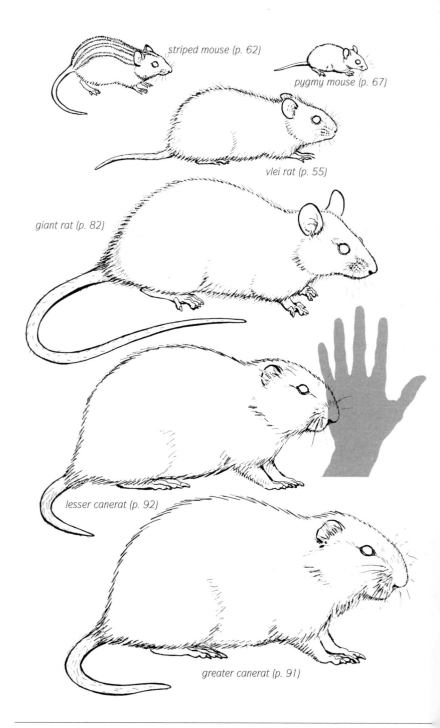

striped mouse (p. 62)

pygmy mouse (p. 67)

vlei rat (p. 55)

giant rat (p. 82)

lesser canerat (p. 92)

greater canerat (p. 91)

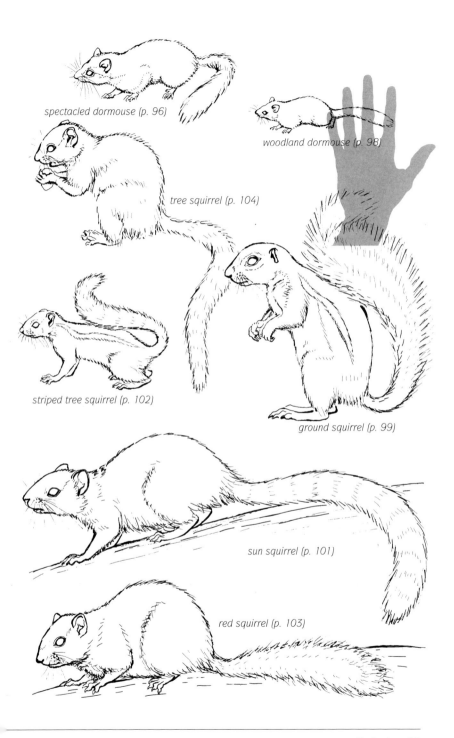

spectacled dormouse (p. 96)

woodland dormouse (p. 98)

tree squirrel (p. 104)

striped tree squirrel (p. 102)

ground squirrel (p. 99)

sun squirrel (p. 101)

red squirrel (p. 103)

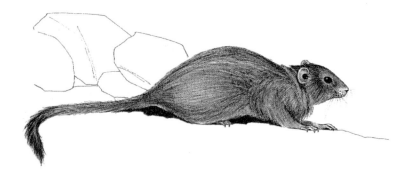

ders, and another pair further back. Head and body length males 17 cm (15,4–21 cm), females 15 cm (13,7–19 cm); tail 14 cm (11,6–17 cm); weight 170–260 g.

Habitat Confined to rocky outcrops, hills and koppies.

Diet Leaves, stems and flowers of grasses, leaves and fruits of other plants.

Life history Litters of two are born in summer.

Behaviour Active during the day, especially in the early morning and late afternoon. Sunbathes in sheltered spots; shelters and gives birth in rock crevices lined with leaves and twigs, and urinates in latrines which stain the rocks yellowish. Lives in pairs or family groups.

Field sign Yellowish or white stains on rocks from urine (also from rock hyrax); droppings are cylindrical with rounded ends (spherical in rock hyrax).

FAMILY GLIRIDAE

DORMICE

Four or possibly five species in the subregion. Dormice have bushy tails and soft, dense, greyish fur. They have four toes on the front feet and five on the hind; four molar teeth on each side of the upper and lower jaws distinguish them from rats and mice, which have three.

SPECTACLED DORMOUSE (NAMTAP)

Gemsbokmuis
Graphiurus ocularis

Description Resembles a small squirrel, silvery grey with whitish underparts (no southern African squirrels are uniform grey). The cheeks and chin and top of the muzzle are white, and there are white patches above the ears, in front of the shoulders, and on the flanks. There is a black mask running from below the ears, around the

eyes and onto the snout. The face and the front legs are sometimes brown. The tail is long and bushy and has a white tip. Largest of the dormice; total length males 25 cm, females 23 cm; head and body length males 13 cm (12–15 cm), females 12,5 cm (12–13 cm); tail males 11 cm (10–12,5 cm), females 10 cm (10–10,5 cm); weight males 83 g (65–85 g), females 55–75 g, up to 96 g when pregnant. *See scale drawing on p. 95.*

Habitat Usually found in rocky areas; also nests in trees and outbuildings. Can be seen in hiking trail overnight huts. It can climb vertical rock surfaces inaccessible to Cape rock elephant shrews and Namaqua rock mice, which live in the same areas.

Diet Insects and other invertebrates, lizards and birds, seeds. Possibly steals honey and larvae from bees' nests.

Life history Litters of 4–6 are born in spring and summer. Females probably breed twice a season. Lives for at least four years.

Behaviour Nocturnal (squirrels are active during the day); a very agile climber among rocks and in trees. Carries food back to the nest. May become torpid for up to a month during food shortages or cold weather.

Conservation Red Data Book: Rare.

The **rock dormouse** (*Graphiurus platyops*), S137, also has dark markings on the face, but its body is lighter grey than that of the spectacled dormouse. The bushy tail has a white tip. Total length 18,5 cm; head and body 11 cm (10,5–13 cm); tail 7,3

cm (6–10 cm); weight 46 g (39–65 g). It occurs in rocky habitats in two areas: a broad strip running approximately southeast to northwest through Namibia, and in northern South Africa, central and east Zimbabwe and western central Mozambique. Nocturnal and solitary, it lives on the ground or sometimes in trees. Eats green vegetation, seeds and insects.

WOODLAND DORMOUSE $\boxed{\text{S138}}$ $\boxed{\text{C}}$
Boswaaistertmuis
Graphiurus murinus

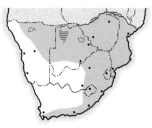

Description A very attractive small rodent resembling a tiny squirrel. Grey or buffy grey (no southern African squirrels are uniform grey), dark around the eyes, white on the lower parts of the face and the chin. The underparts are light grey, the feet are white and the tail is bushy, usually with a white tip. The face and the front legs are sometimes stained brown, apparently from insects that are part of the diet. Total length 17 cm; head and body 9,4 cm (7,8–11,3 cm); tail 7,5 cm (5,8–9,4 cm); weight 28 g (23–34 g). *See scale drawing on p. 95.*

Habitat Widespread in woodland; sometimes lives in roofs and outbuildings.

Diet Eats fruit, insects, and seeds.

Life history Litters of up to three are born in summer.

Behaviour Nocturnal (squirrels are active during the day) and arboreal; lives in holes in trees and under loose bark and often moves into roofs and outbuildings.

The **lesser savanna dormouse** (*Graphiurus parvus*), S 139, is smaller than the woodland dormouse; head and body length 7,5–8,7 cm, but very similar in appearance.

SQUIRRELS

Six indigenous species in four genera. The grey squirrel (*Sciurus carolinensis*), S146, is introduced and occurs in the southwest Western Cape Province.

GROUND SQUIRREL
Waaistertgrondeekhoring
Xerus inauris

 **E** S140 ☼

F   H   0 ⌐

cm

3 ⌐

Description Various shades of cinnamon brown; white on the lower limbs, underparts and sides of the neck. There is a white stripe along the flanks, outlined with darker cinnamon; alternating dark and light stripes run along the bushy tail (in striped tree squirrels there are no stripes on the tail). Each hair on the tail has two black bands (the mountain ground squirrel has three bands). The eyes are large and ringed with white, the ears are very small. The incisor teeth are white (yellow in mountain ground squirrels). The hair on the body, head and limbs is short and bristly. There are four digits on the forefeet and five on the hind, all with long, sharp claws for digging. Females have two pairs of mammae on the belly. The largest of the southern African squirrels; total length males 45,4 cm (41–51 cm), females 44,6 cm (41–49 cm); tail 21 cm (18–24,5 cm); weight males 650 g (511–1 022 g), females 600 g (511–795 g). *See scale drawing on p. 95.*

Habitat Endemic; occurs over most of the south west arid zone where rainfall is 100–500 mm per year, extending eastward in the Free State to areas receiving up to 750 mm. Prefers open ground with sparse bush and grass cover, and needs hard, consolidated ground in which to dig burrows.

Diet Takes a very wide range of vegetable foods: leaves, flowers and seeds, the fruits and runners of tsama melons (*Citrullus lanatus*), berries, bulbs in winter, 'naba' truffles (*Terfezia pfelii*) in mid-winter. Also eats insects, especially termites.

Life history Breeds throughout the year, perhaps at different times in different places; mating in October in the Kalahari. Gestation 42–49 days; litters of 1–4, usually 2. Eyes open at 35 days, first emerges from burrows after 40 days. Females usu-

ally have one litter per year; two if rainfall is exceptionally good. They are preyed on by large raptors, jackals, cats and foxes. Yellow mongooses attack sick or injured ground squirrels.

Behaviour   Active during the day, emerging from the burrow about an hour after sunrise in summer, half an hour later in winter. Less active in windy and wet weather, and stays underground during sand storms. Sunbathes in cold weather, in hot weather lies spreadeagled in the shade and flicks sand onto its back. The long bushy tail is used as a sunshade, which saves 5% of the energy needed to prevent overheating. Climbing is limited to cautious clambering into low bushes.

Shelters in burrows up to about 80 cm deep. It digs its own burrows, takes over or shares those of suricates and yellow mongooses, or takes over and extends whistling rat warrens. Burrows are interconnected into warrens which are continually added to and modified, and often lie under low mounds of excavated soil. Dry grass is gathered to make nests.

Ground squirrels live in colonies of up to 30, which share a warren. Colonies consist of females and their young, with a single dominant individual most active in chasing away strangers. The dominant female may displace others from food with an open-mouthed threat. Nose-to-nose and anal sniffing are used for recognition. Allogrooming, especially between mothers and their young, is common. There may be fights, in which they tail flick and snarl, over food, and when males visit a colony. Youngsters and sub-adults play chase and play fight, giving 'tschip-tschip' calls.

Colonies have home ranges which approximately double in size in winter and spring, when food is scarce. They scent mark with urine, by pressing their anal regions onto the ground, and by rubbing the sides of the muzzle on stones near burrow entrances. Females stay in the colony they were born in; young males disperse as yearlings in late summer. Males visit female groups for mating, stay temporarily and then move on to another colony.

Ground squirrels are extremely alert and vigilant: while above ground they spend 8–14% of their time obviously on the lookout for danger. The alarm signal is a sharp flicking of the tail with its hair erected, and a high-pitched whistle. They squeal-scream when fleeing and badly frightened. Jackals are allowed to approach to within 5 m if the squirrel is near its burrow. Snakes are mobbed and harassed with sideways flicks of the tail until they leave the area. Ground squirrels respond to the alarm calls of birds. They tolerate suricates and yellow mongooses, but drive off slender mongooses. At picnic sites ground squirrels become very tame and easy to observe.
Field sign Warrens with tunnels about 14 cm wide and 11 cm high.

Mountain ground squirrels (*Xerus princeps*), S141, look very similar to ground squirrels but have yellow incisor teeth, and three black bands on the hairs on their tails. (Ground squirrels have white teeth and two bands.) The chromosome number is the same, 2n = 38; chromosome morphology confirms that the two are distinct species. They live in rocky areas running northwest along the western escarpment in Namibia. As far as is known their habits are like those of the ground squirrel.

SUN SQUIRREL S142
Soneekhoring
Heliosciurus mutabilis

Description Variable in colour, usually light brown; in eastern Zimbabwe some are black. The underparts vary from white to brownish or yellow-brown. The long, bushy tail has light and dark bands running across it. There are four toes on the forefeet and five on the hind, all with strong, sharp, curved claws for climbing. The largest arboreal squirrel in the subregion; total length 50 cm (41–56 cm); tail 27 cm (21–30,4 cm); weight 370 g (276–482 g). *See scale drawing on p. 95.*

Habitat Evergreen forest. In areas that are shared with red squirrels, sun squirrels use the higher parts of the canopy.

Diet Eats plant material and insects.

Life history Litters of up to four are born in summer.

Behaviour Active during the day; shelters in tree holes or tangled foliage. Solitary or in pairs. Occasionally forages on the ground. The alarm signal is a clucking call accompanied by tail flicking. Flees to the highest branches and lies along them so as to be invisible from below.

Conservation Like other forest dwellers, sun squirrels suffer from loss of habitat when forests are cleared or replaced by plantations.

STRIPED TREE SQUIRREL

S143 ☼

Gestreepte boomeekhoring
Funisciurus congicus

Description Buffy yellow with a white stripe along the flanks outlined below by a darker band. The tail is distinctly longer than the head and body and is not striped (in ground squirrels the tail is striped, and the same length as the head and body). The underparts are white, tinged yellow near the anus. Females have two pairs of mammae on the belly. The smallest squirrel in the subregion; total length 30 cm, head and body 15 cm, tail 16–17 cm, weight 111 g. *See scale drawing on p. 95.*

Habitat Woodland, especially denser growth with larger trees along watercourses

and on rocky outcrops. Restricted to northwest Namibia in the subregion but is widely distributed further north.

Diet Mainly seeds, nuts and fruit; also some insects.

Life history Litters of two are born in summer, probably with peaks in October and in March; females may have two litters in a season.

Behaviour Active during the day. Shelters in holes in trees, and builds small nests (dreys) of twigs, leaves and grass in the forks of branches. Striped tree squirrels are the only indigenous southern African squirrels that build dreys. Sunbathes lying along branches. Lives mainly in trees but frequently forages on the ground. Excess food is buried in small, scattered caches.

Solitary or in small family groups. The alarm call is high-pitched chattering with tail flicking; bird-like chirps are used to maintain contact between family members. The tail is carried curved over the back like a question mark to provide shade (tree squirrels trail their tails out behind them).

Field sign Nests in the forks of branches.

RED SQUIRREL S144

Rooi eekhoring
Paraxerus palliatus

Description Colour varies widely with locality: lighter in drier areas. The upper parts vary from grizzled dark grey to grizzled black. The underparts, sides of the face, lower limbs and tail are bright reddish, yellowish or auburn, which distinguishes red squirrels from the others in the subregion. The tail is long and bushy. There are four toes on the forefeet and five on the hind, all with sharp, curved claws for climbing. Total length about 40 cm, tail about 20 cm, but size varies with locality and subspecies: head and body averages 18,4–22,5 cm, tail averages 17,6–20,5 cm, weight averages 207–361 g. Females are slightly larger than males. *See scale drawing on p. 95.*

Habitat Forest and woodland with a dense understorey of bushes, small trees and creepers. Where both red squirrels and sun squirrels occur, the red squirrels occupy the lower parts of the vegetation and the forest floor.

Diet Nuts, berries, fruit, roots, buds, bark, lichens and insects, particularly termites.

Life history Mating June–January. Gestation 60–65 days. Births August–March, one or two in a litter. First leaves the nest at 18 days; weaned at 40 days.

Behaviour Active during the day; sleeps in holes in trees or in dense, matted creepers and foliage. Lives in pairs but forages singly except when a female has young that

have just emerged from the nest. Home ranges of a few hectares are marked with urine and anal gland secretion. Males have larger ranges than females. Females aggressively defend the area around the nest when they have young. The resident pair drive away their offspring at the end of their first summer.

Soft murmuring is a contact invitation; hissing, grunting and growling are stress calls that inhibit approach. Clicking, rising in intensity to a trill or warble, signals alertness. When pursued red squirrels flee into heavy cover, or the nest. Unlike other arboreal squirrels they will take cover at ground level.

Field sign Discarded parts of fruits and nuts.

Conservation Like other forest dwellers, red squirrels are in jeopardy from habitat loss and fragmentation of populations. Two subspecies; the **Ngoye red squirrel** (*Paraxerus palliatus ornatus*) and the **Tonga red squirrel** (*P. p. tongensis*) are listed as Vulnerable in the South African Red Data Book.

TREE SQUIRREL

S145

Boomeekhoring
Paraxerus cepapi

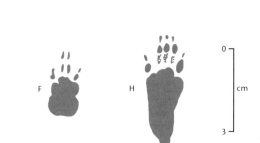

Description The colour of the upper parts varies from pale grey in the west to buffy in the east; some individuals are almost black. The underparts vary from white to yellowish or buffy, or a mixture. The head may be the same colour as the body or may be rusty yellow. In northern South Africa the limbs have a rusty colour. The tail is long and bushy. There are no stripes or bands on the body or tail. Size varies with locality: total length males 34,5 cm (28–58 cm), females 34 cm (29–43 cm); weight males 180 g (76–242 g), females 170 g (108–265 g). *See scale drawing on p. 95.*

Habitat Savanna woodland, in more open areas than the other species of arboreal southern African squirrels.

Diet Seeds, flowers, leaves, berries, fruit and bark of a wide range of plants; acacia gum, lichens, grass, insects. They may eat nestling birds.

Life history Breeds at any time of year, with an October–April peak in births. Gestation 53–57 days; litters of 1–3 (average 2). Emerges from the nest at 20 days, and weans at about 5 weeks. The parents do not provide solid food for the young, even after weaning. Sexually mature at 10 months.

Behaviour Active during the day, especially in the early morning and late afternoon. Sleeps in tree holes lined with grass or leaves. Forages both in trees and on the ground.

Tree squirrels live in groups of one or two adult males or females with subadults and up to seven young. They sleep together, groom one another and anal mark each other. Group members recognise each other by their shared odour. Strangers are chased away from the group's nest hole and feeding areas. Group territories of about half a hectare are defended by adult males and are scent marked by mouth wiping, urination and anal dragging by all group members. A drawn out 'chuck-chuck-chuck' call given while sitting in a prominent position is probably a territorial advertisement.

Predators are mobbed with loud clicking calls that rise in intensity and run together into a harsh rattle accompanied by tail flicking. A high-pitched whistle is an extreme alarm call. Tree squirrels flee to their nest, either directly or via other trees, or they hide in dense foliage or lying along the top of a branch. They climb around the trunks of trees to keep the trunk between them and danger.

A female in oestrus gives a prolonged, loud clicking call similar to the alarm call. She may be chased by several males, including intruders to the territory. For three days after they give birth females leave the nest for only short periods. Males help groom the young. There is a report of a male killing young. Families remain together until the offspring are sexually mature at 10 months old.

Tree squirrels become tame and easy to observe in conservation area rest camps.

Field sign Heaps of discarded shells and food fragments at feeding sites.

MOLE–RATS

Mole-rats are neither moles nor rats; their closest relatives are the hystricomorph rodents such as porcupines. The family is found only in Africa south of the Sahara, and there are six species in three genera in the subregion. All mole-rats have small eyes, small external ears, short legs, short tails and very large, protruding incisor teeth. They live underground, and their feet and incisor teeth are adapted to burrowing. All except the dune mole-rats dig by loosening the soil with their incisor teeth, and kicking it backwards along the tunnel with their feet. Loose soil is pushed up into molehills at the ends of side tunnels running to the surface.

It is while raising mole hills that mole-rats are vulnerable to snakes, carnivores and predatory birds. Since mole-rats rarely emerge above ground the only sign of their presence is usually their mole hills. Much of the burrow system is dug in search of the bulbs, roots and above-ground vegetation that they eat. Many of the bulbs are toxic to most mammals but have no effect on mole-rats. Foraging tunnels are dug when the soil is moist and easy to work. During the dry season mole-rats redistribute soil below ground and plug up disused parts of their burrows.

CAPE DUNE MOLE-RAT

(E) · S129 · ☀ · ☾

Kaapse duinmol
Bathyergus suillus

Description The body is light buff, with the grey bases of the hair showing unevenly. Patches of whitish hair mark the position of the eyes and ear openings, and there is sometimes a white blaze on the forehead. The underparts are dark grey. Each foot has five toes with long claws. There is a single deep groove down the upper incisors. Largest of the mole-rats; total length males 33 cm, females 30 cm; tail 5 cm; weight males 900 g, up to 2 kg, females 670 g, rarely above 1 kg.

Habitat Confined to sandy soil in the southwest of the subregion.

Diet Up to 60% of the diet is green vegetation, the rest roots and bulbs. It can be a serious pest of root vegetables and garden plants.

Life history Litters of up to four young are born between September and December. After weaning pups begin to play fight; this escalates to fighting, and they disperse at about two months old.

Behaviour Adults are solitary, each maintaining its own system of 250–400 m of tunnels. One individual can throw up 500 kg of soil per month into molehills. They

undermine roads and runways and chew through buried cables and pipes. They drum with the hind feet, possibly for reproductive or territorial signalling.

Field sign Burrows up to 20 cm in diameter; molehills up to 75 cm across and 50 cm high.

NAMAQUA DUNE MOLE-RAT

Namakwa-duinmol
Bathyergus janetta

Description Drab or silvery grey on the sides, with a broad dark band down the middle of the back from the neck to the rump. The underparts are dark grey. The eye and ear openings are marked by white hair, the head and face are suffused with black, and there is often a small white blaze on the forehead. The upper incisor teeth are deeply grooved. The tail and hind feet are fringed with long, stiff bristles to assist in pushing soil out of the burrow. Colour and body size vary with locality: near the coast colours are drab and size smaller, 450 g for males, females smaller; inland, colours are more striking, with silvery flanks and black dorsal stripe, and size larger, males 700 g. Total length males 25 cm, females 23 cm; tail males 5 cm, females 4,5 cm.

Habitat Sand dunes or sandy alluvium.

Diet Roots, bulbs and above-ground vegetation.

Life history Litters of 2–7 are born between about September and December.
Conservation Red Data Book: Rare.

COMMON MOLE-RAT

S132

Vaalmol
Cryptomys hottentotus
Cryptomys darlingi

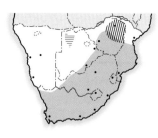

■ *C. hottentotus*
///. *C. darlingi* Distribution in Mozambique is uncertain

Description Buff-grey to slate grey; the underparts are lighter and there is usually, but not always, a small white blaze on the forehead (*C. darlingi* has a larger blaze than *C. hottentotus*). The fur is short, soft and silky. The tail is very short and is fringed with long hair. Males are larger than females. Size and weight vary regionally: animals are smaller in drier areas. Total length 15 cm, tail about 2 cm, weight 50–140 g.

Cryptomys darlingi and *C. damarensis* (see next species) were previously considered to be subspecies of *C. hottentotus* but are now recognised as separate species on genetic grounds.

Habitat Most soils except heavy clay and hard, compacted types.
Diet Roots, bulbs, tubers and the underground stolons of grasses. Food is stored in

chambers close to the communal nest.

Life history Breeding is seasonal but timing varies with locality. In the Western Cape Province one or two litters are born in September–February.

Behaviour Social; colonies of up to 14 share a system of up to 1 km of burrows. Typically there is a single breeding pair in each colony, often the founding pair. Offspring remain in the colony as helpers, caring for their siblings, and do not breed unless they disperse. Helpers extend and maintain the burrow system; if the burrow is opened they soon close it with a plug of soil pushed into place with the hindquarters, and they defend the burrow against other mole-rats. Dispersal occurs only after good rains.

DAMARA MOLE-RAT
S132A ☼ ☾
Damara-mol
Cryptomys damarensis

Description Fawn or very dark brown to black; animals of both colours occur in the same colony. There is a distinctive large patch of white on the head, and there may be white stripes along the middle of the back and belly. The fur is short and thick. The incisor teeth are white and ungrooved. Total length males 16,6 cm (15–20 cm), females 17 cm (15–18 cm); tail 2 cm; weight 160 g (up to 300 g in males). Reproductive animals are largest, and males are bigger than females.

Cryptomys damarensis was formerly classified as a subspecies of *C. hottentotus*.

Habitat Largely restricted to red Kalahari sands.

Diet Underground bulbs, roots and corms, including gemsbok cucumbers (*Acanthosicyos naudianus*) and species toxic to other mammals. Large bulbs and tubers are rarely eaten completely and provide a renewable food source when they regenerate. Food is stored near the nest.

Life history Only one female in each colony breeds. Gestation about 80 days. Up to 3 litters of 1–5 pups per year, at any time of year; weaned at 4 weeks.

Behaviour The most social of southern Africa's mole-rats. Lives in colonies of up to 41 animals founded by a reproductive pair. Offspring remain in the colony as helpers but their reproduction is socially suppressed. Only about 10% ever disperse to found colonies. Colonies fragment if one of the breeders dies.

Intense burrowing follows good rains: one colony of 16 dug 1 km of burrows and threw up 2,5 tonnes of soil in a month. Food discovered at this stage sustains the colony until the next rains. Nests may be as deep as 2 m below ground, where temperature is more stable than at the surface.

Communicates with aggressive snorts and high-pitched squeaks. The reproductive female initiates courtship, which includes drumming with the hind feet. Defensive behaviour is distinctive: rolling onto the back and doubling up with mouth wide open.

CAPE MOLE-RAT

Kaapse-blesmol
Georychus capensis

Description Buff to orange-buff; some individuals are distinctly reddish. Characteristic features are the black markings on the head, white snout and chin, and large patches of white around the ears and eyes and on the forehead. The flanks are greyer than the rest of the body; on the underparts the hair is grey at the base with broad white or buff tips. Total length 20 cm, tail 3 cm, weight 180 g.

Habitat Found in coastal sand dunes and sandy soils, and also the mountains of the Western Cape Province.

Diet Bulbs, roots and tubers; it may become a pest in gardens. Food is stored in a chamber near the nest.

Life history One or 2 litters of up to 10 (average 6) are born in September–December. Young disperse at about two months old.

Behaviour Solitary and territorial; other mole rats are aggressively repelled from entering the burrow. Drumming with the hind feet is used as a territorial signal. In the mating season males and females drum at different frequencies to advertise their sex and reproductive condition.

PORCUPINE

One species in the subregion.

PORCUPINE
Ystervark
Hystrix africaeaustralis

Description Unmistakable among southern African mammals. From the shoulders to the tail the upper parts of the body are covered by long (up to 60 cm) pliable spines and shorter (up to 25 cm) sharp, stiff quills. The only other southern African mammal with spines is the hedgehog, which is much smaller (*see scale drawing on p. 123*) and whose prickles are only up to 2 cm long. There is a crest of long, coarse, black and white hair from the top of the head to the shoulders. The rest of the body and the limbs are covered with short, coarse, flattened black hair, often with white patches on each side of the base of the neck. The end of the short tail carries a rattle of hollow, open-ended quills with narrow, stalk-like bases. The muzzle is heavy and blunt, the eyes and ears small. The legs are short and heavily built, with large feet. Females have one pair of mammae, on the flanks just behind the front legs. Total length males 84 cm, females 86 cm; tail males 13 cm, females 12 cm; weight varies with locality: Free State 12 kg (10–18 kg); Northern Province 15,4 kg (13–17,5 kg); Zimbabwe 18 kg, maximum 24 kg. Females are heavier than males.

Habitat Occurs in all sorts of habitats except the Namib Desert coastal strip.

Diet Eats a very wide range of vegetable material, including fruit, bulbs, roots, bark and seeds. It can be a pest in crops and gardens. Debarks alien syringas (*Melia azedarach*) in preference to white stinkwood (*Celtis africana*), and red syringa (*Burkea africana*) and horn-pod trees (*Diplorynchus condylocarpon*) in preference to acacias. Chews bones for their calcium and phosphorus content.

Life history Only one pair in each group breeds; subordinate females mate but do not conceive. Oestrous cycle 17–42 days; physical contact with a male is necessary for female cycling. Mates May–December. Gestation 94 days. Births August–

January with a peak in January. Litters of 1–3 (half of litters are single) are weaned at 10–20 weeks. They are mature at 9–18 months and full-grown at 1 year. Porcupines are preyed on by lions in the Kalahari, and at least one pride in the Kruger NP specialises in killing them.

Behaviour Nocturnal, sheltering during the day in caves, rock crevices or burrows taken over from springhares or aardvarks, and adapted. Travels up to 16 km in a night's foraging.

The basic social unit is a monogamous pair with their current litter, but larger groups (up to 14 in one case) may share a burrow. Pairs are bonded by daily mating. Groups have a home range of up to 400 ha, part of which is defended as a territory. Ranges are scent marked, more heavily by males than by females. Youngsters forage under the protection of their parents up to an age of at least 5,5 months but have also been seen foraging alone at 2,5 months.

When a porcupine is threatened it erects its crest, spines and quills, especially on the side facing the threat. It growls, rattles its quills, stamps its feet and shakes its tail to rattle the hollow quills at its tip. If approached it rushes backwards or sideways at its attacker, trying to stick quills into it. The quills are not barbed, and the porcupine cannot shoot them, but they are only loosely rooted in the skin, so they pull loose and stay in the target. Scenes of confrontation are littered with detached quills.

Field sign Detached quills, diggings, debarked trees and roots, tooth marks 1,5 cm wide on food remnants and bones (no other rodent leaves such wide marks). Droppings are rounded, 2–3 cm across, or cylindrical, 4–7 cm long, stuck together in clumps, black and often containing fibres from roots and bark.

SPRINGHARE

The Pedetidae includes only one species, whose relationship to other rodent species is uncertain.

SPRINGHARE/SPRINGHAAS
Springhaas
Pedetes capensis

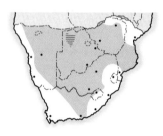

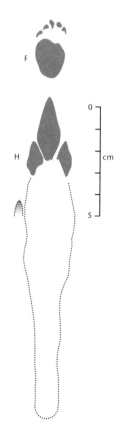

Description The over-all impression is of a miniature kangaroo, reddish buff on the head, back, and flanks; white or white washed with yellow on the underparts and the underside of the tail (except in northeast Zimbabwe, where the underside of the tail is black). The tail is long and has a broad, bushy, black tip. The head is small, the eyes are large, and the ears are long and pointed. The hind legs are very long and strongly developed. The front feet have five curved claws; the hind feet have four large, sharp-edged triangular claws. In a dazzling light the eyes shine very brightly, and springhares can be recognised by the up-and-down movement of their eyes as they bob their heads and then move away. Total length 80 cm (76–86 cm); tail 43 cm (35–46 cm); weight 3,1 kg (2,9–3,9 kg). *See scale drawing on p. 123.*

Habitat Widespread; its main habitat requirement is sandy soils. It occurs in dry areas but not in true desert. Under favourable conditions springhares can reach densities of four per hectare.

Diet Grass leaves, seeds and underground stems; bulbs and corms. A selective feeder with a preference for freshly sprouted grass leaves; may be a pest in crops.

Life history Gestation 72–82 days. Single young (twins in less than 1% of births) are born at any time of year, with a peak in July and August in the Free State.

Females can give birth 3–4 times a year. Young remain in the burrow and are suckled until nearly fully grown at 6–7 weeks old. Springhares fall prey to several mammal predators, including African wild cats, leopards, caracals, brown hyaenas, lions, cheetahs and ratels. They are also popular as human food.

Behaviour Very strictly nocturnal, sheltering during the day in burrows that they dig themselves and not emerging until about an hour after sunset. Burrows are up to 46 m long, with 2–11 entrances, which the resident plugs with soil while it is inside, and an escape tunnel running to just below the surface. Each springhare has its own burrow but several animals may congregate on patches of good grazing.

Field sign Burrows 20–25 cm in diameter plugged with soil during the day. Shallow, crescent-shaped diggings for roots, etc. Droppings are pale, flattened and squarish with a groove across the end, about 2 cm long. Tooth marks 8 mm across.

O R D E R
LAGOMORPHA

FAMILY LEPORIDAE

RABBITS AND HARES

In the subregion the family Leporidae includes two species of hares, five species of red rock rabbits, and the riverine rabbit. Hares are long-legged fast runners, and their young are born fully furred, mobile and with all their senses developed. Rabbits are less fleet of foot, they shelter in burrows or under cover of rocks, and their young are born blind and relatively helpless in fur-lined nests. There are also differences in the incisor teeth, the chromosomes and the morphology of the sperm.

CAPE HARE

S122 C

Vlakhaas
Lepus capensis

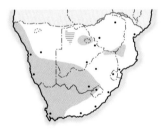  

Description Colour varies with locality. Towards the south and west the upper parts are light buff, finely speckled with black, the sides of the nose and the cheeks are tinged with yellow, the nuchal patch on the nape of the neck is brownish pink. The underparts are pinkish buff, or the belly is pure white with ochre-buff bands separating the white from the colour of the flanks (underparts in scrub hare are white with no ochre-buff band). The tail is black on top and white underneath. In north-east Botswana the colour is lighter; the upper parts are pale grey, speckled with grey, the sides of the nose, cheeks and nuchal patch are light grey, the underparts are white with an ochre yellow margin, and the black on top of the tail is less distinct. The fur is soft and woolly, the ears are very long and the eyes are large. The hind legs are very long and strong, with large feet. The tail is short. The upper incisor teeth are narrower than in scrub hares. Size varies with locality. In the Western Cape Province total length 60 cm (55–62 cm); tail 12 cm (10–14,5 cm); weight 2 kg (1,7–2,5 kg). In the Makgadikgadi Pan area, Botswana, total length 48 cm (44–54 cm); tail 9 cm (7–11 cm); weight 1,65 kg (1,36–2,33 kg). Females are slightly heavier than males.

Habitat Open grassland or grassland with light scrub; prefers more open habitat than the scrub hare, and even occurs in desert. At least seasonally it is independent of water. *See scale drawings on pp. 123, 182 and 329.*

Diet Grass, preferably short and green. In the Karoo, it browses bushes in winter when grass is in short supply.

Life history Gestation 42 days. Litters of up to 3 (average 1,6) are born above ground at any time of year, with a peak in summer (October–February in Botswana, July–December in the Free State). Taken by carnivores from small spotted cat upwards, and by large raptors.

Behaviour Active from dusk to dawn and occasionally during the day in cool, overcast weather. During the day it rests in forms (see Field sign) in patches of thicker cover or under bushes. Solitary, although small groups may congregate on patches of rich grazing. A female on heat may be attended by several males who fight for mating rights. When pursued by a predator a hare runs straight until the predator is just behind it, and then dodges suddenly to the side. This is why hares run for hundreds of metres in front of vehicles and appear to dive under the front wheels when the vehicle gets close. Cape hares use holes dug by other species to escape from predators, behaviour which has not been recorded for scrub hares.

Field sign Forms, small patches of flattened vegetation or bare soil showing the impression of the fore and hind parts of the body, in the shelter of long grass or bushes. Small heaps of pellets about 10 mm long, slightly flattened blunt ovals, pale coloured and rough surfaced.

SCRUB HARE
Kolhaas
Lepus saxatilis

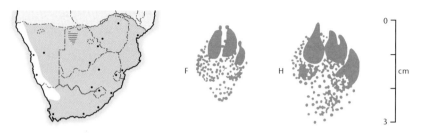

Description Greyish or buffy, with fine black speckles; the underparts are pure white (pinkish white or white with ochre-buff bands in the Cape hare); the nuchal patch on the nape of the neck is orange-buff; the short, fluffy tail is black on top and white underneath. The fur is soft and woolly. The eyes are large, and the ears are very large, especially in animals from the southwestern Cape (ear length 14,4 cm), decreasing to 10 cm in the Kruger NP and northeastern Zimbabwe. The hind legs are long and strong; the hind feet are very large and have long hair between the pads. The incisor teeth are wider than in Cape hares. Total length 40–60 cm, weight 1,5–4,5 kg, size decreases from southwestern Cape (mean weight of males 3,19 kg) northeastwards to Zimbabwe (2,04 kg) and Kruger NP (1,92 kg); females are slightly larger than males. *See scale drawing on p. 123.*

Habitat Savanna woodland, mixed grass and scrub; avoids areas of open grass, and is not found in true desert.

Diet Grass. Prefers fresh young growth.

Life history Gestation 42 days. Up to three young (usually two) are born at any time of year with a peak in summer (September–February). Taken by carnivores from African wild cat and black-backed jackal upwards, and by large raptors.

Behaviour Active from dusk to dawn; during the day it rests in forms (see Field sign) in patches of thicker cover or under bushes. Solitary, although small groups may congregate on patches of rich grazing.

A scrub hare that detects a potential predator while it is still at a safe distance moves off with a rocking-horse action that flashes the white underside of the tail. This may be a signal to the predator that it has been detected and has lost the element of surprise that it needs to make a kill. When pursued by a predator the hare runs straight until the predator is just behind it, and then dodges suddenly to the side. This is why hares run for hundreds of metres in front of vehicles and appear to dive under the front wheels when the vehicle gets close.

Field sign Forms, small patches of flattened vegetation or bare soil showing the impression of the fore and hind parts of the body, in the shelter of long grass or bushes. Small heaps of pellets about 10 mm long, slightly oval and flattened, pale coloured and rough surfaced. In the spoor the marks of the pads of the hind feet are obscured by the long hair between them.

RED ROCK RABBITS
Genus *Pronolagus*

Five species in the subregion. Two of them, which do not yet have common names, are recent divisions of Smith's red rock rabbit (*Pronolagus rupestris*), based on genetic and skull characteristics. Red rock rabbits can be distinguished from hares by their stockier build, smaller ears, and tails which are not white underneath. They live in rocky areas, and so have a patchy distribution within the areas shown on the maps. They are active at night, and shelter during the day in deep rock crevices. They are solitary, but may share restricted areas of rocky habitat and congregate in areas of good grazing. Several males may gather when a female is on heat. They eat grass, with a preference for young growth. They defecate in middens up to 1 m across and 10 cm deep. The droppings are flattened and slightly oval, 10 mm across, medium brown when fresh, with a rough surface (klipspringer droppings are elongated, dassie droppings spherical).

SMITH'S RED ROCK RABBIT

Smith se rooiklipkonyn
Pronolagus rupestris
Pronolagus saundersiae
Pronolagus barretti

\\\ *P. rupestris*
'/// *P. saundersiae*
≡ *P. barretti*

Description All three species are rufous brown, grizzled with black; the rump and hind legs are bright rufous, the sides of the face are grey, the underparts are pinkish buff and the nuchal patch on the nape of the neck is rufous. *P. rupestris* has a black or black and dark red tail, *P. saundersiae* has a deep red tail, and *P. barretti* has a light sandy tail and a sandy undertone to its fur. Total length 53 cm; head and body length 45 cm (38–54 cm); tail 8,6 cm (5–11,5 cm); weight 1,6 kg (1,4–2 kg).

Life history One or two young are born in summer.

NATAL RED ROCK RABBIT

Natalse rooiklipkonyn
Pronolagus crassicaudatus

Description Rufous brown, grizzled with black. The rump and the backs of the hind legs are bright rufous, the underparts are rufous buff and the forehead and the sides of the face are grey. This species can be recognised by the off-white band that extends from the chin along the lower jaw and upwards to the nuchal patch at the nape of the neck, which is brown or grey. The tail is ochre-brown, short and not bushy. Largest of the red rock rabbits: total length 57 cm; head and body length 51 cm (46–56 cm); tail 6,5 cm (3,5–11 cm); weight 2,6 kg (2,4–3 kg). *See scale drawing on p. 123.*

JAMESON'S RED ROCK RABBIT

E S126 **(**

Jameson se rooiklipkonyn

Pronolagus randensis

Description Rufous brown, grizzled with black. The rump and the backs of the hind legs are lighter. The head is light grey flecked with brown, which contrasts with the colour of the body. The nuchal patch on the nape of the neck is rufous, and the underparts are pinkish buff. The tail is large and bushy (short and not bushy in the Natal red rock rabbit), and is ochre-brown with a black tip. Total length 56 cm; head and body 46 cm (42–50 cm); tail 10 cm (6–13,5 cm); weight 2,3 kg (1,8–3 kg).

Life history One or two young are born at any time of year.

rock dassie (p. 125)

springhare (p. 114)

Cape hare (p. 116)

Natal red rock rabbit (p. 121)

riverine rabbit (p. 124)

scrub hare (p. 118)

hedgehog (p. 34)

porcupine (p. 112)

RIVERINE RABBIT

Rivierkonyn / oewerkonyn
Bunolagus monticularis

Description Grey, grizzled with black; the flanks are tinged rufous, the chest and belly are tinged yellow and the eyes are ringed with yellow. A diffuse black band along the side of the lower jaw, broadening out and disappearing towards the base of the ear, a greyish tail, and hairy feet are characteristic of this species. The ears are much larger than red rock rabbits', almost as large as hares'. Total length 52 cm; head and body length 43 cm (34–47 cm); tail 9 cm (7–11 cm); weight 1,7 kg. *See scale drawing on p. 123.*

Habitat Restricted to dense riverine scrub along seasonal rivers in the central Karoo.

Diet Green grass in summer and the leaves of shrubs in winter.

Life history Litters of one or two are born in shallow, fur-lined burrows at any time of year except the coldest winter months.

Behaviour Nocturnal and solitary; during the day it lies up in a form, a shallow, unlined depression in the ground.

Conservation Southern Africa's most endangered mammal. Its habitat is being cleared for agriculture and attempts at captive breeding and reintroduction to a protected area have not yet been successful. Riverine rabbits are not very fast runners, and so they are vulnerable to domestic dogs. Red Data Book: Endangered.

ORDER
HYRACOIDEA

FAMILY PROCAVIIDAE
DASSIES / HYRAXES

Three species in the subregion: two live in rocky areas and one in trees. Their digestive systems are unique: bacteria ferment cellulose in a large sac at the end of the small intestine, and in a double caecum. Dassies are sometimes called rock rabbits, but they are not even distantly related to rabbits, and can easily be distinguished from them by their short, rounded ears. Their closest relatives are the elephants and dugongs, but even this relationship is very distant.

They all have a chunky, compact build with a short neck and legs, and no tail. There is a pair of large, pointed incisor teeth in the upper jaw (triangular in males, rounded in females), and two pairs in the lower jaw. The ears are short, and barely show above the fur. The soles of the feet are padded with glandular tissue which keeps them moist for better grip. The front feet have four toes, the hind feet three, all of them with nails which form a grooming claw on the inner toes of the hind feet. In the middle of the back is a dorsal spot of longer hair, overlying a patch of glandular skin. The colour of the spot varies within and between species.

ROCK DASSIE / ROCK HYRAX   S290 ☼
Klipdas / dassie
Procavia capensis

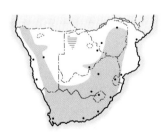

F   H

0
cm
5

Description   Colour varies with locality: light grey in the south; darker, slightly reddish brown in the north; paler and yellower in northern Namibia. Looks darker when the coat is fluffed up in the cold, exposing the dark underfur, and glossy when the coat is sleeked down in hot conditions. Long, black, tactile whiskers are scattered throughout the coat. Behind the ears there is a buffy patch. The dorsal spot is usually black (dorsal spot cream, yellowish or reddish in yellow-spot rock dassie, white

or off-white in tree hyrax). The penis is 20–25 mm from the anus (60–70 mm in yellow-spot rock dassie). Females have one pair of mammae on the chest and two pairs on the belly (yellow-spot rock dassie sometimes has no mammae on the chest; number of mammae is variable in tree dassie). Total length 54 cm (45–60 cm); weight males 3,7 kg (3,2–4,7 kg), females 3,4 kg (2,5–4,1 kg). Males are larger than females, and the tips of their incisor teeth show below the upper lip. The Kaokoveld rock dassie (formerly *Procavia welwitschii,* S291) is now recognised as a subspecies, *Procavia capensis welwitschii.* There are two genetic groups within what is now *Procavia capensis* and a review of their taxonomy is overdue. *See scale drawing on p. 123.*

Habitat   Occupies a very wide range of habitats from sea level to the high Drakensberg, and from high rainfall areas in the east and south to the Namib Desert. It occurs on the fringes of forest but not in forest itself. Its only definite requirement is for shelter among rocks; drains, culverts and similar structures provide adequate substitutes, allowing it to live in the suburbs of some cities. It is independent of water as long as it can eat green or succulent vegetation, otherwise it has to drink.

Diet   Takes a wide range of vegetation including grass, forbs, shrubs and trees. Prefers easily digested foods but can utilise low quality forage and plants that are poisonous to domestic stock.

Life history   Reproduction is triggered by day length. In the far southwest, mating February, births September–October, progressively later further north; in the former Transvaal, mating May–July, births December–February; in Zimbabwe, mating August–September, births March–April. Gestation 230 days (very long for an animal this size). Two young per litter in females at 2 years, 4–6 per litter at 5 years and older. Young are born fully furred and active, first take solid food at a few days old, and are weaned by 1–5 months. They continue growing for at least 3 years; females are sexually mature at 16–17 months, males at 28–29 months. Potential lifespan 15 years; rarely older than 8 years in the wild. They are eaten by black eagles (*Aquila verreauxii*), caracals and leopards. Small stock farmers who kill predators are plagued by dassies instead.

Behaviour   Active during the day, feeding in the morning and afternoon, and resting in shelter to avoid the midday heat. Sometimes feeds on moonlit nights. Food is cropped with the cheek teeth. Spends only 5% of the time feeding, interacting and moving around, probably as a way of saving energy and avoiding predators. Also saves metabolic energy by allowing body temperature to fall by as much as 3 °C and then warming up by basking in the sun with the coat fluffed up to expose the dark underfur.

Rock dassies are exceptionally agile, the soft, moist pads of their feet providing a secure grip even on smooth rock. They also climb trees to reach the foliage.

Colonies of 3–17 females and their young are controlled by a territorial male, sometimes with another male on the periphery. Group size depends on the availability of shelter. Males without territories are solitary. Territorial males monopolise access to breeding females. Subadult males leave their groups at 15 months. Males are aggressive and use their sharp incisor teeth to inflict serious wounds on each other, and on females. Fights over territories and the females they contain may be fatal; territorial take-overs usually occur at the end of the mating season when the breeding males are in poor physical condition.

Juveniles form nursery groups. Where rock hyraxes and yellow-spot hyraxes live together their young form mixed species nursery groups for which adults of either species act as sentinels. Adults of either sex may kill youngsters.

Faeces accumulate in piles at latrine sites. Urinates in specific spots, and dried urine produces white streaks on rocks, sometimes accumulating into substantial amber deposits which at one time were used in folk remedies.

The alarm call is a squeal, and a bark for immediate danger. Growls and tooth grinding are aggressive signals. The hair on the dorsal patch is raised, and the odour of the gland's secretion released, during aggression and courtship.

Field sign Middens of roughly spherical, rough-surfaced, dark droppings about 1,5 cm in diameter (klipspringer pellets are elongated, rock rabbit pellets are slightly flattened). White streaks on rocks from dried urine.

YELLOW-SPOT DASSIE / YELLOW-SPOT HYRAX S292 ☼
Geelkoldas
Heterohyrax brucei

Description Colour varies with locality: in the south of the range, dark brown tinged red on the upper parts, pale yellow on the underparts, with a creamy buff or reddish ochre dorsal spot. In Zimbabwe, grey tinged with brown on the upper parts, white underparts, and a yellowish dorsal spot (dorsal spot black in rock dassie, white or off-white in tree dassie). Slightly lighter on the face, with distinct white spots above the eyes (face the same colour as the body in rock hyrax). Long, black tactile whiskers are scattered through the coat. The penis is 60–70 mm from the anus (20–25 mm in rock dassie). Females have one pair of mammae on the chest and two pairs on the

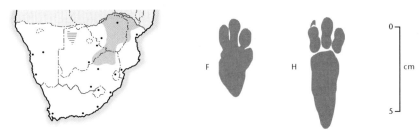

belly, or just the two pairs on the belly (rock dassie always has one pair on the chest and two on the belly). Total length 50 cm (46,5–56 cm); weight 3 kg (2,3–3,6 kg).

Habitat Rocky areas. Often lives in mixed colonies with rock dassies.

Diet Takes a wide range of vegetation; browses more than the rock dassie.

Life history Litters of two are born in March–April. Breeds at the same time as rock dassies in the same area. Young are born fully furred, with eyes open, and fully mobile. They are preyed on by black eagles (*Aquila verreauxii*), caracals and leopards.

Behaviour Studied in less detail than rock dassies, but what is known shows behaviour to be similar in the two species. Juveniles form nursery groups, which may be mixed with rock dassies where the two species both occur. Adults serve as sentinels. Gives repeated, long (1,5 second) shrill calls in sequences up to 5 minutes long.

Field sign Indistinguishable from rock dassies.

TREE DASSIE / TREE HYRAX
Boomdas
Dendrohyrax arboreus

S293 R (

Description Grey with a brown tinge, slightly darker in high rainfall areas. The dorsal spot is white or off-white (black in rock dassie, cream, yellowish or reddish in yellow-spotted rock dassie). Slightly lighter on the head, with white fringes around the ears and pale patches above the eyes. The underparts are white or creamy white. The coat is much longer and woollier than in the other dassies, and does not have

long, tactile whiskers. The eyes do not shine brightly in a beam of light. Females have one or two pairs of mammae on the belly, and sometimes one pair on the chest. Total length 47,5 cm (43–52 cm), weight 1,5–3,5 kg.

Habitat Evergreen and riverine forest (rock dassies do not penetrate beyond forest fringes); may occur in suburban gardens. Three separate populations: in central Mozambique, southern KwaZulu-Natal, and Eastern Cape.

Diet Browses on a wide variety of tree leaves (55 species in the Eastern Cape). The composition of the diet varies with availability of different species.

Life history Gestation 7–8 months (very long for an animal this size). Litters of 2–3; breeding season unknown.

Behaviour Nocturnal and solitary, sheltering during the day in holes in large trees. Arboreal and a nimble climber, but not as agile as the rock dassies. Defecates and urinates in middens in tree holes or on the ground. Its most distinctive call is a wailing scream; also gives a cackling bark, growls and grinds its teeth. Much more likely to be heard than seen.

Field sign The droppings are small rounded pellets, clumped into cylindrical clusters about 5 cm long and 2 cm thick. They are deposited in middens in tree holes or on the ground at the base of trees.

Conservation Like all forest dwellers, tree dassies suffer from loss of habitat to development and agriculture. Selective felling of large trees deprives them of their nesting holes. Red Data Book: Rare.

ORDER

PROBOSCIDEA

FAMILY ELEPHANTIDAE

ELEPHANTS

One species in the subregion, two in the world. Both are threatened by loss of habitat as growing human populations encroach on their living space.

AFRICAN ELEPHANT

S289 ☼ ☾

Afrikaanse olifant
Loxodonta africana

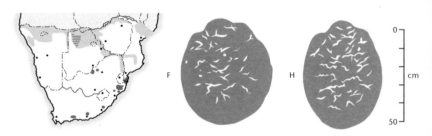

Description Enormous and unmistakable. The skin is naked, rough and grey-brown, but very often coloured by mud and dust. The head is very large, carried on a short, thick neck. The nose and upper lip are enormously elongated into the muscular, mobile trunk with the nostrils and two 'fingers' at its tip. Most, but not all, adults have a pair of curved tusks, which are very large incisor teeth, growing from the upper jaw. Some adults (nearly all of the females in Addo Elephant NP) lack tusks, some have only one. The eyes are small relative to the huge size of the animal. The ears are very large, flat and roughly triangular, often with tears and holes in them. On each side of the head, roughly half way between eye and ear, is the opening of the temporal gland, whose secretion sometimes makes a dark streak down the face. The legs are thick columns to bear the weight of the body and head. The front feet are roughly circular, with five blunt toenails; the hind feet are oval, with four blunt toenails. The soles are padded, allowing silent movement. The tail is thin, up to 1,5 m long, and has a whisk of long, thick hairs at the end. Females have one pair of mammae, low on the sides of the chest, just behind the forelegs. Shoulder height males, Hwange NP 3,5 m, Etosha NP 3,45 m, Kruger NP 3,4 m, females 2,7 m (up to 2,9 m); weight males up to 6 tons; a female from Gonarhezhou NP, Zimbabwe 3,8 tons; 2,5–2,8 tons and up to 3,2 probably typical. The tallest bull ever measured was 4 m at the shoulder with a guessed weight of 10 tons, from Angola.

Besides the male's penis and the female's mammae, a number of features distinguish the sexes: males are larger, 1,3 times as tall and twice as heavy as cows; they typically have thicker tusks and wider heads. In profile males have a more rounded forehead, and a more curved outline to the back (see p. 132). Both sexes have a thick flap of skin hanging between their hind legs.

An elephant's height can be estimated from the size of its footprints. For females shoulder height is approximately 5,5 times the length of the hind footprint. For males shoulder height is approximately 5,8 times the length of the hind footprint.

The heaviest reliably weighed tusks are 102,3 kg and 107,3 kg, from near Mt Kilimanjaro. The heaviest tusks from the subregion are 84,1 kg and 83,2 kg, from Mozambique. Tusks recovered from the Kruger NP 'magnificent seven' bulls weighed 50–58 kg.

Habitat Historically, elephants had a very wide habitat range; present habitats are constrained by human encroachment. In the subregion they are typically found in tree savanna, woodland and grassland near rivers, flood plains and similar areas providing food, water and shade. They move into forest, but do poorly if they have to stay there without access to grassland, as in the Knysna forests. They are dependent on water but can move up to 80 km from it. Their ability to move long distances

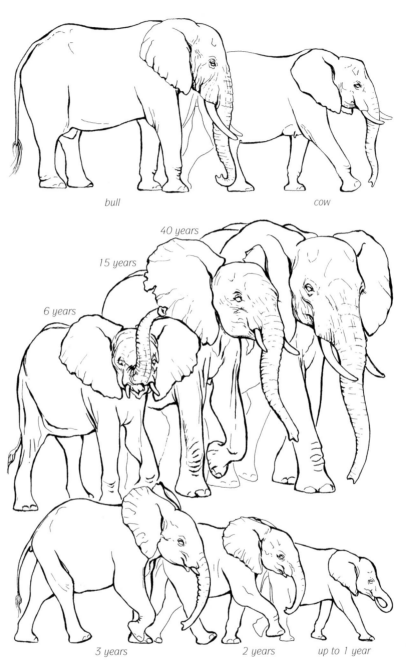

bull

cow

40 years

15 years

6 years

3 years

2 years

up to 1 year

size and age classes

allows them to use several different habitats within a wide area, and to move through habitats that provide no resources, e.g. arid rocky areas between food and water in the Kaokoveld.

Diet Elephants eat any plant material: grass, forbs, the leaves, branches, bark and roots of trees, fruit, seeds, pods, wood, reeds and sedges, etc. In Hwange NP 165 species of plant are eaten by elephants. They are very unselective: when browsing acacias they swallow more wood than leaves.

In summer grass forms the bulk of the diet, replaced in winter by woody plants. In Hwange NP grass is 98% of the diet in February; woody plants make up more than 90% of the diet from April to November. Seeds, pods and fruit are taken in season. They eat soil, salt encrustations and rocks to obtain sodium and trace elements.

Intake is about 150 kg (wet weight) per day. Only about 40% of the dry matter is assimilated, leading to the production of 100 kg of dung per day by a 10-year-old female. This makes elephants a major channel for cycling nutrients from plants to detritus.

Elephants and crops cannot co-exist.

Life history Breeds throughout the year, with more births in early summer, following a higher frequency of mating during and just after the wet season two years previously. Cows are in oestrous for 3–6 days. Gestation 22 months. One young at a birth, rarely (1% of births) twins. Birth weight 120 kg, shoulder height 90 cm. Wean at 3–8 years, just before the birth of the next calf. Calves are vulnerable to lions and spotted hyaenas, and are carefully protected by their mothers and relatives. Their permanent tusks erupt at 18 months in males, 27 months in females. Mean inter-birth interval 3,5–5,5 years. Females stay in their family groups, males move out at 12–13 years. Females are sexually mature at 9–18 years, males at 7–18 years. Potential lifespan is 60 years. In exceptional cases adult elephants may fall victim to predators but these are always, or nearly always, animals that are sick or injured. The only significant cause of violent death for elephants is shooting by humans.

Behaviour Active throughout the day and night, alternating feeding (which occupies about 18 hours of the day) with movement, resting and drinking. Rests in shade at midday. Elephants of all ages lie down to sleep.

Food is picked up or plucked with the trunk, passed to the mouth and chewed only roughly. The trunk is dextrous enough to pick up single seeds, and strong enough to uproot trees. It contains 6 pairs of muscles, divided into over 100 000 units. Trees may be pushed over, bark is chiselled off with the tusks, and roots are dug up with the feet and tusks. As the cheek teeth are worn away they are replaced from behind in a series of six in each half of each jaw. Once the sixth tooth is worn the elephant cannot chew its food properly, and it slowly starves to death.

Elephants drink by sucking 4 litres of water into the trunk and emptying it into the mouth. If water and food are close together elephants drink at least once a day, but if they have to they can go for 3–4 days between drinks. Water intake is 120 litres a day for an adult bull; in Hwange NP elephants drink 80% of the available water. They prefer clean water, and will drink direct from the inlet pipe at pumped waterholes. If no surface water is available they dig in river beds, making large holes that other species also use, or deep narrow wells in which only an elephant's trunk can reach the water.

Highly social. The nuclear social unit is a cow with her calves. These units fuse into groups of 2–10 closely related females — the family group — led by the oldest and biggest cow (the matriarch). Family groups may join others temporarily in herds of up to 100. Exceptionally more than 1 000 elephants of both sexes and all ages may amalgamate. After puberty at about 14 years, males live outside the female social structure in unstable, loosely bonded groups of 2–4, exceptionally up to 20–30, and move back into female herds only in search of cows in oestrous.

Communication is by touch, smell, sight and sound. The trunk combines touching and stroking with sniffing at the mouth, temporal gland and genitals. Reproductive condition in both males and females is signalled by odour (see below). Spreading and flapping the ears, head shaking, kicking up dust, standing tall and mock charging are used to intimidate other elephants, and other species including people. In a serious charge the ears are held back against the neck and the trunk is tucked up under the chin. Elephants are very vocal, producing a wide variety of squeals, screams and high-pitched trumpeting which are audible to humans. However, about three quarters of their vocal communication uses frequencies too low for humans to hear, commonly down to 14 vibrations per second. The upper harmonics of these calls are the 'tummy rumbles'. Some infrasonic calls are very loud, 110 decibels, and carry for at least 5 km.

Elephants show an unexplained fascination with their dead: even old elephant bones are carefully investigated and carried around.

An area's bulls have a dominance hierarchy. From the age of 25 bulls periodically go into musth as their testosterone levels rise to six times the usual level. Musth becomes more regular and lasts longer as bulls age, then periods become shorter after 45. Musth bulls wander widely in search of oestrous females, joining female herds, checking their members and consorting with cows that are close to oestrous. Their temporal glands swell and produce a sticky secretion, they dribble urine continuously (up to 400 litres per day) with the penis sheathed, staining the penis sheath and the inside of the back legs dark green, and generating a strong, sharp odour. They walk with their heads high and become very aggressive towards other males, which avoid them. They give loud (up to 110 decibels) contact calls; part of one call sounds like water sloshing in a pipe. Musth bulls are highly favoured as mates and oestrous females do their best to attract them. Females follow musth bulls' urine trails, an oestrous female's group companions rumble in chorus, females answer musth bulls' calls, and when a musth bull moves into a breeding herd the females back towards him and urinate to demonstrate their sexual status. The odour of a female's urine changes 2,5 weeks before oestrous.

Musth bulls will fight to the death over access to females. In the restricted area of

Addo Elephant NP musth bulls kill young males often enough to slow the growth of the population.

By the time she is ready to mate an oestrous female is being followed by a high-ranking, preferably musth, bull. She stops running away, the bull puts his trunk on her back, levers himself upright against her, supporting himself on his back legs, and she backs towards him. Copulation takes 45 seconds. Mating may be repeated 3 or 4 times over about 24 hours and a cow may mate with more than one bull.

Cows do not necessarily leave their herd to give birth. Other females may gather around and help clean the membranes off the baby. Babies can stand and walk within an hour of birth. They suck with their mouths, not their trunks. Females rarely allow calves other than their own to suck.

Elephants are not territorial. Home range size varies with habitat: 126–1 000 km^2 in Kruger NP, 5 800–8 700 km^2 in northwest Namibia. Bulls have larger ranges than cows: in Kruger NP 200–1 700 km^2. In northern Namibia, daily movements are determined by the localities of food and water. During severe droughts elephants move an average of 54 km in 24 hours, with a maximum of 68 km.

An elephant's ears make up 20% of its total skin surface area, and up to 12 litres per minute of blood flows through the network of large blood vessels just under the thin skin on their back surfaces. By flapping its ears an elephant can cool the blood flowing through them by at least 3 °C, shedding up to 60% of the 4 kW of metabolic heat that it generates. There are no sweat glands in the skin, but the skin is not waterproof and so water evaporates from it to provide additional cooling. Under extreme heat stress elephants stick their trunks down their throats, suck up water and spray it over their heads and backs.

Field sign Faeces are roughly spherical, very coarse and fibrous with undigested fragments of wood and bark (rhino faeces are comparable in size but are more cylindrical). Demolished trees and bushes; elephants leave ragged ends on branches, black rhinos cut them neatly at a 45° angle. Mud smears on trees and rocks above 1,8 m can only be made by elephants. Holes dug in river beds.

Conservation Southern African elephant populations are the most secure on the continent. The elephant population of South Africa increased from only 120 in 1920 to 8 589 in 1991, of which 7 278 were in the Kruger NP. The area in which elephants occurred increased from 1 000 km^2 to 26 000 km^2. Elephant numbers in fenced areas increase by 6,7% per year; at present the only ways to avoid overpopulation and subsequent ecological degradation are to continuously increase the area of land in national parks and reserves at the same rate as the elephant population grows, or to kill elephants.

Even at the continental level, and taking into account the dangers of poaching, elephants are much more secure than wild dogs, cheetahs, rhinoceroses and less glamorous species such as riverine rabbits. Elephants are one of the hunter's big five, and ecotourism's big seven. Their Red Data Book classification is Out of Danger. CITES: Appendix I.

ORDER
PERISSODACTYLA
ODD-TOED UNGULATES

Two families in the subregion, with two species in each. They are large herbivores which carry most of their body weight on the third toe of the foot.

FAMILY EQUIDAE
ZEBRAS

Two species in the subregion, Burchell's zebra and mountain zebra. There are two subspecies of mountain zebra, the Cape mountain zebra and Hartmann's mountain zebra, which are considered separately.

CAPE MOUNTAIN ZEBRA

Kaapse bergsebra
Equus zebra zebra

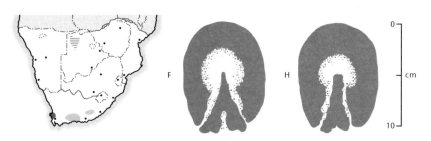

Description A black and white striped pony; it cannot be confused with anything except other zebras. The stripes on the flanks do not extend onto the belly, which is white with a single stripe along the middle (belly is striped in Burchell's zebra). The legs are distinctly striped all the way down (stripes fade out on lower legs of Burchell's zebra). The stripes run crossways on top of the rump (diagonally and lengthways in Burchell's). The stripes are clearly contrasting black and white (Burchell's usually has shadow stripes dividing the white stripes on the rump). Each individual has a unique stripe pattern. The muzzle is black outlined with chestnut. The ears are larger than in Burchell's zebra. There is a short mane down the back of the neck, and a distinct dewlap underneath. The tail has a whisk of long hair on the end. Females have a pair of mammae between their hind legs. Shoulder height males

1,27 m, females 1,24 m; weight males 250–260 kg, females 234 kg (204–257 kg). *See scale drawings on pp. 139 and 221.*

Habitat Mountainous areas of the Eastern and Western Cape Provinces. Prefers grassland to scrub, and is not found in riverine bush. In the rainy season it lives on plateau grassland, and moves onto slopes in the dry season.

Diet A grazer, browsing rarely. Selects for species, but takes both stem and leaf. Preferred feeding height is 4–8 cm. Foals up to an age of 14 weeks eat the faeces of adults to inoculate their guts with microorganisms.

Life history Gestation 364 days. Single foals are born at any time of year, with a peak in spring and early summer in the winter rainfall regions, and in summer in the semi-arid, summer rainfall regions (Mountain Zebra NP). First grazes at a few days old; weaned at 10 months, before the birth of the next foal. Females first foal at average 5 years (between 3 years 3 months and 8 years 9 months); males are sexually mature at 5 years, full grown and first breed at 7 years. Lifespan is at least 25 years. All Cape mountain zebras are in conservation areas where the only large predators are leopards, and they suffer no significant predation.

Behaviour Most active during the day, alternating bouts of grazing with resting; avoids harsh weather by sheltering in kloofs and shallow caves. Drinks twice a day, with a strong preference for clean water.

The basic social unit is the breeding herd of a stallion with up to five mares and their offspring. New herds are formed when young stallions acquire young females that have just left the herd that they were born in. Old herd stallions may be displaced by younger challengers in violent conflicts.

Stallions run in the rear when herds flee from danger, and walk at the front when they go down to water. Home ranges are 3,1 to 16 km², not defended as territories.

Dominance among the mares of a herd is maintained largely by threats: pulling back the ears, lowering the head and baring the teeth. Mothers aggressively drive other zebras away from their newborn foals. High ranking mares may kill foals of low ranking mares.

Young males leave the herds that they were born in when they are 2–3 years old, and join bachelor groups in which there are dominance hierarchies. Young females leave their natal herds when they first come into oestrous. They will not join a herd controlled by a stallion that is related to them.

Field sign Dust baths. The dung is kidney-shaped lumps, 5 cm or more across, characteristically with a crack across the middle, often loosely stuck together.

Conservation Cape mountain zebras almost became extinct in the 1930s. The Mountain Zebra NP was proclaimed specifically for the protection of the few that survived, and after a shaky start during which numbers in the park shrank to only three, they began to increase in numbers, and have now been translocated to other reserves. Red Data Book: Vulnerable. CITES Appendix I.

HARTMANN'S MOUNTAIN ZEBRA

S297

Hartmann se bergsebra
Equus zebra hartmannae

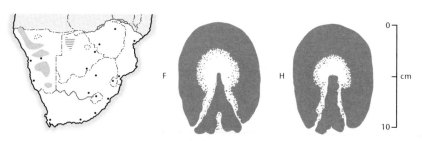

Description Very similar to the Cape mountain zebra, but the stripes on the rump are more even in width. Slightly larger than Cape mountain zebras: shoulder height 1,5 m; weight males 298 kg, males older than 7 years 336 kg, females 276 kg. *See scale drawing on p. 221.*

Habitat Occurs where mountains and lowlands meet, using the two areas according to the availability of food. Dependent on water.

Diet Grazers.

Life history Gestation 362 days. Single foals are born at any time of year, with a November–April peak. Mothers drive other females away from their newborn foals so that mother and young imprint only on each others' stripe patterns and odour.

Burchell's zebra

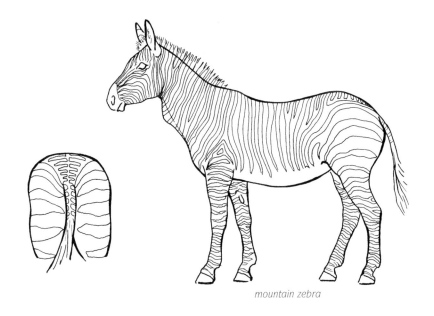

mountain zebra

Foals start grazing after only a few days, and wean at 10 months. Mares first breed at three years. Preyed on by lions, spotted hyaenas, leopards and cheetahs.

Behaviour Grazes mostly in the early morning and late afternoon, resting in shade during the midday heat. Dust-bathes regularly. Drinks at least once, and in the dry season twice a day. If surface supplies dry up, it will dig for water. May make movements of up to 100 km to reach grazing after local rain.

The basic social unit is the breeding herd of a stallion with up to four mares and their foals. Stallions fight fiercely when assembling a herd. There is a dominance hierarchy among a breeding herd's mares. Young males are driven out of the herds by their mothers at an age of 12–14 months. Males with no mares form bachelor herds with dominance hierarchies established by inhibited fighting. Larger, older animals have higher rank. Young females that leave their natal herd before they are sexually mature join bachelor herds. Aggregations of up to 30 or 40, including both breeding herds and bachelor groups, may form temporarily.

Meetings between herd stallions are tense, with stamping, sniffing and lateral displays with arched neck and lashing tail. Stallions protect their herds from predators by running in the rear of the herd as they flee, and kicking and biting attackers.

Stallions investigate mares' reproductive condition by sniffing and flehmen of their urine and genitals. Females urinate more frequently as they come into oestrus, but repel premature sexual advances by kicking backwards.

Foals groom their mothers but grooming between adults has not been recorded.

The alarm calls are a sudden snort or a two-syllable 'kwa-ha'. Submission is signalled by squealing. Soft lip smacking is a contentment and short-range contact call.

Field sign Dust baths. The dung is kidney-shaped lumps, 5 cm or more across, characteristically with a crack across the middle, often loosely stuck together.

Conservation This subspecies is secure. CITES Appendix I.

BURCHELL'S ZEBRA / PLAINS ZEBRA

Bontsebra (Bontkwagga)
Equus burchelli

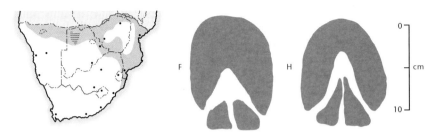

F   H

0

cm

10

Description A black and white striped pony. Can be mistaken only for mountain zebra. The stripes on the flanks run on to the belly (belly is white with a single stripe along the middle in mountain zebra). Stripes fade out on lower legs (distinctly striped all the way down in mountain zebra) and run diagonally and lengthways on top of the rump (crossways in mountain zebra). On the rump there are usually chestnut or yellowish shadow stripes in the middle of the white stripes (not in mountain zebra). In KwaZulu-Natal and Etosha NP the stripes on the rump are less distinct. Each individual has a unique pattern, and aberrant patterns occasionally occur. The muzzle is black. Ears are smaller than in mountain zebra. There is a short mane down the back of the neck, and no dewlap. The tail has a whisk of long black hair on the end. Females have one pair of mammae between their hind legs. Somewhat bigger than mountain zebra: shoulder height males 1,35 m (up to 1,37 m); weight males 320 kg (290–340 kg), females 260 kg. *See scale drawings on pp. 139 and 221.*

Males are a little larger than females and have a narrow black stripe running vertically between their hind legs; in females this stripe is wide.

Habitat Open woodland, scrub and grassland. Strictly dependent on water and rarely moves more than 12 km from it. Very widely translocated.

Diet Prefers short, green grass but will readily take tall, coarse growth. Occasionally browses, and will eat the fire-scorched leaves and twigs of mopane (*Colophospermum mopane*) and round-leaved kiaat (*Pterocarpus rotundifolius*). Being unselective bulk feeders, zebras are less sensitive to food quality than other large herbivores, and can maintain body condition on very poor forage.

Life history Oestrous lasts up to 5 days; gestation 360–390 days. Single foals are born at any time of year, with a peak in summer. In Kruger NP 85% of births are between October and March. Birth weight 30–35 kg. A foal stands after about 10 minutes, walks after half an hour and can run after an hour. It starts eating grass within a few days and weans at 11 months. Lions and spotted hyaenas take adult zebras; foals are taken by lions, spotted hyaenas, leopards and cheetahs. In southern Africa they stand their ground to wild dogs. Zebra provide 16% of lion kills in Kruger NP, 29% in Savuti, and 80% of spotted hyaena kills in the dry season in Savuti.

Behaviour The main periods of activity and grazing are the cooler early morning and late afternoon. Drinks at least once a day, with a strong preference for clean water. If the water is muddy it may scrape a hole into which clean water seeps, or try to skim cleaner water from the surface. Home ranges cover 110–220 km² in Kruger NP. Considerable distances are covered (up to 160 km in Etosha NP) to reach grazing.

The basic social unit is the breeding herd of a stallion with an average of four or five mares (Kruger NP) and their foals. Stallions fight viciously for control of females. Males that do not hold breeding herds join bachelor groups of up to 15, with dominance rank depending on age. Groups are bonded by mutual grooming. Aggression from herd stallions keeps bachelors on the fringe of areas in which zebras occur.

When herd stallions meet they sniff nose to nose, rub their cheeks together and sniff each other's genitals, stamp their forefeet and toss their heads. Submission is signalled by lowering the head, holding the ears back and making chewing movements. Dominance and threat are signalled by holding the head high with ears cocked forward or turned inwards and back, showing the teeth, and chasing.

Males check their mares' reproductive condition by sniffing and flehmen of their urine. Receptive females stand with their legs straddled, their tails to one side and the mouth wide open with lips drawn back. The vulva swells and discharges mucus. Mature mares signal oestrus more subtly than do fillies. Copulation is repeated once every 1–3 hours for about a day.

The alarm call is a high-pitched 'kwa-ha', from which the old name quagga comes. If threatened by predators, herds flee in tight bunches. Top speed is 55 km/h. Herd stallions defend their groups by running in the rear as they flee, kicking and biting attackers. Mares defend their foals similarly. Predators are much more successful if they can separate a zebra from its herd, and the contrasting black and white stripes may allow zebras to see each other more clearly in the poor visibility of a night hunt.
Field sign Dust baths. The dung is kidney-shaped lumps, 5 cm or more across, characteristically with a crack across the middle, often loosely stuck together.

RHINOCEROSES

Two species in the subregion. Both are seriously threatened by commercial poaching for their horns.

SQUARE-LIPPED RHINOCEROS / WHITE RHINOCEROS   S295 ☼ ☾
Witrenoster
Ceratotherium simum

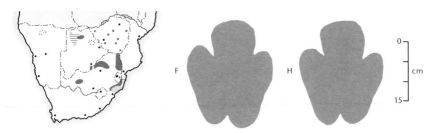

Description The second largest land mammal. The skin is rough, dark grey-brown (same colour as hook-lipped rhino), and appears naked, but has a scattering of coarse bristles. The muzzle is broad, the lips wide and square (upper lip pointed in hook-lipped rhino), and the front of the base of the front horn is straight (round in hook-lipped rhino). The head is long in proportion to the neck, and is carried low (short and carried high in hook-lipped rhino). The ears have small points and a sparse fringe of hair (rounded and thickly fringed in hook-lipped rhino). The neck is massive, with a distinct hump at its base and on the shoulders (no hump in hook-lipped rhino). The body is barrel-shaped and low-slung on short, sturdy legs with three toes on each foot. The tail is 1 m long and has a tuft of dark hair at the tip. Females have a pair of mammae between their hind legs. Shoulder height up to 1,8 m; weight males 2–2,3 tonnes, females 1,3–1,6 tonnes. Only one square-lipped rhino has ever actually been weighed, a young male of 2,13 tons. Maximum horn length from the subregion 1,58 m; horns grow at 2,5–6,6 cm per year. *See scale drawing on p. 153.*

Males have a thick fold of skin running down between the backs of the hind legs. Horns tend to be longer and thinner in cows. Adult females often have a calf at foot.
Habitat Requires grassland, thick cover and water close together, and prefers flat or gently undulating terrain. The most important feature for survival of rhinoceroses is protection from poachers.
Diet A grazer; grass forms 99% of the diet, with a preference for short, fresh growth. It is selective as to species eaten, but takes both leaf and stem. Sometimes eats soil to obtain minerals.

Life history Gestation 16 months. Single calves are born at any time of year, with peaks in March and July in KwaZulu-Natal. Birth weight 40 kg. Wean at 12–18 months, sometimes as late as 2 years, and stay with the mother for 2–3 years. Sexually mature at 4–5 years; males usually first mate after establishing a territory at 12 years old. Average inter-birth interval 22 months to 3,5 years. The sex ratio at birth is heavily skewed: 173 males to 100 females. Lifespan 40–45 years: 30% of deaths, and 50% of male deaths, are due to fighting. Calves very occasionally fall prey to lions and spotted hyaenas. Adults are killed by poachers. Translocated elephants have caused problems by killing square-lipped rhinos: at least 17 incidents are known in Pilanesberg NP. This is also recorded, but very rare, for resident elephants in the Kruger NP.

Behaviour Active at any time of the day or night, but tends to avoid the midday heat and cold weather by lying up in cover. It spends about 50% of the time feeding. Grass is cropped short between the 20 cm wide lips; the rhino takes a series of bites, swinging its head in an arc, then steps forward and repeats the process, keeping its head low. It drinks in the late afternoon and into the night, every day if water is freely available, but can go four days between drinks in dry periods when it must walk further to water. Wallows in water and mud to cool down and to remove parasites. Rubs on trees, rocks and termite mounds; rocks and stumps develop a polish from long use.

Females and their young live in overlapping home ranges of 6–8 km² where food is abundant, increasing to 10–15 km² under poorer conditions; in Kruger NP the average home range is 23 km² (7–45 km²). On patches of good grazing small amicable groups are formed.

Mature bulls are territorial and solitary but tolerate other males in their territories as long as they behave submissively and keep away from females. Territories cover 0,75–2,6 km² in Umfolozi; 6,2–13,8 km² in Kruger NP; 5–11 km² in Kyle NR, Zimbabwe. Only territorial bulls spray urine backwards onto bushes. Borders are marked with faeces deposited in middens. After defecating a bull kicks the faeces around and gouges the soil of the midden with his hind feet; young males kick only weakly, and females do not kick at all. Neighbours may share a midden, and square-lipped rhino middens may also be used by hook-lipped rhinos. Neighbours meeting on their common boundary rub their horns on the ground and stand head to head pushing sideways against each other's horns. Bulls who have no water in their territories leave every 3–4 days to drink, passing through other bulls' territories as they go. If confronted they squeal and shriek and hold their ears back to demonstrate their submission, and are usually allowed to proceed. When off their territories bulls urinate in the same way as subordinates. Fights are usually over territory or females. They involve horn sparring, shoulder ramming and hooking at the body, and can cause fatal injuries. The skin is 25 mm thick to provide protection during fights. Bulls that are supplanted by challengers may be allowed to remain on their old territories as long as they behave submissively.

Bulls check the reproductive condition of cows passing through their territories by sniffing and flehmen, and try to stop cows that are coming into oestrous from leaving the area. Initial advances are aggressively rebuffed, and herding and courtship may go on for two weeks. Copulation lasts up to 30 minutes; they mate only once, with multiple ejaculations, and may stay together for 2–6 days afterwards.

Cows give birth in heavy cover. Calves are not fully mobile for about three days; during this time they stay hidden while the mother grazes nearby. Calves walk in front of the mother (behind in hook-lipped rhino).

Eyesight is not particularly acute but hearing and scent are very sensitive. Communication is by sound and visual signals: snorting and snarling with the ears back is a signal to keep away, panting is an invitation to move closer. Squealing and shrieking are submissive signals but also occur during fights and when a bull is herding a female into his territory. Calves also squeal when frightened.

Square-lipped rhino are more even-tempered than hook-lipped rhino, but cows with calves are fiercely protective and must be avoided. They can charge at 40 km/h.
Field sign Spoor is indented at the back (no indentation in hook-lipped rhino). Faeces are dark and contain undigested grass fragments (twigs in hook-lipped rhino faeces). Middens. Mud smears on trees, termite mounds and rocks; polished rubbing spots.
Conservation In May 1994 there were 6 750 square-lipped rhinos in Africa, of which 6 376 were in South Africa, 98 in Namibia, 134 in Zimbabwe, 33 in Swaziland and 18 in Botswana.

up to 3 mths

3 mths–1 yr

1–3,5 yrs

3,5–7 yrs

F

H

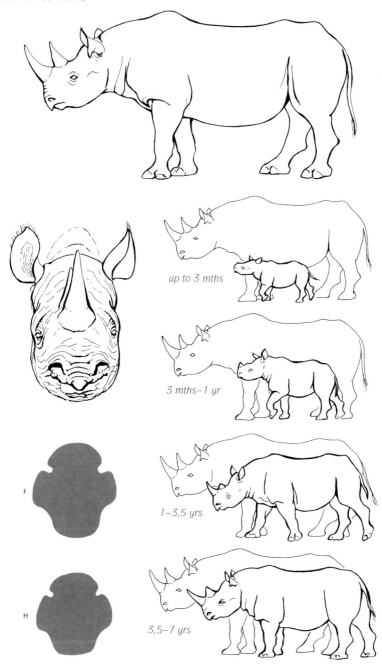

up to 3 mths

3 mths–1 yr

1–3,5 yrs

3,5–7 yrs

F

H

In 1929 there were 150 square-lipped rhinos in the Umfolozi-Hluhluwe area. Over the rest of southern Africa they had been exterminated. Strict protection in the Natal reserves and parks allowed the population to recover to 650 in 1961. The first major translocation was of 97 rhino to the Kruger NP in 1963 and 1964, and square-lipped rhino numbers have continued to increase as animals have been translocated throughout the subregion and further north in Africa. There are now about 2 000 square-lipped rhino in the Umfolozi-Hluhluwe complex. When properly protected, translocated square-lipped rhinos breed well: in Kruger NP there are at least 1 500 and numbers are increasing by 6–9% per year.

Poaching pressure is so heavy that square-lipped rhino only survive if they are in securely fenced, heavily patrolled areas with armed guards and cooperation from people living in the area. CITES: Appendix I.

HOOK-LIPPED RHINOCEROS / BLACK RHINOCEROS
Swartrenoster
Diceros bicornis

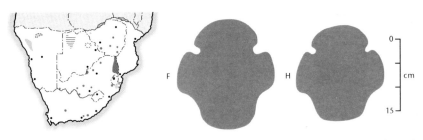

Description   Large and robust. Dark grey-brown (same colour as square-lipped rhino) but often coloured by dust or mud. The skin looks naked, but has a sprinkling of coarse bristles. There are two horns of top of the nose, the front one has a rounded base (base of front horn of square-lipped rhino is straight). The upper lip is triangular and muscular, and is used to grasp branches while feeding (lips square in square-lipped rhino). The head is short relative to the neck, and is carried high (long relative to neck and carried low in square-lipped rhino). The ears are rounded (narrower in square-lipped rhino), with a fringe of hair that is often lost in animals from areas which experience regular frost. There is no distinct hump on the shoulders. In the lowveld and Kwa-Zulu Natal, but not in drier areas, the flanks are usually marked by darker, sometimes bloody, patches caused by parasitic worms (does not occur in square-lipped rhino). The legs are short and sturdy, with three toes on each foot. The tail has a tuft of coarse hair at the tip. Females have a pair of mammae between their hind legs. Shoulder height 1,4–1,65 m; weight males 708–1 022 kg, females 718–1 194 kg). Maximum horn lengths from the subregion: front 105 cm, rear 52 cm;

'iorns grow at 4–6 cm per year. *See scale drawing on p. 153.*

Males have a thick fold of skin running down between the backs of the hind legs. Horns tend to be longer and thinner in cows. Adult cows often have a calf at foot.

Hook-lipped rhinos in KwaZulu-Natal, Zimbabwe and Mozambique are *Diceros bicornis minor*; in the Northern Cape and Namibia they are the bigger *D. b. bicornis*. Addo Elephant NP has populations of *D. b. michaeli* translocated from Kenya, and *D. b. bicornis* in the Suurberg section.

Habitat Woodland with thickets and permanent water is typical habitat, but it also occurs under arid conditions. Under present circumstances the principal habitat requirement is protection from poachers.

Diet Browses leaves and shoots; also eats fruit. In arid areas it obtains water by eating succulents, even such unpalatable types as *Euphorbia virosa*.

Life history Gestation 15 months. Single young are born at any time of year. Birth weight 40 kg. A calf can move with its mother after three hours, but may be left hidden in cover for the first week. It starts browsing after a few weeks, weans at about 12 months, sometimes as late as 19 months, and stays with its mother until 2–4 years of age, when the next calf is born. Average interval between births 2,5 (2–4) years. Females first calve at 6–12 years, males mature at 8 years. Potential lifespan 30–40 years. Calves are taken by lions and spotted hyaenas; adults are killed by poachers. Claims that dehorned females cannot protect their calves from hyaenas do not stand up to critical examination.

Behaviour Active for 30–50% of the day and 90% of the night. Avoids the midday heat by lying up in shade. Drinks in the afternoon. In northern Namibia, may move

over 10 km to water at night and drink only once every 2–3 days. It will dig for water if surface supplies dry up. Females may come to water without their calves, presumably to avoid predators. Wallows in water and mud to cool down and remove parasites. Rubs on rocks, trees and termite mounds.

Twigs and branches up to 1 cm thick are grasped with the upper lip and cut off by the cheek teeth at a 45° angle. Preferred feeding height is 0,5–1,2 m, maximum reach is 1,5 m. If food is out of reach it will pull down branches up to 17 cm thick by hooking the front horn over them.

Usually solitary, except for females with calves, and males courting females, but may form small temporary groups. Home ranges cover 500 km² in Namibia, 4–7 km² in Hluhluwe. Females ranges overlap; males have exclusive ranges. Both sexes defecate in middens and kick the dung around. Hook-lipped and square-lipped rhinos may use the same midden. Only mature bulls spray urine onto bushes.

Bulls investigate females' reproductive condition by smelling and flehmen of their urine. The cow aggressively rebuffs the bull's early approaches, and he will follow her around for up to six days. Copulation lasts 20–40 minutes. Bulls fight fiercely for access to oestrous females. Fighting is the main cause of death in 8–10 year old males. Overstocking an area with hook-lipped rhino leads to 2–3 year old subadults being killed by adults.

Calves are born in heavy cover, and stay hidden for up to a week. They walk behind their mothers (square-lipped rhino calves in front), but may flee in front of their mother.

The sense of sight is not particularly acute; scent and hearing are very sensitive. Of uncertain temper; hook-lipped rhino females with calves are extremely dangerous and should be avoided.

Field sign Neatly pruned bushes with twigs trimmed off at 45°. Spoor has no indentation at the back (indented in square-lipped rhino). Dung contains undigested twigs with ends cut at 45°. Middens. Mud smears on trees, termite mounds and rocks; polished rubbing spots.

Conservation In 1994 there were 2 550 hook-lipped rhinos in the whole of Africa, a decline of 97% in 25 years. South Africa had 897, Zimbabwe had 381, Namibia 583, Mozambique 45, Swaziland 4, and Botswana 4. Only five countries on the continent have populations of more than 100.

Translocated hook-lipped rhinos can breed well: there are 300 in Hluhluwe-Umfolozi and 57 translocated to the Kruger NP have increased to over 200, with numbers increasing at 9% per year. Poaching pressure is so heavy that, except in Namibia, they only survive if they are in securely fenced, heavily patrolled areas with armed guards. Their status is much less secure than that of elephants, which receive much more attention. Red Data Book: Vulnerable, has deteriorated to Endangered. CITES: Appendix I.

O R D E R
ARTIODACTYLA
E V E N - T O E D
U N G U L A T E S

Most members of this order stand on the tips of their third and fourth toes, which are covered by horny hooves. Hippos stand on their second to fifth toes. There are four families in the subregion: the SUIDAE, pigs; HIPPOPOTAMIDAE, hippopotamus; GIRAFFIDAE, giraffe; and BOVIDAE, the buffalo and 33 species of antelope.

All members of the order are basically herbivorous. The Bovidae and the giraffe are ruminants: they have complex, four-chambered stomachs and they re-chew their food, the process known as rumination or chewing the cud. The pigs and hippopotamus have simple stomachs and do not ruminate. The ruminants have no upper incisor teeth; instead they have a tough pad that the lower incisors close against. Pigs and hippos have at least one pair of upper incisor teeth.

FAMILY HIPPOPOTAMIDAE

HIPPOPOTAMUS

Two species in Africa, one of which occurs in the subregion.

HIPPOPOTAMUS   S302   R   (
Seekoei
Hippopotamus amphibius

Description The skin is dark grey, smooth and naked, pink around the eyes and lips and in the folds. The head is massive with an enormous broad muzzle up to 50 cm wide, and a huge mouth in which the upper and lower canine teeth and incisors are enlarged into tusks. The upper and lower canines work against each other, keeping the tips sharp. The eyes and ears are small, set far back and high on the head. The

Artiodactyla **151**

neck is short and thick, with heavy folds of skin, especially in mature bulls. The body is an elongated barrel shape, carried on short, stocky legs. Each foot has four toes with thick nails. The tail is short and flat and is fringed at the end with thick, stiff bristles. Females have one pair of mammae between the hind legs. Shoulder height males 1,5 m (1,3–1,7 m), females 1,44 m (1,1–1,6 m); weight males 1,5 tonnes (970 kg–2 tonnes), females 1,32 tonnes (990 kg–1,7 tonnes). Length of lower tusk above the gum: males 22 cm (12,5–31 cm), females 14 cm (7,5–20 cm); lower tusks up to 50 cm above the gum are known. *See scale drawing opposite.*

Mature males are larger than females, and have much thicker necks with heavier skin folds, and larger tusks.

Habitat Needs water which is at least 1,5 m deep in which to submerge; can survive temporarily in mud holes. If the water that it rests in is brackish, it needs fresh water as well for drinking. Preferred feeding areas are lawns of short grass within 1–2 km of water, but it is able to travel up to 30 km to reach grazing.

Diet A grazer; 95–99% of the diet is grass. Prefers freshly sprouted, short growth and selects palatable, nutritious species. Under conditions of severe food shortage it will take floating water plants, and eat elephant dung. It can do serious damage to crops and gardens. Plays with floating carcases but eats very little, if any, of the meat. Intake up to 13 kg per day, approximately half what is expected from body size.

Life history Gestation 225–227 days. Single young are born at any time of year, with a May–June peak in KwaZulu-Natal; in Kruger NP 70% of births are in October–March with a peak in January–February. Birth weight 30 kg. Begins grazing at 6–8 weeks; weans at 8–14 months. One birth every 2–3 years. Females mature at 5 years, males at 6–8 years. Lifespan 35 years (females). Populations can grow at 8% per year under ideal conditions. Crocodiles take young hippos in the water; lions take young hippo and rarely adults.

Behaviour Spends the day resting in or near water to keep cool, protect the skin from sunburn, and avoid biting insects. Leaves the water to sunbathe on the banks, especially during overcast cool weather in summer, and warm sunny weather in winter. Hippo sweat contains a red pigment that acts as a sun screen. In water it stands

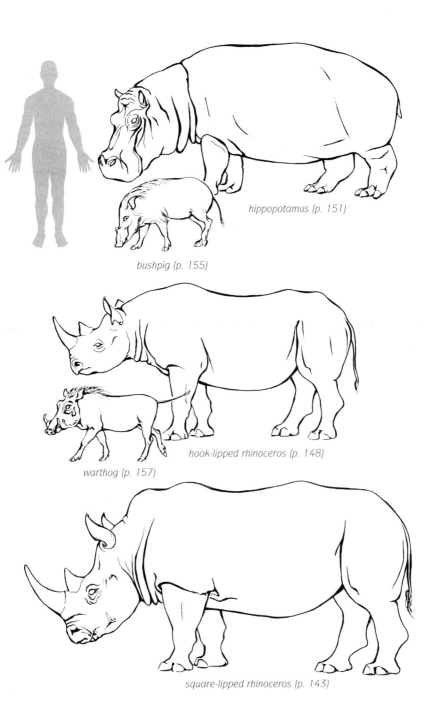

hippopotamus (p. 151)

bushpig (p. 155)

hook-lipped rhinoceros (p. 148)

warthog (p. 157)

square-lipped rhinoceros (p. 143)

or lies on the bottom with only the top of the back and the ears, eyes and nostrils exposed; babies use their mothers as rafts in deep water. It can swim on the surface or under water, and walk along the bottom, staying submerged for up to 6 minutes. Both ears and nostrils can be closed to stop water getting in. As it surfaces it exhales with a series of grunts.

At dusk it moves out of the water to feed for 7–8 hours. Grass is cropped with the hard edges of the wide lips, leaving a short smooth lawn. Overpopulation leads to serious habitat degradation from overgrazing, trampling and erosion. Usually feeds within 2–3 km of water; may travel up to 30 km to feed and wander long distances. One walked nearly 1 800 km from Lake St Lucia to the Keiskamma River.

Lives in schools of up to 30, containing females and their offspring, young males, and a single dominant bull that defends the school's stretch of water as a territory in order to monopolise access to the cows. If suitable water is restricted several schools may occur close together. Territories do not extend away from water. A bull may hold a territory for as long as 12 years. Neighbouring bulls meeting on their boundary stare at each other, turn, and spray dung and urine.

Fights over territory and females are savage: the tusks are used to stab and slash at the opponent, leaving serious wounds even in the 6 cm thick skin on the neck. Battle injuries may be fatal but even in the filthy water that most hippos live in the wounds rarely become infected. Losers are driven out of the territory. Young males are driven out by the dominant bull at about six years old; females stay in the school. Dominant bulls sometimes kill youngsters; whether these are the offspring of other bulls has not been determined. Mothers and babysitters defend their offspring against these infanticidal attacks.

Dominant bulls and maybe others scatter dung and urine by wagging their tails as they defecate. Scattered dung can build up into heaps where hippo paths leave the water. When the bull approaches another hippo it urinates and defecates into the water and the bull tests the water with his vomeronasal organ. If he finds a female in oestrous a brief courtship that involves yawning and sparring precedes mating in the water. The female submerges completely, coming up for breath at intervals. Hippos are the only southern African land mammals that mate in the water.

The most characteristic call is a series of one long roaring grunt and several short ones produced as it surfaces; it also roars, screams, croaks, clicks and whines. Calls transmit through water as well as through air; underwater croaks are probably a short-range contact call. Calls are loud, up to 120 decibels, and probably include sounds below the frequency limit of human hearing.

Yawning displays the tusks and is a dominance signal and sign to intruders of other species, including humans, to keep away. It also occurs in play fights and sparring between young animals.

Females give birth in dense reedbeds or similar cover. Calves are introduced to the herd at 10–14 days. Other females act as babysitters. Females with young are very aggressive. Calves suckle under water, coming up for breath every few seconds.

Young hippo are playful, indulging in play fights and pushing contests.

On three occasions hippos have been seen to rescue animals of other species from drowning or attacks by crocodiles. The motivation behind this is a mystery. They have also been seen to attack and kill animals of other species.

Hippos are the most dangerous wild mammals in Africa. If frightened on land a hippo charges back to the safety of the water, and anything in the way is likely to be trampled. In the water, females attack to defend their babies, and dominant bulls attack to defend their females. If at all possible stay away from hippos.

Field sign Hippo trails wear into two parallel ruts. Dung heaps near paths.

Conservation Development near water deprives hippos of feeding grounds. Abstraction of water from rivers deprives them of resting places. In conservation areas they prosper and sometimes have to be harvested to prevent damage to their habitat. Red Data Book: Rare. CITES Appendix II.

FAMILY SUIDAE

PIGS

Two species in the subregion.

BUSHPIG

S299 ☾

Bosvark

Potamochoerus porcus

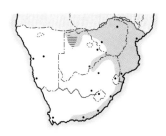
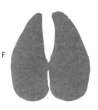
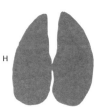
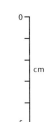

F H cm

Description The body is compact and robust, with a short neck and long head tapering to a blunt snout, and covered by coarse hair (the warthog has a sparse coat of bristles). Colour varies from reddish to dark brown; some are nearly black. There is a crest of long, yellowish hair along the top of the neck and back, and a thick patch of off-white or yellowish hair near the angle of the lower jaw, sometimes extending along the lower edge of the jaw. The ears are high and pointed, with long tufts of hair at the tips, and a fringe of white or yellowish hair on the outer edges. The head is narrower than a warthog's, and except in a few old males, there are no warts on the side of the face. The canine teeth do not rise above the snout as in warthogs. The legs are short, there is a cloven hoof on each foot, and a pair of false hooves just behind them. Females have three pairs of mammae on the belly. Total length males 1,55 m (up to 1,73 m), females 1,46 m (up to 1,54 m); tail males 40 cm (up to 43 cm), females 36 cm (up to 43 cm); weight males 62 kg (46–82 kg, exceptionally to 130 kg), females 59 kg (48–66 kg). *See scale drawing on pp. 153 and 329.*

Newborn young are reddish brown with yellow or buffy stripes running along the body; at three months the stripes fade, leaving them bright orange rufous, at six months the crest becomes white and the face paler.

Habitat Forests, thickets, dense growth along rivers, reedbeds and tall grass, and similar dense cover. It is dependent on water. Moves out of its dense refuges to feed if necessary, but habitat requirements make its distribution very patchy.

Diet Omnivorous: roots for rhizomes, bulbs, tubers, roots, insect larvae and pupae, earthworms; eats fallen fruit, birds' eggs and nestlings. May do serious damage in crops. Readily takes carrion and occasionally kills snakes, frogs, rats, and lambs and kids. Fruit is the preferred food and makes up 40% of the diet when available in summer and autumn; bulbs and woody roots are taken in winter.

Life history Gestation four months. Litters of up to 8 (usually 3–4) are born between October and January in KwaZulu-Natal, November–February in Zimbabwe. Birth weight 700–800 g. Weaning is probably at six months, when the piglets are driven out of the sounder by the parents. Females first give birth at two years old. Lifespan 15 years. Bushpigs are taken by the larger carnivores and allowing these predators to remain in an area can go a long way to controlling crop-raiding pigs.

Behaviour Mostly nocturnal. In farming areas where it is hunted as a pest it becomes strictly nocturnal. In winter when food is scarce it is more likely to be active during the day. Social, living in groups known as sounders of 2–12 (usually 6–8),

with a dominant boar and sow, other sows, juveniles and piglets. The dominant boar leads the sounder, protects the piglets and drives other sounders away from feeding grounds by displaying with his shoulder crest raised, tail wagging and jaws snapping, pawing the ground and throwing up dust and clods of earth. Encounters may escalate to head pushing but serious fighting is rare. Males that do not hold sounders live solitarily or in bachelor groups. Aggregations of up to 30 pigs occasionally form.

Sounders have large home ranges which are not defended as territories, and they will move up to at least 4 km to reach feeding grounds. Faeces are deposited in middens, scent marks are produced by glands on the feet, and dominant boars gouge the bark of trees with their tusks.

Soft grunting is a short-range contact call. The sounder's boar gives a resonant grunt as an alarm call, causing his sounder to scatter into heavy cover. They run with their tails down (warthogs run with tails up).

Bushpigs are the largest animals in the subregion to build nests. Sows bite off grass and pile it into heaps up to 3 m across and 1 m high, looking like small haystacks. They burrow into the heap to have their young. Apart from suckling them, the sows leave the care of piglets to the dominant boar.

Food is detected mainly by smell. Typically forages in damp, soft soil, rooting with the tough disc at the end of the muzzle. Readily wades in water to reach aquatic plants, and can swim strongly. Wallows in mud to cool down.

The lower canine teeth are sharpened by wearing against the upper ones and they form effective weapons, capable of inflicting fatal damage on dogs, and serious wounds on humans. Wounded or cornered bushpigs are very dangerous.

Field sign Droppings are segmented cylinders looking rather like dried figs, up to 8 cm in diameter, sometimes in middens containing up to 40 (average 10) droppings. Patches of soil churned up by rooting. Tusk marks on bark.

Conservation Bushpigs are displaced by intensive development, but benefit from the planting of crops as long as heavy cover remains nearby. They are very difficult to control; electric fencing is reasonably effective in keeping them out of crops. They carry African swine fever and movement of their carcasses is restricted by legislation to protect commercial pig farming.

WARTHOG
Vlakvark
Phacochoerus aethiopicus

S300 ☼

Description The body is compact and robust, with a short neck and long, heavy head tapering to a blunt snout. The wrinkled grey skin is sparsely covered by coarse bristles (the bushpig has a coat of coarse hair). There is a crest of long black, brown or yellowish bristles on top of the neck and back. The ears have rounded tips (point-

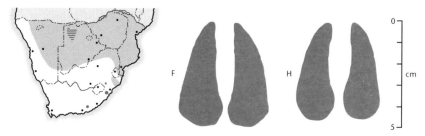

F   H   0

cm

5

ed tips with tassels of long hair in bushpig) and the small eyes are set high on the head. Beneath each eye, on the side of the head, is a prominent lump, the so-called wart. Males have another pair of warts further down the snout. The canine teeth form prominent tusks, growing outwards then curving upwards and over the top of the snout; the upper canines are longer and thicker than the lower ones, which are kept sharp by contact with the upper set (tusks much smaller in bushpig). Along the bottom edge of the jaw is a fringe of bristles growing sideways, often white and curving upwards to give the impression of tusks. The snout is broad, especially where the tusks are rooted in the skull, and it ends in a broad oval pad. The legs are short; each foot carries a cloven hoof with a pair of false hooves close above it. The tail is thin and has a tuft of bristles at its tip; it is carried upwards as the warthog runs (tail carried downwards in bushpig). Females have two pairs of mammae. Head and body length males 1,3 m (1,16–1,44 m), females 1,2 m (1,1–1,3 m); shoulder height males 68 cm (61–72 cm), females 60 cm (54–66 cm); weight males 80 kg (59–104 kg), females 56 kg (44–69 kg). *See scale drawing on p. 153.*

Males are larger, have broader heads and larger, straighter tusks than females, and have two pairs of 'warts' on the sides of the head. Their scrotums are prominent.
Habitat Open woodland, grassland, vleis, floodplains.

Diet The bulk of the diet is grass; everything from seeds to roots and underground stems is eaten. Also takes fruit, bark and invertebrates, occasionally carrion, and is known to kill rats, frogs and snakes. May become a nuisance raiding garbage cans in rest camps and stealing cattle food. Babies eat their mother's dung to inoculate their guts with bacteria. Eats bones, soil and stones to obtain minerals.

Life history Oestrus lasts 3 days; gestation 167–175 days. Breeding season and litter size vary with locality. In KwaZulu-Natal, peak of matings in May, litters of up to 5 (average 3,6), peak of births in October; in Zimbabwe, litters of up to 8 (average 3), births September–December; in Kruger NP births late October–December. In a rapidly growing population in the Eastern Cape, average litter size is four. Birth weight varies widely: 480–850 g. First takes solid food at 2–3 weeks, weaned at 6 months. Sexually mature at 1,5 years, less than 1 year in rapidly growing populations. Sustained population growth of 45% per year can be achieved. Young warthogs are eaten by carnivores from jackal size upwards, large raptors and pythons. Adults are taken mainly by lions and spotted hyaenas. Warthogs supply 12–15% of the diet of lions, leopards and wild dogs in Kruger NP and 13% of the diet of lions in Savuti.

Behaviour Usually active during the day, but there is at least a little activity at night, even in winter. Shelters in large holes, usually abandoned aardvark burrows; also uses small caves, overhangs in river banks, erosion gulleys, and drain culverts. Holes are modified by digging with the forefeet. Warthogs enter their holes backwards so that any pursuer has to face their tusks. One warthog may use the same hole for a few nights running but there is no long-term use of particular holes, and they may be shared with other species. Holes are warm refuges from night-time cold; during the midday heat warthogs lie in shade.

The hard edge of the muscular snout is used for rooting, backed up by the tusks. Because its neck is so short a warthog often goes down onto its knees when grazing or rooting. Grass seeds are combed off the stems with the teeth. It eats both meat and stomach contents from carcases, and has been seen chasing wild dogs and chee-tahs off their kills. Digestion is not particularly efficient and food quality needs to be high. Warthogs are one of the first species to lose body condition during droughts: 80–90% of juveniles under a year old died in the 1982–83 drought in the Kruger NP.

Wallowing in mud is used to cool down and remove parasites; also rubs on rocks, trees and similar surfaces, leaving mud smears lower than most produced by rhino. Warthogs are often seen in groups on areas of good grazing, but their social organi-sation is very loose, and most associations between individuals are temporary. Females are more gregarious than males. The most common grouping is a sounder of a mature boar with one or two females and their piglets. Family groups may stay together for two years. Young males form temporary bachelor groups.

Home ranges of 63–374 ha (average 174 ha) are scent-marked with urine, and by wiping the lips and preorbital glands on trees and similar surfaces, but are not defended as territories. Males mark more frequently than females. Where home ranges overlap, meetings are usually friendly, with recognition by mutual sniffing, and perhaps a bout of mild head pushing. Group members groom each other. Mature boars dominate young males and sows. The contact call is a soft grunt from an adult, a whistling squeal from a piglet.

Females on heat stand and walk with a hunched posture. A boar detects when a female is on heat from the smell of her urine and courts her by approaching with a springy walk, rolling his hips, with his tail cocked up or wrapped along his flank. He champs his jaws, salivates profusely and grunts rhythmically. He rests his chin on her rump and if she is receptive she backs towards him and brief mating follows.

Males compete for females by displaying with mock charges, pawing the ground, and erecting their manes. They fight by wrestling head to head, which escalates to striking with the tusks. The warts under the eyes are protection against these blows.

Being active only in daylight provides some protection against nocturnal predators. Young warthogs suffer heavy predation but the adults, especially males, are likely to respond aggressively to attacks from carnivores. The lower canines are kept sharp by abrasion against the upper tusks, and are very effective defensive weapons. Only lions and groups of spotted hyaenas regularly prey successfully on mature warthogs. When fleeing, warthogs hold their tails up (bushpigs hold the tail down). The alarm call is a snort-grunt.

Baby warthogs are very sensitive to cold and wet, and they sleep on a raised shelf at the back of the burrow, which keeps them out of any water that runs into the hole.
Field sign Holes. Dung is soft, flattened segments, stuck together in rough, often misshapen cylinders, with a distinctive unpleasant smell when fresh. Mud smears low down on trees and rocks. Rooting in both hard and soft ground (bushpig only in soft ground). Trees scraped with tusks. Mud wallows.
Conservation In South Africa warthogs and raw warthog meat may not be removed from the African swine fever area under legislation to protect commercial pig farming from African swine fever. Research into the potential of warthogs for sustainable meat production should be a high priority.

FAMILY GIRAFFIDAE

Two species in Africa, the okapi (*Okapia johnstoni*) and the giraffe. Only the giraffe occurs in the subregion.

GIRAFFE

S303

Kameelperd
Giraffa camelopardalis

Description Unmistakable because of its height and long neck and legs. Covered with irregular patches of fawn, chestnut brown, dark brown or nearly black, on an off-

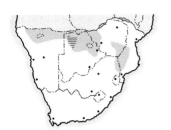
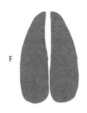

white or buff background. There is a pair of short, thick horns on top of the head, covered with hairy skin except at the tips. Mature bulls and some old cows have at least one bony protrusion in the middle of the forehead, and there are sometimes extra lumps on the head in other places. There is a mane of stiff, dark brown hair down the back of the neck, and a whisk of long, dark hair on the end of the tail. Each foot has a cloven hoof. Females have two pairs of mammae between their hind legs. Measurements from Botswana: shoulder height males 3 m (2,5–3,5 m), females 2,74 m (2–3 m). From South African lowveld: shoulder height males 3,3 m (3,1–3,5 m), females 2,8 m (2,7–2,9 m); weight males 1 200 kg (973–1 400 kg), females 828 kg (700–950 kg). Maximum head height males 5,5 m, females 4,5 m; maximum weight males 1 930 kg, females 1 180 kg. *See scale drawing on p. 164.*

Males are larger than females, and often darker. They have thicker horns, and have a lump on the forehead, which most females lack. The horn tips are bald in males and old females, hairy in younger females.

Habitat Woodland; it does not occur where the canopy is closed, and uses grassland only for travelling. Independent of water if fresh green food is available. Can occur in very arid areas by using vegetation and water along drainage lines. Very widely translocated.

Diet A nearly exclusive browser, taking leaves, fresh shoots, flowers, pods, and fruits from trees such as monkey oranges (*Strychnos madagascariensis*) and sausage trees (*Kigelia africana*). Acacias are the most important source of food. Eats soil to obtain minerals, and very commonly chews bones, especially in areas where the soil is deficient in phosphorus. This habit makes it vulnerable to anthrax and botulism, whose spores persist in carcases and bones.

Life history Gestation 457 days (the only ruminant with gestation longer than a year). Single young are born at any time of the year; twins (stillborn) recorded only once in the wild. Birth weight 100 kg, shoulder height of newborn 1,5 m. Begins eating plants at 2 weeks, weans at 6–8 months. Interval between births 16–25 months. Sexually mature at 4–6 years. Lifespan up to 20 years (females). Numbers can increase by 18% per year where there are no predators. Lions are the main predators, driving giraffe into gullies, over rocky areas, or onto tar roads to make them lose their footing.

Behaviour Most active in the early morning and late afternoon, but also feeds at night in bright moonlight. During the heat of the day stands in shade; at night it is

more likely to rest lying down, sleeping for only a few minutes at a time.

Twigs and branches are pulled into the mouth with the very long and dextrous tongue. Leaves are removed from thorny branches by combing them between the teeth. Freshly grown twigs are nipped off, chewed and swallowed thorns and all, aided by large quantities of sticky saliva. Ends of branches may be brought within reach by chewing at the branch lower down until it bends sufficiently. The thorns on acacia trees slow down a giraffe's feeding; cows feed for 12 hours a day and bulls for

9–10 hours, each tree is browsed for only 2–5 minutes. When feeding on flowers of knobthorn (*Acacia nigrescens*) pollen is carried from tree to tree.

Giraffe can reach up to about 5,5 m, and nearly 90% of feeding is done above the reach of competing browsers such as kudu. Bulls tend to feed at full stretch, with their necks more vertical and their heads tipped upwards. Cows feed with their heads tipped downwards and their necks angled forward. Bulls' extra reach cuts competition with cows for food, but makes them less able to keep watch for predators while feeding, and in Kruger NP lions kill 1,8 times as many bulls as cows.

Giraffe will drink if water is available, but can survive without it. The forelegs are straddled and the knees bent in order to get the head down low enough. Elastic-walled blood vessels in the neck protect the brain from the changes in blood pressure caused by raising and lowering the head. While drinking they are very vulnerable, and will not drink if suspicious of danger.

Females, calves and juveniles occur in herds of up to about a dozen, exceptionally up to 60, with only very loose social ties, and a flexible membership. Young males may form small bachelor groups; mature bulls are nearly always alone, except when they join a female herd for mating.

Home ranges are about 25 km² in the lowveld, 80–120 km² in less productive areas. Young males spar by neck wrestling, twining their necks together and trying to push the opponent off balance. Neck twining also occurs in courtship and as a preliminary to serious fights. Mature bulls fight for dominance by striking at the opponent's legs and body with the head. The length of the neck makes the blows look slower than they are, but the sounds of the impacts can be heard from 100 m away, and broken jaws and necks, and combatants being knocked unconscious, have been recorded. High-ranking bulls intimidate subordinates by standing with their necks nearly vertical to exaggerate their height and bulk.

Males are very mobile, moving from herd to herd searching for females on heat. Females urinate as a bull approaches, and he tests the urine by flehmen and sniffing. If a cow is coming into oestrus he stays with her until displaced by a higher ranking challenger. Courtship involves sniffing and licking, nudging with the head and resting the head on the female's back. Copulation itself is very brief.

Cows leave the herd to give birth in cover. Calves can stand within an hour, and lie hidden for 1–3 weeks. They may form nursery groups with an old female as a guard while their mothers graze up to 3 km away. Social bonds between mother and calf persist past weaning until the birth of her next offspring. Calves suffer heavy predation; first year mortality is 48% in the South African lowveld.

Giraffe are usually silent. They bellow, grunt or snort when alarmed, as when confronted by lions, and moo in distress. The heavy hooves are defensive weapons and can cripple or kill even lions.

Fleld sign Browsing by giraffe prunes trees into an hourglass shape. Their droppings are dark pellets, 2 x 3 cm, tapered at one end and blunt at the other, more scattered than those of antelope due to the long drop.

giraffe (p. 160)

elephant (p. 130)

ANTELOPE AND BUFFALO

presented in the subregion by the buffalo and 33 species of antelope. The family livided into eight subfamilies.

SUBFAMILY ALCELAPHINAE

'x species in the subregion: black and blue wildebeest, two hartebeests, the ssebe, and the bontebok and blesbok, which are subspecies of *Damaliscus dorcas*.

BLACK WILDEBEEST
Swartwildebees
onnochaetes gnou

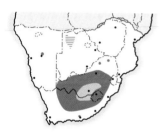  

Description   Mature males are dark brown, appearing black; youngsters and females are lighter brown, new-born calves fawn. The head is large and the muzzle heavy, with wide nostrils. There is a tuft of stiff black hair on top of the muzzle, a black beard, a long fringe running underneath the neck to between the forelegs, and a stiff mane on the back of the neck. Both sexes have horns, which grow downward and forward from bosses on the forehead and then hook sharply upwards into a distinctive pitchfork shape. In calves the horns grow straight up, beginning to curve at about nine months. A hump on the shoulders gives the back a sloping appearance, and the hindquarters are less heavily developed than the forequarters. The tail resembles a horse's and its long white hair hangs almost to the ground. Females have one pair of mammae between their hind legs. Shoulder height males 1,2 m, females 1,15 m; weight males 160 kg, up to 205 kg, females 130 kg, up to 145 kg. *See scale drawing on p. 173.*

All the tufts, fringes and manes are better developed in mature bulls. Males have longer, thicker horns than females.

Habitat   Open karoo and grassland where water is available, preferring areas of short grass for both feeding and good visibility.

Diet An unselective grazer with a preference for short grass; grass provides 94% of the diet in the Free State.

Life history In the Free State, mating mid-March to end April; single calves are born mid-November to early January. In KwaZulu-Natal, mating March, calving November–December. Gestation 253 days. Birth weight 14 kg. Calves can follow their mothers soon after birth, begin grazing before a month old, and are weaned at about six months. Females first mate at 16 months, first calf at 2 years. Males are sexually mature at 16 months and first mate at 3 years.

Behaviour Most active in the early morning and late afternoon; rests in the middle of the day in the open, not seeking shade like most animals. Males spend longer feeding than females because territorial bulls have extra energy demands, and bachelor herds occupy areas of poor grazing.

Three sorts of social unit: female herds of adult and subadult females and calves, bachelor herds of subadult and adult males, and territorial adult bulls. In the Free State, female herds contain an average of 28 and bachelor herds 21. Female herds are strongly attached to home ranges; bachelor herds move around. The social tolerance of males in bachelor herds contrasts with the aggressiveness of territorial bulls.

Prime bulls hold territories throughout the year. They mark their areas with scent from preorbital and interdigital glands, and with middens of urine and faeces, usually pawing the ground before defecating. They paw and horn the ground, and can often be recognised by the mud and broken vegetation sticking to their horns. They display their status with a stiff-legged trot and give a loud, high-pitched honking call, described as *ge-nu*, from which they get their species name, and a loud sharp 'hic' accompanied by an upward jerk of the chin.

In the breeding season territorial bulls herd females onto their territories and check their reproductive condition by sniffing and flehmen.

Calves 2–3 months old group together in crèches within the herds.

Field sign Droppings are dark pellets, sometimes in clusters. Middens and bare, trampled patches on territories.

Conservation The black wildebeest is endemic to South Africa and was on the brink of extinction at the turn of the century, by which time the hundreds of thousands that occurred in the central, northern and northeastern Cape, Free State, southern Transvaal, and Natal at the foot of the Drakensberg had been reduced by hunting, disease and habitat loss to agriculture to about 550 in the Free State and southern Transvaal. Under protection instituted in the 1930s, numbers increased to about 12 000, and black wildebeest have subsequently been widely translocated.

BLUE WILDEBEEST

Blouwildebees
Connochaetes taurinus

Description Adult males are dark grey with a silver sheen, black on top of the muzzle and on the forehead, with a russet tinge to the forehead and darker stripes on the sides of the neck, shoulders and chest. Females and juveniles are browner and have more russet on the forehead; calves up to 5–6 months old are fawn all over. There is a mane of long hair on the back of the neck, and a fringe along the throat. The tail has a long whisk of black hair at the end, reaching nearly to the ground. Both sexes have horns, growing sideways from bosses on the forehead, then hooking upwards and inwards. Horns of juveniles grow straight up, and begin to grow sideways at eight months. Females have one pair of mammae between their hind legs. Shoulder height males 1,4 m (1,23–1,6 m), females 1,26 m (1,17–1,34 m); weight males 240–250 kg, females 180–215 kg. *See scale drawing on p. 173.*

The horns of males are heavier than those of females, grow from a much heavier boss, and usually extend further sideways than their ears. The penis sheath breaks the curve of the belly in males.

Habitat Open woodland, scrub and grassland. Needs access to water or space to migrate to fresh pasture: where fences prevent migration it is seldom found more than 15 km from water. Not found in large numbers where the winters are cold. Very widely translocated.

Diet A grazer, preferring fresh growth less than 10–15 cm high; bite width is 6,5 cm and it does not select for species or parts. Can survive without water by eating wild melons such as tsamas (*Citrullus lanatus*).

Life history In KwaZulu-Natal, mating in April and August with births peaking in December and April–May. In Kruger NP mating in April to early June with births from mid-November to December, tailing off in January. In the southern Kalahari mating

in April–June, births in December–January. Gestation 250 days. Births are synchronised, with a sharp peak to saturate predators. Birth weight 22 kg. Weans at 8 months, but up to 16 months if the mother loses her next calf. Females have their first calf at two years, and breed annually. Lifespan 15 years. Being so numerous, blue wildebeest are an important source of food for all the larger carnivores. In Kruger NP they make up 15% of spotted hyaena kills and 14% of lion kills. In the southern Kalahari they provide 18% of hyaena kills and 37% of lion kills. Also taken by crocodiles.

Behaviour Most active during the day, with peaks of grazing in the early morning and late afternoon. Avoids the midday heat by standing or resting in shade, especially if water is not available; if there is no shade it stands to face the breeze, cooling the blood that flows through the horn bosses. Half of the time spent grazing is after dark. Drinks daily if water is available; more willing than most animals to drink muddy water, but avoids saline water.

Social structure varies with locality and in some areas changes seasonally. When food and water are available, females and calves live in herds with fixed home ranges. Outside the breeding season males who do not hold territories may mix with female herds, producing group sizes of up to 30. Average group size in the southern Kalahari is 12, in KwaZulu-Natal 15–19. As food and water become less available herds move off their home ranges and may amalgamate into herds of tens of thousands.

The home range of a cow and calf in the Kalahari with no access to permanent water was 2 700 km^2, compared to 917 km^2 for one with access to permanent water, but moving in search of food. Home ranges are three times larger during droughts. Males have smaller ranges than females, 38–420 km^2, and stay closer to water, probably so that they meet more females coming in to drink.

Will move to distant rainfall, possibly in response to the sound of thunder or the sight of lightning. The high shoulders and long front legs are an adaptation to moving long distances at a canter, which is faster than walking, and uses less energy than trotting. Migration to water in late winter has been blocked by veterinary cordon fences in Botswana, leading to an almost 90% decline in numbers from 100 000 in the 1970s, and by boundary fencing in the Kruger NP, with similar declines in one subpopulation originally of 750.

Mature bulls hold small mating territories; only those with territories can mate. Territories are fixed in sedentary populations, and move with the herds in migratory ones. Neighbours interact on their boundaries with tail swishing, horn tossing, pawing and horning the ground, and brief horn clashing. Intruders are chased out. In serious fights the combatants go down on their knees and wrestle with their horns. Territorial bulls can be recognised by their often being alone, by the mud which sticks to the body and horns after they have rolled in it or horned the ground, and by their holding their heads higher then the others when in a herd. Territories are marked by rubbing preorbital gland secretion, which has a sharp, tarry smell, onto the ground, trees, rocks and other wildebeest. Glands between their front hooves mark the ground as they walk.

Territorial males are solitary unless they have a female herd on their ground. Males without territories mix with female herds outside the breeding season, but are driven out by territorial bulls during the rut. Territorial males herd females and check their reproductive condition by sniffing and flehmen. Cows coming into oestrus are courted by persistent following and mounting attempts and by the male's rearing up onto his hind legs. Unreceptive females avoid courting males by running away or lying down. Mounting and copulation occur as soon as the female stands for them, and may be repeated at short intervals. Females may mate with other bulls in quick succession.

Females usually move out of the herd to give birth. Calves can run within five minutes, and keep pace with adults after a day. Females suckle only their own calves; others trying to steal milk are repelled by a sweep of the horns. They defend their calves against predators.

Field sign The droppings are pellets, 2 cm long, pointed at one end and blunt at the other; sometimes in middens on trampled, bare patches in territories.

Conservation Secure as a species, but in southern Africa the wildlife spectacle of large-scale migrations has been destroyed by fences. Thrives in ranches, reserves and parks with artificial water, sometimes to the detriment of species needing taller grasses. Translocations in South Africa were formerly restricted by legislation because blue wildebeest were suspected of transmitting *snotsiekte* (malignant catarrhal fever) to domestic stock.

LICHTENSTEIN'S HARTEBEEST

S307 ☼

Mofhartebees / Lichtenstein se hartebees
Sigmoceros lichtensteinii

Description Yellowish tawny with an indistinct reddish-tinged saddle from the shoulders to the base of the tail. There may be a dark area behind the shoulder where pre-orbital gland secretion is rubbed on the flank. The chin, the front of the lower parts of the limbs and the brush of longer hair on the tail are black. The base of the tail, the rump and the top of the hind legs are white. The head is long and narrow. Both sexes have lightly ridged, sharply bent horns (horns heavily ridged in red hartebeest, not sharply bent in tsessebe). There is a distinct hump on the shoulders. Females have one pair of mammae between their hind legs. Shoulder height 1,24 m (1,2–1,36 m); weight 170 kg (157–204 kg), females from Zimbabwe 125–177 kg. *See scale drawing on p. 173.*

Habitat Savanna, especially where open woodland meets grassland. Dependent on water.

Diet A selective grazer, favouring fresh growth. Strongly attracted to regrowth after a burn, when it also eats ash and burned grass, presumably for their mineral content.

Life history Gestation 240 days. Single young are born in September. Birth weight 15 kg. Females first calve at two years. Preyed on by large carnivores.

Behaviour Forms small herds of females and young or bachelor males, with up to 12 members, exceptionally up to 16. Larger numbers may congregate where grazing is good. Non-territorial males live alone or in bachelor groups.

Mature bulls are territorial throughout the year, holding areas of 2,5 km².

Territories are marked with dung piles, preorbital gland secretion, dug up soil and vegetation thrashed with the horns. Territorial bulls often stand on higher ground for better visibility. During the mating season females are herded onto the territories and males are chased out. Males court by approaching with the nose pointed forward and the tail held out horizontal; they may rub their preorbital glands on the female's rump.

Calves are mobile shortly after birth, but usually lie in the open while the mother grazes nearby.

The alarm call is a 'sneeze-snort'.

Field sign Horned up patches of soil, thrashed bushes.

Conservation The status of the population in Mozambique is uncertain following the civil war in that country. The species is widely distributed further north in Africa. A few have been translocated from Malawi to Kruger NP.

RED HARTEBEEST

Rooihartebees
Alcelaphus buselaphus

Description Colour varies from rich reddish brown to yellowish fawn, with a darker saddle from the shoulders to the base of the tail, broadening out over the rump. The saddle is more distinct in males. The top of the muzzle and the forehead are black, there is a black stripe on the front of the shoulders, continuing down onto the forelegs, and black high on the hind legs (Lichtenstein's hartebeest lacks these mark-

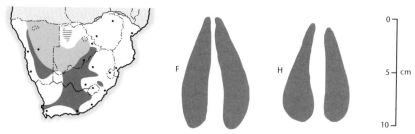

F   H

0
5 cm
10

ings). All the black markings are glossy and iridescent. The rump is pale yellow or off-white (same colour as body in tsessebe). There is a brush of longer, black hair on the tail. The preorbital glands are well developed and open onto a black patch just in front of the eyes. The head is narrow, its length exaggerated by the bony pedicel from which the horns rise straight up, flare outwards and forwards and then bend sharply backwards. Both sexes have horns, heavily ridged almost to the tips (ridges less heavy in Lichtenstein's hartebeest; horns not sharply bent in tsessebe). There is a distinct hump on the shoulders, and the outline of the back slopes down to the rump. Females have one pair of mammae between the hind legs. Total length males 2,2 m, females 2,1 m; tail 47 cm; shoulder height males 1,3 m (1,24–1,4 m), females 1,25 m (1,2–1,3 m); weight males 152 kg (137–156 kg), females 120 kg (105–136 kg). *See scale drawing opposite.* Males are taller than females, more richly coloured and more distinctly marked, with much thicker horns.

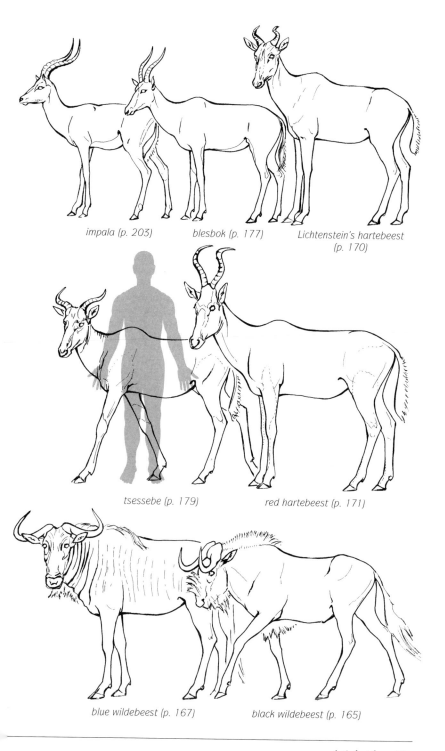

impala (p. 203)   blesbok (p. 177)   Lichtenstein's hartebeest
(p. 170)

tsessebe (p. 179)   red hartebeest (p. 171)

blue wildebeest (p. 167)   black wildebeest (p. 165)

Habitat Open grasslands and semi-arid bush savanna, to a lesser extent open woodland. Avoids denser woodland except when passing through. Independent of water, but will drink if it is available. Very widely translocated.

Diet A selective grazer and browser. The diet in Botswana is all grass, in former western Transvaal 56,5% grass and 44,4% browse, in the Free State 40% browse. Selects for species, and for leaf over stem. If no water is available eats melons and digs for tubers.

Life history Mating is triggered by short day length. In the northwest Free State and Botswana, mating March–April with 80% of births in October–November. In the Free State and KwaZulu-Natal, mating peaks in February, births peak in October. In the southern Kalahari, mating January–March, births August–October. Gestation 8 months. Begins grazing at 2 weeks; weaned at 7–8 months. Cows first calve at three years. Breeds annually. Lifespan 15–16 years. Taken by the larger carnivores, but its open habitat and speed make it difficult prey. Calves provide 6% of leopard kills in the Kalahari Gemsbok NP.

Behaviour Most active in the early morning and late afternoon. Rests in shade in the summer, in the open in the winter, but is heat tolerant and can graze all day if necessary.

Very mobile and will move long distances to where rain has fallen. The long forelegs allow an energy-saving canter. Highly adapted to hot arid conditions; the metabolic rate is low, and blood going to the brain is cooled by heat exchange with blood coming from the nasal membranes.

Forms small herds of up to 20, larger herds of a few hundred on areas of good grazing, and aggregations of thousands in Botswana before migration routes were blocked by veterinary cordon fences.

In the Free Sate mature bulls defend territories of 100–400 ha throughout the year and control harem herds of females and juveniles of both sexes. Non-territorial males form bachelor herds in unfavourable habitat. In the southern Kalahari bulls are territorial only for breeding. Females have home ranges of 320 km², and males 230 km² in good years, five times as large during droughts. Some adult males are solitary. Territories are defended by fierce fighting involving charges, horn clashing and horn wrestling, when both combatants go down onto their knees for better leverage. Fighters' horns may jam together, in which case both are doomed. Territories are marked with preorbital gland secretion, by thrashing vegetation with the horns, and by defecating and urinating in middens. Neighbours display on their boundary by posing sideways on, tossing their heads, horning the soil, and horn fencing.

Bulls check females' reproductive condition by sniffing their genitals; courtship consists of approaching with head stretched forwards and ears lowered, and nudging with the snout. Copulation is brief and repeated.

A fast runner, reaching speeds of 60–70 km/h; stots in stiff-legged zig-zags. Calves that cannot keep up with a fleeing herd drop flat on the ground in an attempt to avoid detection.

Females leave the herd to give birth. A newborn calf lies hidden in tall grass while its mother grazes; she returns at intervals to clean and suckle it.

Field sign Vegetation damaged by territorial bulls' horn thrashing. Dung middens. Horned up soil. Dung pellets are 1,5 cm long, tapered at one end and blunt at the other.

Conservation Drought and fences have reduced the red hartebeest population of the Kalahari from 100 000 to 30 000.

BONTEBOK

Ⓔ **S309** **R** ☀

Bontebok

Damaliscus dorcas dorcas

Bontebok are one subspecies of *Damaliscus dorcas*; the other is the blesbok (*D. d. phillipsi*).

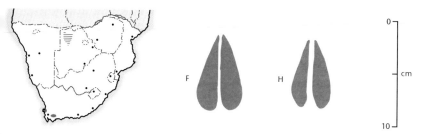

Description Rich dark brown on the upper parts, darker on the sides of the head, flanks, top of the rump and upper parts of the limbs. The dark patches at the tops of the legs have a purple sheen. There is a brown stripe down the front of the forelegs. Pure white on the rump (paler than body but not white in blesbok), lower limbs, base of the tail and underparts. Males have a conspicuous white scrotum. The white blaze from the forehead to the nostrils narrows sharply between the eyes but is usually (80% of animals) not broken (blaze usually broken by bar of brown in blesbok). Calves are fawny brown with indistinct darker markings, and darker on the face. Both sexes have horns, strongly ridged except at the tips, uniformly black (straw coloured on ridges in blesbok), the males' thicker than the females'. Females have one pair of mammae between the hind legs. Shoulder height males 90 cm, weight males 61 kg (59,6–63,6 kg); females are smaller and lighter.

Habitat Natural habitat is a mixture of grassland and low scrub in the fynbos zone 50–200 m above sea level; widely translocated to other areas of grassland with scrub and woodland. Needs grass, shelter and permanent water.

Diet An almost exclusive grazer; prefers short grass.

Life history Breeding is triggered by short day length. Mating January to mid-

March, tailing off into April. Gestation 238–254 days. Single lambs are born September–February, most in September–October. Females first calve at three years old. The conservation management of bontebok keeps them away from large predators, but some lambs may be lost to caracals, jackals and feral dogs.

Behaviour Active during the day. Shelters amongst trees and bushes; in very hot weather stands facing the sun with head lowered.

Mature males (at least 3 years old, usually 5) hold territories of 4–28 ha throughout the year. Territories are marked with dung middens scattered throughout the area. The holder lies in the central midden to pick up the smell of his territory. Occupation is advertised by standing tall in a prominent position. Bushes are thrashed with the horns, and grass stems are scent-marked with the secretion from the preorbital glands. Fights are ritualised and do not progress beyond inhibited horn clashing.

Females and young of the year live in herds of up to eight which move through the male territories. Females have a dominance hierarchy maintained by threats and horn clashing. Young males leave mixed herds at a year old and join a bachelor herd. Females usually stay in the herds they were born in. Bachelor herds are larger than the mixed herds and contain males of all ages, including old, deposed territory holders, and a few immature females.

In the mating season territorial rams herd females and display with head stretched forward and tail curled upwards. They investigate the females' reproductive condition by sniffing their genitals; they do not show flehmen.

Field sign Thrashed bushes. Dung pellets are 1,5 cm long, with a short point at one end, blunt at the other, sometimes in middens on territories.

Conservation By 1927 there were only 120 bontebok left. In 1931 the first Bontebok National Park, containing 22 bontebok, was proclaimed near Bredasdorp. Numbers increased and despite translocations the original park became overpopulated, highlighting the unsuitability of the habitat. The park was reproclaimed near

Swellendam and 84 bontebok were transferred in 1960, of which 61 survived. They have subsequently prospered there, in provincial reserves, and on private land, and have been widely translocated. Reckless disregard for the integrity of the subspecies gene pool has led to their introduction to farms where blesbok also occur, and the two subspecies have interbred. It is very important that stocks of pure bontebok be identified as such and carefully kept free of blesbok genes. Red Data Book: Rare.

BLESBOK

Blesbok
Damaliscus dorcas phillipsi

Blesbok are one subspecies of *Damaliscus dorcas*; the other is the bontebok (*D. d. dorcas*).

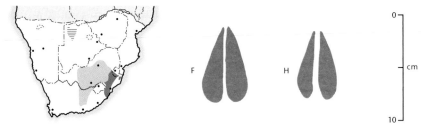

Description Reddish brown on the upper parts with an indistinct paler saddle. Dark brown on the outer surfaces of the legs. Pale on the rump (pure white in bontebok). The white blaze from forehead to nostrils is broken in most animals by a narrow bar of brown between the eyes (narrow but not broken in 80% of blesbok). Calves are dull buffy. Both sexes have horns, strongly ridged except at the tips, straw coloured on the ridges (uniformly black in bontebok), the males' thicker than the females'. Females have one pair of mammae between the hind legs. Shoulder height 95 cm; weight males 70 kg, females 61 kg. *See scale drawing on p. 173.*

Habitat Highveld grassland with permanent water; does not naturally occur in the Karoo, which was a barrier between blesbok and bontebok distributions. Very widely translocated.

Diet A grazer, but will take some browse. Prefers short grass, especially growth flushed by fire. Selects for species in older grass, and for growth stage in short grass. Preferences change seasonally.

Life history Breeds in response to short day length. Mating March–May; gestation 246 days. Peak in births November–December, continuing into January. Birth weight 6–7 kg; wean at 4 months. Black-backed jackals take newborn calves. Females are sexually mature at 2–3 years. Lifespan 13 years. Populations can grow at 20% per year.

Behaviour Most active in the early morning and late afternoon. Rests in shade during the midday heat; shelters in thickets on winter nights. In very hot weather it may stand facing the sun, head down. Drinks at least once a day.

Social organisation changes seasonally. During the mating season harem herds of 2–25 adult females are herded by mature rams onto territories of 1–4 ha (Gauteng), or 5–10 ha (KwaZulu-Natal). Males without territories form large bachelor herds. In winter, rams leave their territories and herds of up to a few hundred form, containing both sexes and all ages. Rams start to re-establish territories in October.

Territories are marked with dung middens, in which the resident lies to pick up the smell of his area. Both sexes and all ages deposit preorbital gland secretion on grass stalks, which are then stroked with the horns, picking up a deposit of secretion between the ridges. Secretion from glands between the front hooves is deposited while walking and when territory residents paw the ground and scrape dung. Standing sideways on to intruders, foot stamping, horn swinging and digging up soil with the horns advertise territory occupation, and territories are defended by vigorous bouts of horn clashing, which can become serious, and are sometimes fatal.

Territorial rams herd females by circling them with head stretched forward and tail curled up. Reproductive condition is checked by smelling their genitals, with no use of flehmen. Newborn calves can stand within a few minutes and run with the mother after 20 minutes. Mothers chase other blesbok away, and will only suckle their own calf. Calves separated from their mothers bleat loudly, mothers answer with deep grunts. Social bonds between mother and calf weaken when the calf is about six months old, but a loose association between a mother and her female offspring may last for two years.

Blesbok are popular for game ranching because they can be contained by standard stock fencing.

Field sign Dung middens, horned up soil. Dung pellets are 1,5 cm long with a short point at one end, and blunt at the other.

TSESSEBE

S310   R   ☼

Tsessebe
Damaliscus lunatus

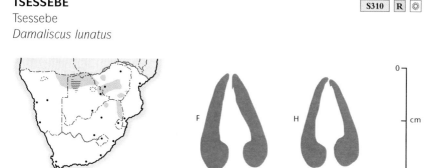

Description Reddish brown with a purplish sheen. The muzzle, top of the head, lower parts of the shoulders, and upper parts of the legs are suffused with black. Yellowish white on the inner sides of the hind legs and the belly. The legs below the knees are brownish yellow, with a brown stripe down the front of the forelegs. The tail is brown with a whisk of longer black hair. Newborn calves are light brown. There is a distinct hump on the shoulders, and the outline of the back slopes down to the rump. The head is long and narrow, thickening at the muzzle. Both sexes have horns, ridged almost to the tips. Females have one pair of mammae between their hind legs. Total length males 2,2 m (2,1–2,3 m), females 2,13 m (1,9–2,3 m); tail 43 cm (36–52 cm); shoulder height 1,25 m (1,1–1,34 m); weight males 140 kg, females 126 kg. *See scale drawing on p. 173.*

Males and females are very difficult to tell apart.

Habitat Open woodland; grassland bordering woodland. Prefers areas where there is good visibility at head height and therefore does not do well in tall grass, dense scrub or bush. Dependent on water. Widely translocated.

Diet A grazer. Preferred feeding height is below 60 cm, down to 5–10 cm. Selects leaf over stem. Prefers fresh growth, and is attracted to burnt areas.

Life history Mating peaks in March–April; births October–December, with a November peak. Gestation 235–245 days; birth weight 10–12 kg. Males are sexually mature at 3–4 years, females at 2–3 years. Lifespan 15 years.

Behaviour Drinks at least once a day unless the grass is very lush and green. Breeding herds consist of females and their young, with a territorial bull. Males without territories form bachelor herds. Territories cover 200–400 ha. Breeding herds contain up to 21 animals, usually 3 or 4; bachelor herds contain up to 31 animals, average 8. Up to 200 may congregate on good grazing.

Territorial rams patrol their areas, marking with faeces and with a sticky clear pre-orbital gland secretion, manoeuvring the tip of a grass stem into the opening of the gland just in front of the eye; they also rub their faces on the soil or on termite heaps, horn up the soil and smear mud on themselves with their horns, and mark with glands between their front hooves by pawing the ground. Females also horn the ground, smear mud on themselves, and mark with preorbital gland secretion, but less frequently than the bulls. Territorial possession is advertised by standing prominently on a patch of raised ground. Trespassers are challenged by head shaking and rearing up. Fights involve horn clashing with the combatants going down onto their knees, and at higher intensity, locking horns and wrestling.

A territorial bull herds his females by parading in front of them with his head up and nose pointing forward, and his ears held downwards against the sides of his neck, taking exaggerated high steps with his front legs. Bulls act as sentinels, snorting if a predator is detected, and chasing jackals and hyaenas.

Young males are evicted from breeding herds by territorial bulls at about a year old, between September and January of the year after they were born. They join bachelor herds on the periphery of the territorial area.

Tsessebe are very fast runners, and they avoid predators by fleeing and then standing to watch for pursuit, a habit which makes them vulnerable to hunting with firearms. Calves follow their mothers from an early age, lying down in small groups in the open while the herd grazes. One or two adults may stay near the calves as sentinels.

Field sign Horned up soil. Droppings are 2 cm long with a long taper at one end, blunt at the other.

Conservation Tsessebe are particular about habitat, and thrive only with appropriate veld management. They do not do well where there is bush encroachment. Red Data Book: Rare.

DUIKERS

Three species in the subregion.

BLUE DUIKER
Blouduiker
Philantomba monticola

S311 R

Description The smallest southern African antelope. Colour varies with locality: in Zimbabwe dark smoky brown, darker on the head and rump, with a distinct bluish sheen; in Eastern Cape Province and KwaZulu-Natal dark brown, reddish on the limbs; in coastal Mozambique upper parts rusty brown, dark smoky brown on the middle of the back, darkening towards the tail, legs light chestnut. Underparts white. The preorbital glands open as long slits just in front of the eyes. Both sexes have short, straight horns, growing backwards in the plane of the face, ridged at the base and smooth at the tips. Females have two pairs of mammae between the hind legs. Total length males 65 cm (62–68 cm), females 66,5 cm (58,5–71 cm); tail 7,5 cm (7–8,5 cm); shoulder height males 30 cm, females 32 cm; weight males 4 kg (3,8–4,2 kg), females 4,7 kg (4,6–4,9 kg). *See scale drawing on p. 182.*
Habitat Forest, thickets and dense coastal bush. Independent of water.
Diet Fruit is the preferred food; also eats freshly fallen leaves.

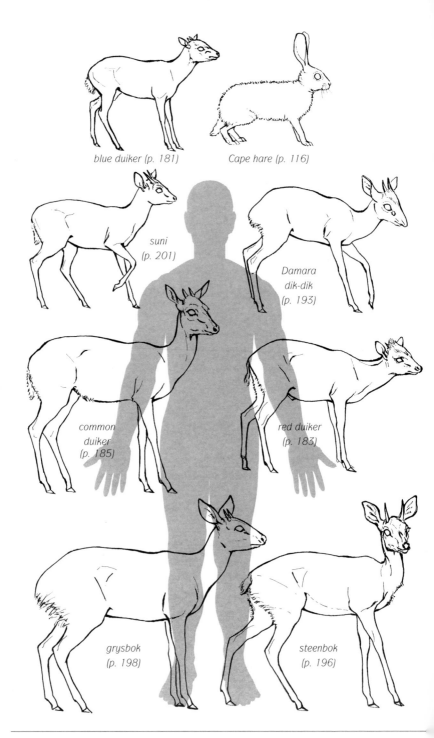

blue duiker (p. 181)

Cape hare (p. 116)

suni (p. 201)

Damara dik-dik (p. 193)

common duiker (p. 185)

red duiker (p. 183)

grysbok (p. 198)

steenbok (p. 196)

Life history Gestation seven months. Single young are born at any time of the year, with a peak in October–November. Females first give birth at 1,5–2 years. Lifespan 6–7 years. Preyed on by leopard and caracal; in Tsitsikamma 27% of leopard scats and 7% of caracal scats contained blue duiker remains.

Behaviour Most active in the early morning and late afternoon–evening, spending the night and up to half the day inactive.

Solitary, except for females with lambs, and mating pairs. Holds territories of 0,5–1 ha whose boundaries are marked by scraping bark with the horns, and scent-marking by rubbing the preorbital glands on branches. Uses well-worn trails through vegetation, which makes it vulnerable to snares.

Avoids predators by freezing motionless, suddenly dashing away when approached closely.

Field sign Worn trails. Scars on tree bark on territory borders. Middens containing dung pellets 0,5 cm long, tapered at one end, hollow at the other.

Conservation Like all forest dwellers, blue duikers suffer habitat destruction and fragmentation of populations. They are heavily poached with dogs and by snaring. Red Data Book: Rare. CITES Appendix II.

RED DUIKER

S312   R   ☼

Rooiduiker
Cephalophus natalensis

Description Deep chestnut red, paler on the flanks and underparts (flecked with white in grysbok and Sharpe's grysbok); tawny on the sides of the head, sides of the neck and the inner surfaces of the upper limbs, white on the throat. In Mozambique more orange on the upper body. The large preorbital glands open through long, narrow slits in front of the eyes. There is a tapering tuft of long hair on top of the head (no tuft in grysbok and Sharpe's grysbok). Both sexes have short, straight horns, growing backwards in the plane of the face, grooved lengthwise near the base (rings and ridges run across in other small antelope), smooth towards the tip. The short tail has a whitish tip. Females have two pairs of mammae between their hind legs. Total length 88 cm (81–95 cm); tail 10 cm (7–12,5 cm); shoulder height 42 cm (38–48

cm); weight 12 kg (10–13 kg). *See scale drawing on p. 182.*

Habitat Forest, thickets, thickly wooded ravines and dense coastal bush in warm, moist areas.

Diet A browser; also eats freshly fallen leaves, fruit and pods.

Life history Gestation 210 days. Single lambs are born at any time of year, possibly with a spring–summer peak in KwaZulu-Natal. Females first lamb at 18–24 months. Lifespan 8–9 years.

Behaviour Most active in the mid-morning, late afternoon and early evening. Inactive at night and for up to 70% of the day.

Solitary, in male–female pairs, females with a lamb, or pairs with a lamb. In KwaZulu-Natal it lives in overlapping home ranges: males 3–9,5 ha, females 2–17,5 ha; may be territorial in other areas. Defecates in middens used by more than one animal.

Avoids predators by freezing motionless and dashing away when closely approached.

Field sign Dung pellets are 0,5 cm long, tapered at one end, hollow at the other, deposited in middens.

Conservation Like all forest dwellers, red duikers suffer habitat destruction and fragmentation of populations. They are heavily poached with dogs and by snaring. Red Data Book: Rare.

COMMON DUIKER / GREY DUIKER

Gewone duiker
Sylvicapra grimmia

 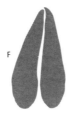 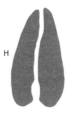 

F   H

0
cm
3

Description Upper parts vary from greyish buff to reddish yellow. Underparts are usually white, but may be grey or tinged reddish. Black or dark brown down the front of the forelegs. The forehead is usually darker and redder than the upper parts of the body; a black band on top of the muzzle runs a variable distance from the nostrils, sometimes reaching as far as the forehead. The large preorbital glands open into a narrow slit in front of the eyes. The horns are short and straight, growing back in the plane of the face, heavily ridged at the base, smooth towards the tips. Typically only males have horns, but horned females are known and in some areas are common. There is a tuft of dark brown or black hair on top of the head. The tail is dark on top, white underneath. Females have two pairs of mammae between their hind legs. Total length 1,1 m (1–1,26 m); tail 14 cm (10–20 cm); shoulder height 51 cm; weight males 18,7 kg (15,3–21,2 kg), females 20,7 kg (17–25,4 kg). *See scale drawing on p. 182.*

Habitat Scrub and bush, woodland with an understorey of bushes, grassland with patches of bush or dense grass, forest fringes. It penetrates desert along drainage lines, and can survive in agricultural areas as long as some cover is available. Habitat requirements are cover and browse; it is independent of water as long as there is green food.

Diet Browses a wide range of broad-leaved forbs, trees and bushes; also eats fruit, pods and seeds, roots, bark, flowers, fungi, caterpillars and even nestling birds. In arid areas wild melons are eaten for their water content. It may be a problem in crops, orchards, vineyards and plantations.

Life history Gestation probably 5–6 months. Single lambs, very rarely twins, are born at any time of year, possibly with a peak in summer. Birth weight 1,6–1,9 kg. Full grown at 7 months; females first mate as early as 8–9 months, and give birth at 1 year. Lifespan 8–11 years. Important prey for medium-sized and large carnivores; 13% of leopard and cheetah kills in the Kruger NP. Also taken by pythons, and baboons eat lambs.

Behaviour Most active in the early morning and late afternoon, extending into the night; becomes more nocturnal if disturbed or hunted. Rests in the cover of bushes or dense grass.

Solitary (87% of sightings in KwaZulu-Natal), or a female with a lamb, rarely in male–female pairs. Territorial in KwaZulu-Natal, but this is very likely to vary with locality and habitat. Scent-marks are produced by the preorbital glands and glands between the front hooves. Mating system probably varies with locality and habitat from monogamous pairs to males with more than one female.

Avoids predators by lying quietly or freezing motionless and dashing away at the last moment if approached closely. Runs with a distinctive diving, zig-zag motion from which comes the name duiker, Afrikaans for diver. Uses its horns and sharp back hooves as defensive weapons. The alarm call is a nasal snort; if caught bleats loudly, a sound that attracts other duikers, and calls mothers to assist lambs.

Lambs can run within a day of birth, but remain hidden in heavy cover, with the mother returning to suckle and clean them.

Field sign Droppings are 1 cm long, 1 cm across, with a short point at one end, blunt or slightly hollow at the other, sometimes in middens.

SPRINGBOK AND DWARF ANTELOPE

Eight species in the subregion, in two tribes: the ANTELOPINI with one species, the springbok, and the NEOTRAGINI, or dwarf antelope, with seven: klipspringer, Damara dik-dik, oribi, steenbok, grysbok, Sharpe's grysbok, and suni.

SPRINGBOK

S314

Springbok
Antidorcas marsupialis

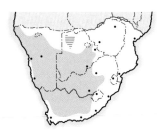

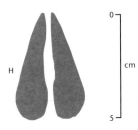

Description Distinctive among southern African antelope. Bright cinnamon brown upper parts, bright white underparts, with a chocolate brown stripe along the flanks. White on the face and muzzle, with a red-brown stripe running through the eyes to the corner of the mouth. The rump is white, the tail is thin, white near the base with a tuft of dark hair at the tip. From the rump to about half way up the back there is a crest of long white hair, usually folded out of sight into a narrow pouch along the middle of the back, flared open during the pronking display (see Behaviour). The ears are long, narrow and pointed. Both sexes have lyre-shaped horns, ridged in the lower two-thirds, smooth where the tips curve inwards and back. Females usually have one pair, occasionally two pairs, of mammae between their hind legs. Measurements from Botswana: total length 1,5 m (1,4–1,6 m); tail 25 cm (14–21 cm); shoulder height males 75 cm, females 60 cm; weight males 41 kg (33–48 kg), females 37 kg (30,4–44,5 kg). Larger in Namibia (males 42–59 kg, females 32 kg) and in Kalahari Gemsbok NP (males 46 kg, females 35 kg); smaller in South Africa (males average 31,2 kg, females 26,5 kg). Mature males are slightly bigger than females, their horns are distinctly thicker, and they have thicker necks. *See scale drawing on p. 235.*

Habitat Arid and semi-desert scrub and grassland, Karoo. A true desert antelope, able to survive indefinitely without drinking. Very widely translocated. When translocated to areas with heartwater disease (transmitted by the bont tick, *Amblyomma hebraeum*) hardly any survive.

Diet A versatile feeder, changing diet according to availability, and selecting for nutrients. Typically grazes in summer and browses more in winter and during droughts. Eats grasses, forbs, bushes, seeds, pods, fruits and flowers, and digs for roots and bulbs. Will eat plants that are unpalatable and toxic to other species. Wild melons and cucumbers are eaten for their water content, and soil for minerals.

Life history Gestation 24 weeks. Single young are born at any time of year with peaks varying with locality, apparently in relation to the timing of rainfall. Peaks of births in September–October in Gauteng, Northern Cape, central Karoo, Northwest Province, Western Cape and Eastern Cape (early summer rain); in December–January in northern Namibia and throughout the Kalahari (midsummer rain); in July in Namaqualand (winter rain). Begins grazing at two weeks, weans at two months. Females first mate as early as 7 months; males are sexually mature at 16 months, but do not secure territory and mate until at least 2,5 years old. Lifespan 10 years. In the southern Kalahari it makes up 87% of cheetah kills, 13% of lion, 65% of leopard and 6% of spotted hyaena kills. In Etosha NP it is the main prey of spotted hyaenas, and 97% of cheetah kills. Jackals and martial eagles (*Polemaetus bellicosus*) take lambs; caracals may take adults. Adult males suffer twice as much predation as females.

Behaviour Active at any time of the day and night; at night in the Kalahari in summer moves onto dry river beds and pans where the hard surface gives better footing for escape from predators. Grazes with the white rump towards the sun to reflect heat; the white underparts reflect heat from the ground. In summer avoids midday heat by standing in shade if any is available; in cold weather in winter lies in the sun, and spends the night in the dunes where it is warmer.

Lives in mixed herds of about 10–50, and up to 200. May form aggregations of up to a few thousand. Within historical times springbok migrated in tens or hundreds of thousands, probably in response to drought in the Kalahari and Karoo. During the mating season territorial rams chase other males out of the herds, which then consist only of females and juveniles. Adult males without territories form herds of up to 50.

Breeding rams hold territories of 25–70 ha in Northwest Province; 1–17 ha or about 300 m of river bed in Kalahari Gemsbok NP. Rams stay on their territories even when the rest of the local springbok have left in search of food, but will vacate them in periods of extreme food scarcity. Territories are marked with middens of dung and urine; a ram defecates in a low crouch and urinates on the pellets in a stretched posture, made more obvious by the stripe along the flanks. Territorial rams thrash bushes with their horns and horn up vegetation, sometimes collecting a 'head dress' of tangled vegetation. Intruding males are chased away from females. Fights over territory and females are fierce: opponents clash horns, lock horns and wrestle, trying to wrench each other off balance. Deaths occur from horn wounds, broken necks and horns jamming together, and battle injuries such as gouged eyes and damaged legs make combatants more vulnerable to predators. Fights between established neighbours are ritualised. Young males spar by brief horn clashing and wrestling; females use horn hooking as a threat.

Only territorial males breed. Females moving into the territory are herded, and their reproductive condition checked by sniffing and flehmen of their urine and genitals. Courtship involves herding while giving deep grunts, close following and tapping between the female's hind legs with a foreleg. Several mounting attempts are necessary before momentary penetration is achieved; the female may not even stand still. Mating may be repeated, and females may mate with more than one male. Rams also court and try to mount females that have just given birth.

Springboks' most distinctive and striking behaviour is pronking, which includes stiff-legged jumps up to 2 m high with the head high or tucked down, bouncy running, enormous leaps up to 3 m high, and a variety of exaggerated gaits. The crest of white hair on the back may be flared open, producing a visual signal and releasing scent from glands at the roots of the hair. Pronking seems to signal mild uneasiness, for instance about the possible presence of a predator, or general excitement such as when a herd comes to water or before a thunderstorm. Sudden alarms cause herds to scatter by jumping or sprinting away. Top speed is 88 km/h. The alarm call is a whistling snort. Lambs cannot match an adult's speed until they are a month old. For the first two days they lie tightly in the cover of bushes or grass clumps.

Field sign Dung middens in territories. Dung pellets are 1–1,5 cm long with short, sharp points, sometimes squashed and stuck together.

Conservation Springboks' potential for producing meat in arid areas without the ecological degradation caused by sheep and goats should be a high priority for research. The spectacle of large-scale migrations has been destroyed by fences and loss of range to agriculture.

KLIPSPRINGER

Klipspringer
Oreotragus oreotragus

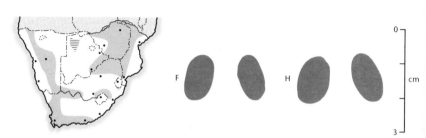

Description Colour varies with locality: in the southern Western Cape Province the upper parts are yellow speckled with brown; in northern South Africa bright yellow speckled with black, and in western Zimbabwe greyer and duller. The underparts are white. The hairs of the coat are short, flattened, springy and harsh, providing insulation from heat and cold. The muzzle is short and sharply tapered. Large black patches just in front of the eyes mark the openings of the preorbital glands. The body is stocky, the legs short with small hooves, which have rubbery centres and hard rims to provide grip on rocks. The tail is very short. In southern Africa only males have horns, rising from above the eyes, short and with a slight forward curve, ridged on the bottom third, smooth towards the tips. Females have two pairs of mammae between the hind legs. Total length males 86 cm (82–92 cm), females 90 cm (88–100 cm);

tail 8 cm (6,5–9 cm); shoulder height 60 cm; weight males 10,6 kg (9,1–11,6 kg), females 13,2 kg (10,5–16 kg). *See scale drawing on p. 192.*

Habitat Confined to rocky areas, which makes its distribution patchy. Independent of water. Sometimes moves out onto flatter areas to feed.

Diet A strict browser, taking leaves, shoots, fruit and flowers of a wide range of trees, bushes and forbs, according to availability. Chews bones and eats soil to obtain minerals.

Life history Gestation uncertain, probably five months. Single young are born at any time of year. Breeding may be influenced by food availability. Birth weight 1,13 kg. Weans at 4–5 months; horns first visible at 6 months; full grown at 1 year. Females first lamb at 1,5–2 years. Lifespan eight years. Preyed on by caracals, leopards, spotted hyaenas and baboons; large eagles and black-backed jackals take lambs.

Behaviour Active in short spells during the day, and for at least part of the night. Shelters from both heat and cold by lying among rocks or in clumps of bushes.

Lives in male–female pairs with young of the year; occasionally a male with two females. Groups of up to six may congregate at a patch of rich feeding. Pairs stay close together and follow each other around; they are bonded by grooming each other.

Strictly territorial, and very faithful to the territory; one male was resighted in his original area after eight years. Territory size varies with habitat; 8 ha in KwaZulu-Natal, 15 ha in the Karoo, 45 ha in the arid Northern Cape Province. Males advertise occupation of territory by standing prominently on rocks for long periods, probably also watching for predators. Territories are marked with large dung middens and by small blobs of black, sticky preorbital gland secretion with a sharp tarry smell on twigs and stiff grass stems. Both sexes mark, males more than females, and males usually over-mark female marks. Males horn bushes. Fights over territory are fierce and damaging, and therefore rare; intruders retreat as soon as confronted by a resident.

Very agile and surefooted on rocks (klipspringer is Afrikaans for rock jumper) and able to outpace any ground predator over rocky ground. The hard edges of the hooves provide grip, and the tiptoe stance allows klipspringers to stand with all four feet almost touching on small areas.

The alarm call is a loud whistle, given while standing prominently on a rock or boulder. This alerts the mate, who also stands and whistles, while telling the predator that it has been detected and has lost the element of surprise.

Lambs lie hidden for 2–3 months, and stay close to the adults once they become mobile. They learn what to eat by watching their mothers.

Field sign Dung middens up to 1 m across and 10 cm deep; the pellets are 0,5–1 cm long, 0,5 cm across, tapered at both ends (more elongated than droppings from rock rabbits, dassies and mountain reedbuck, which share the habitat). Blobs of black preorbital gland secretion on the tips of twigs.

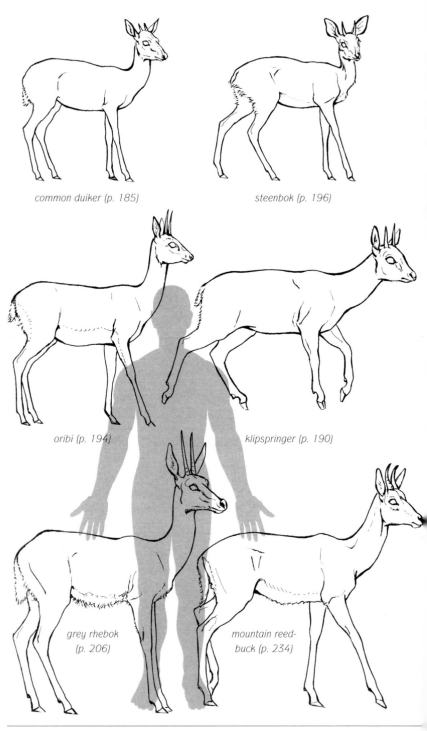

common duiker (p. 185)

steenbok (p. 196)

oribi (p. 194)

klipspringer (p. 190)

grey rhebok
(p. 206)

mountain reed-
buck (p. 234)

DAMARA DIK-DIK

Damara dik-dik
Madoqua kirkii

Kirk's dik-dik from East Africa is the same species.

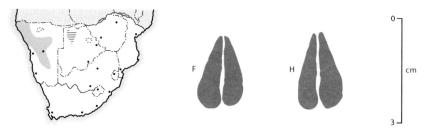

Description A tiny antelope; grizzled yellowish grey on the upper parts of the body, pale rusty on the face and top of the head, richer rusty on the shoulders and flanks. Pure white on the underparts. There is a tuft of long, orange-brown hair on the forehead (hair tufts on the top of the head between the horns or ears in duikers). The eyes are ringed with white and have large preorbital gland openings just in front of them. The snout is bulbous and pointed, with the tiny nostrils at its tip. The tail is very short, the hind legs are long. Only males have horns: short, straight, rising from high on the forehead, and growing backwards in the plane of the face; heavily ringed at the base, smooth towards the tips. Females have two pairs of mammae between the hind legs. Total length 64 cm (58–69 cm); tail 5 cm (3,2–5,6 cm); shoulder height 40 cm; weight 5,1 kg (4,6–5,5 kg). *See scale drawing on p. 182.*

Habitat Dense woodland and thicket with plenty of low shrubs but little grass, on stony ground or hard clay, with 75–500 mm rain per year. Benefits from removal of grass through overgrazing by game or cattle. Penetrates into desert along drainage lines. Not found on rock outcrops (klipspringer habitat). Independent of water.

Diet Browses on shoots, stems, twigs, leaves, fruits and flowers of a wide range of

woody plants and forbs. Eats small quantities of the leaf tips of grasses during the rainy season (December–April). Also takes freshly fallen leaves and fallen fruit.

Life history Gestation six months. Juveniles, pregnant females, and courtship have all been recorded in February. Seasonality of births in response to food supply is expected but unconfirmed. Preyed on by leopards, caracal and large raptors; medium-sized raptors such as African hawk eagles (*Hieraaetus fasciatus*) take lambs.

Behaviour Active at dawn, in the late afternoon, at dusk, and during the night. Stands or lies in shade during the hottest part of the day.

Selects the most nutritious plant parts, at least partly by smell; the mobile snout is extended to sniff for the preferred parts, and it may stand on its hind legs if browse is out of reach. It will drink if water is available, but can survive without. The swollen snout and tiny nostrils are probably means of reducing the loss of water by evaporation, and the urine is 11 times as concentrated as the blood.

Solitary, in pairs, or families of three. Occasionally up to six together in the dry season (April–August). Males' horns enable them to dominate females. Pairs stay together for life in territories of 3,5 ha; each partner chases away intruders of the same sex. Faeces are deposited in middens, usually at path junctions. Males sniff the midden, scratch at it with a forefoot, defecate, urinate, and then wipe preorbital gland secretion onto nearby vegetation. Females do the same without the scratching. Males defecate and urinate on top of the faeces and urine of females and juveniles; they also rasp the ringed bases of their horns on low branches. Neighbouring males display on their boundary by making horn stabbing movements while standing about half a metre apart.

The alarm call is a sharp whistle. May stot, drawing the legs up close under the body at each jump and giving a short whistle each time the feet touch the ground. Longer whistles are probably contact calls.

Young lambs lie hidden in patches of thick cover. Mothers visit to suckle and clean them at about six-hour intervals.

Field sign Paths through undergrowth with dung middens at junctions.

ORIBI

S317 | V | ☼ | ☾

Oorbietjie
Ourebia ourebi

Description Upper parts of the body yellowish rufous, underparts pure white, extending about a third of the way up the flanks (white on underside of steenbok barely extends onto flanks). The coat is long and woolly, with a tendency to curl (smooth and sleek in steenbok). There is a white stripe down either side of the muzzle, and white crescents above the eyes. Preorbital glands open onto dark patches in front of the eyes and there are dark glandular patches below the ears.

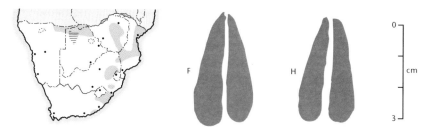

Proportionately, the neck is longer and thinner, the ears smaller than in steenbok. The tail is short and black on top (tail same colour as body in steenbok), white underneath. Only males have horns, rising from the top of the head with a slight forward curve, strongly ridged at the base. Females have two pairs of mammae between the hind legs. Total length 1 m (0,97–1,15 m); shoulder height 59 cm (51–63,5 cm); weight 14,1 kg (7,5–17,4 kg). *See scale drawing on p. 192.* Females are slightly bigger than males.

Habitat Requires an open habitat with short grass and patches of heavy cover. Does not occur in woodland, except near grassland. Suitable habitat, and therefore the oribi, is patchily distributed. Independent of water. Heavy grazing and trampling by cattle or game improves thickly grassed habitats for oribi.

Diet A selective grazer with a strong preference for freshly flushed grass. Seasonally selects grass flowers. Also browses on forbs and trees, and eats leaves and corms of succulent *Watsonia densiflora*.

Life history Mating April–June in KwaZulu-Natal; gestation 210 days. Single young are born mostly November–January in KwaZulu-Natal, November–December in former Transvaal, October–December in Zimbabwe. Birth weight 2,3 kg, weans at 3–4 months. Females probably first lamb at two years. Lifespan 13 years.

Behaviour Active day and night, grazing for about a third of the day and resting in patches of thicker grass or among bushes. Prefers to graze on areas last burnt within a year.

The basic social unit is a territorial ram and one or two females and their young. Single adults of either sex also occur. Groups are larger where the habitat is richer, congregating in groups of up to about a dozen on patches of good grazing. Male territories cover 49 ha in KwaZulu-Natal, 34 ha in former Transvaal; territories are smaller in richer habitats. Both males and females stay on their home territory unless forced off by lack of suitable food.

Rams advertise their territorial status by standing prominently, patrolling the borders, and pronking with an exaggerated rocking horse action.

Territories are heavily marked with urine and faeces; black preorbital gland secretion is deposited on stiff grass stems which may be bitten off at a convenient height before marking. Males scratch then defecate and urinate on spots where females have done the same, and mark a nearby stem with the preorbital gland. There are also scent glands below the ears, below the knees and hocks, between the hooves of all four feet, and in the groin. Some faeces are deposited in communal middens near pathways. Males defend territories vigorously, and fights may be fatal; consequently intruders flee rather than challenging a resident.

Very alert, keeping its head up even when resting; selects spots where higher ground gives good visibility. The alarm call is a snorty whistle. Often flees for a couple of hundred metres, then stops and watches for pursuit; may stot with a rocking horse action. In long grass it keeps its head high, and jumps every few paces to watch for pursuit. A soft, repeated whistle is a contact call.

Lambs lie hidden for 8–10 weeks, and lie tight with their heads down if approached.

Field sign Bitten-off grass stems with black secretion on top. Droppings are 1 cm long with a short narrow point at one end, sometimes in middens.

Conservation Oribi habitat is fragmented, and populations are small and consequently susceptible to local extinction. Habitat is lost to bush encroachment, arable crops, forestry, and badly managed agriculture with overgrazing and annual burning of large areas. Oribi are vulnerable to free-roaming dogs. Red Data Book: Vulnerable.

STEENBOK

S318 ☼ ☾

Steenbok
Raphicerus campestris

Description Reddish brown to rich, glossy brick red on the upper parts; white on the underparts, barely extending onto the flanks (white extends about a third of the way up the flanks in oribi). The neck is shorter and proportionately thicker than in

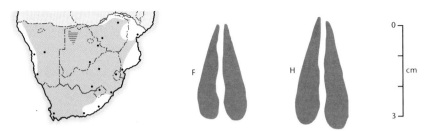

oribi. Very large ears. A black Y on the forehead and a tapering black stripe on top of the muzzle occur in some animals. The preorbital glands open onto black patches in front of the eyes. The tail is short and the same colour as the body on top (black on top in oribi), white underneath. Only males have horns, rising from the top of the head, nearly straight, smooth almost to the base where they are lightly ringed, sometimes with irregular changes in thickness. Females have two pairs of mammae between their hind legs. Total length 85 cm (77–92 cm); shoulder height 52 cm; weight males 10,9 kg (3,9–13,2 kg); females 11,3 kg (9,6–13,2 kg). *See scale drawing on p. 192.*

Habitat Grassland with thick patches of taller grass or bushes for cover; open woodland. Penetrates into desert along watercourses. Avoids forest, dense woodland, and rocky areas. Can survive on farmland and even in peri-urban areas. Independent of water as long as green food is available; probably has to drink when forage is poor.

Diet Graze and browse, probably according to local and seasonal availability. In Botswana grass and broad-leaved plants are each about half of the diet. In Zimbabwe 70% is browse and 30% grass; in Kruger NP only 0,2% of feeding time is spent eating grass. Browse includes leaves and fine stems of forbs and woody plants, berries, fruit and pods; in the Kalahari it digs for tubers and bulbs and eats melons for water.

Life history Gestation 168–173 days. Single lambs are born throughout the year with a November–December peak in Zimbabwe; possibly two seasonal peaks each year. Birth weight 0,9 kg. Females mature at six months, first lamb at one year old. Lifespan eight years. Steenbok are an important source of food for medium and large carnivores: in Kruger NP they make up 13% of cheetah kills and 22% of spotted hyaena kills; in Kalahari Gemsbok NP 1% of cheetah and spotted hyaena kills, 6% of leopard kills. Predation by feral, free roaming and poachers' dogs is a problem on farms and near settlements.

Behaviour Active day and night; time spent feeding at night increases in the dry season. A very selective feeder, often looking as if it is grazing when it is selecting forbs from amongst grass. Almost all feeding is below 60 cm.

Mostly solitary, less commonly in pairs: in Kruger NP 75% of females are solitary; in KwaZulu-Natal 78% of either sex are solitary, 16% in pairs; in Kalahari Gemsbok NP 85% are solitary. Home ranges cover 0,3 to 1 km² in the Kalahari, 0,6 km² in Namibia, 0,5–0,7 km² in Kruger NP. Whether home ranges are territories is uncertain and probably varies with locality and habitat. Faeces and urine are mixed with soil by scraping with the forefoot both before and after elimination; they are not, or not always, buried in the process. Although steenbok have preorbital glands they have not been seen to use them. Glands between the hooves of all four feet presumably mark home ranges as the steenbok walks around, and may add scent when dung is mixed with soil.

Avoids predators by lying tight in thick cover. Sprints away if approached closely, making long leaps every few paces, then drops out of sight into a patch of cover or stops and watches for pursuit. If there is no other cover it will hide in large holes in the ground such as aardvark tunnels. Lambs lie hidden for 3–4 months.

Field sign Faeces mixed with soil (not necessarily buried); the pellets are shiny, long and thin, 1 cm x 0,5 cm, with a narrow point at one end.

Conservation Steenbok can survive close to human development and on farms, but small local populations are susceptible to habitat loss, poaching and over-hunting, and attacks by dogs.

GRYSBOK (CAPE GRYSBOK)

Ⓔ | S319 | Ⓒ | ⛰

Grysbok

Raphicerus melanotis

Description Stands and moves with a hunched posture, like a duiker. The hindquarters are higher than the shoulders, the neck short. Reddish brown, sprinkled with white (no white in steenbok, oribi or red duiker). Yellowish brown on the face, neck, legs and flanks; buffy on the underparts (underparts white in oribi and steenbok). Ears large, greyish on the back. Pale rings around the eyes. The tail is short and the same colour as the body (black on top in oribi). There are small false hooves on the hind legs (absent in Sharpe's grysbok). Only males have horns: short, sharply tapered spikes, lightly ridged at the base, growing from between eyes and ears, slightly for-

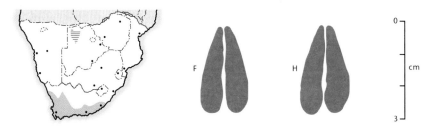

ward of the plane of the face. Females have two pairs of mammae between the hind legs. Total length 78 cm (72–82 cm); tail 5,5 cm (4–7 cm); shoulder height 54 cm; weight males 10 kg, females 10,5 kg (8,8–11,4 kg). *See scale drawing on p. 182.*

Habitat Thick scrub and bush, including fynbos. Survives close to suburban developments in coastal towns of the Western Cape.

Diet A grazer; also browses on leaves and fruit. May become a problem in vineyards by eating young shoots.

Life history Most mating March–June; gestation 180 days. Births throughout the year with a September–December peak. Most of the areas inhabited by grysbok contain few predators, as a result of human influence. Probably taken by leopards and caracals; one report of an attack on a lamb by a large grey mongoose.

Behaviour Mostly nocturnal; becomes active at dusk. Solitary, rarely in mating pairs, or females with lambs. Males hold territories of 1,5–4,8 ha, females have home ranges of 1 ha. Both sexes urinate and defecate in middens. Adult males scent mark with preorbital gland secretion.

Field sign Large middens up to 1 m across and 10 cm deep; the pellets are 1 cm long, tapered at one end, blunt at the other.

Conservation Possibly subject to local extinctions as patches of bush and fynbos are isolated and destroyed by human development.

SHARPE'S GRYSBOK
Sharpe se grysbok
Raphicerus sharpei

S320 R (☵

Description Stands and moves with a hunched posture, like a duiker. The hindquarters are higher than the shoulders; neck short. Rich red-brown (redder than grysbok), sprinkled with white (no white in steenbok, oribi or red duiker). Yellowish brown on the sides of the face, forehead, upper parts of the muzzle and outer parts of the limbs. Buffy on the underparts (underparts white in oribi and steenbok). Ears large, greyish on the back. Pale around the eyes. The tail is short and the same colour as the body (black on top in oribi). There are usually no false hooves on the hind legs (present in grysbok). Only males have horns: sharply tapered spikes, lightly ridged only at the base, growing from between the eyes and ears, in the plane of the face. Females have two pairs of mammae between the hind legs. Total length 75 cm (71–80 cm); tail 6 cm (4,5–7 cm); shoulder height 45–50 cm; weight males 7,3 kg (6,8–8,9 kg), females 7,7 kg (6,4–8,9 kg).

Habitat Dense, low scrub and grass; avoids thick, pure grass. Regrowth after logging provides good habitat. Found in rocky areas as long as there is dense cover.

Diet Mainly browse, but also eats some grass; diet in southeastern Zimbabwe is

70% broad-leaved plants, 30% grass. Browse includes fruit and berries.

Life history Gestation 210 days; single lambs are born throughout the year.

Behaviour Mainly nocturnal; also active at dawn and dusk. Shy and secretive. Solitary, in pairs, or females with lambs. Lies concealed in thick cover. If closely approached it moves off in a slinking run (duikers bound, steenbok sprint with intermittent leaps).

Field sign Large middens up to 1 m across and 10 cm deep; the pellets are 1 cm long, tapered at one end, blunt at the other.

Conservation Red Data Book: Rare.

SUNI

S321 V

Soenie

Neotragus moschatus

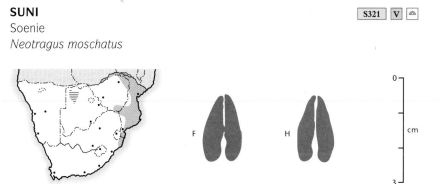

Description A tiny antelope; rich reddish brown, lightly flecked with buff, darker down the middle of the back. White on the underparts (underparts buff in Sharpe's grysbok). Dark reddish brown on the forehead and top of the head. Whitish patches above the eyes, large dark slits in front of the eyes where the preorbital glands open. Broad, rounded ears. The tail is short, the same colour as the body on top and white underneath, which shows at the edges. Only males have horns, rising from just behind the eyes (further back in grysbok, duiker, oribi and steenbok), lying back in the plane of the face (more upright in oribi and steenbok), flattened in cross section, heavily ridged for most of the length (smooth in other small antelope). Females have two pairs of mammae between their hind legs. Total length 70 cm (66–73 cm); tail 10 cm (9–11 cm); shoulder height 35 cm; weight males 5 kg (4,5–5,2 kg), females 5,4 kg (5,1–5,9 kg). *See scale drawing on p. 182.*

Habitat Dry woodland with thickets and underbrush; scrub and bush along rivers and drainage lines. Independent of water. Habitat is damaged by increased browsing by nyalas.

Diet Eats mainly fallen leaves, flowers and fruit, but will also browse and eat mushrooms.

Life history Gestation seven months. Single young are born throughout the year.

Females first lamb at 20 months. Eaten by eagles, carnivores, and pythons; poaching with snares kills more suni than predators do.

Behaviour Active at any time, mainly in the early morning and late afternoon. Lies up in thickets during the hottest part of the day.

Both sexes are territorial; male territories overlap those of females, which may overlap with each other. Usually seen singly (77% of sightings in KwaZulu-Natal); sometimes in pairs (12%), a female with lamb, or a pair with a lamb. Rarely up to four females with one male. Territories cover 1–4 ha in good habitat, 4–10 ha in poor habitat. Scent marks of preorbital gland secretion are deposited, mostly by the male, on stems and twigs bitten off to 1,5–3 cm, in feeding areas rather than along paths. Glands between the hooves mark pathways as the suni walks. Both sexes contribute urine and faeces to communal middens. Middens are probably not territorial markers, but if a strange suni uses one the territorial male over-marks the deposit and scratches up the midden with his forefeet.

Shy and wary; freezes if disturbed, then jumps away. Runs for cover if alarmed, with a high-pitched 'chee-chee'.

Field sign Trails through undergrowth. Black blobs of preorbital gland secretion on short stems and twigs. Droppings are 0,5 cm long, tapered at one end, blunt at the other, in middens.

Conservation Dependence of suni on dense habitat makes them susceptible to habitat loss when bush is cleared for development, or numbers of nyala increase. Killings by domestic and feral dogs are a problem. Use of trails makes them vulnerable to poachers' snares. Red Data Book: Vulnerable.

SUBFAMILY AEPYCEROTINAE

One species, with two distinct subspecies.

IMPALA AND BLACK-FACED IMPALA

S322 ☼

Rooibok en swartneus-rooibok
Aepyceros melampus

Impala are *Aepyceros melampus melampus*, black-faced impala are *A. m. petersi*.

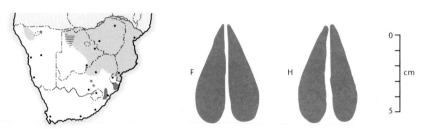

Description Rich, glossy, chestnut brown, darker on the back and upper flanks, paler on the legs and lower flanks. White on the underparts and buttocks and the underside of the tail. There is a black stripe down the top of the tail, and two black stripes down the buttocks, separating the brown and white areas. Black tufts just above the ankle of the hind legs are unique to this species. There are white patches above the eyes, and white on the tip of the muzzle. The ears are large, with small black tips, or more extensive black in black-faced impala. There is a black patch in the middle of the top of the head, and the top of the muzzle is variably darker brown in impala, extensively black in black-faced impala. Only males have horns, long and lyre-shaped, strongly ridged on the lower two thirds, smooth towards the gently tapering, sharp tips. Females have two pairs of mammae between their hind legs. Impala: total length males 1,6 m (1,4–1,8 m), females 1,55 m (1,44–1,6 m); tail males 30 cm (24–33 cm), females 27 cm (22–30 cm); shoulder height males 90 cm, females 85 cm; weight males 54,5 kg (47–66 kg), females 41 kg (32–52 kg). Black-faced impala shoulder height 90 cm; weight males 63 kg, females 50,4 kg. *See scale drawing on p. 213.*

Habitat Open woodland; bush encroachment improves habitat for impala. Dependent on water: in Kruger NP stays within 8 km (usually within 1,6 km) of water.

Diet A very selective grazer and browser, including flowers, fruits, pods, bark and fallen leaves, according to the availability of different food types, which changes with season and locality. Grass is preferred if available; in Kruger NP it is 90% of the diet in January, 37% in July; 33% in Zimbabwe, 80% in KwaZulu-Natal. 80% of feeding is below 40 cm.

Life history Breeding is stimulated by shorter day length, peaking at the dark phase of the moon in autumn (May in Kruger NP, April–May in KwaZulu-Natal). Gestation 194–200 days. Breeding and birth seasons are short, but occur at different times in different localities; births peak in November in the Zambezi Valley, December in southwest Zimbabwe and northern South Africa, early December in KwaZulu-Natal, end December–January in northern Namibia (black-faced impala). Single lambs, one set of twins recorded in black-faced impala. Birth weight 5 kg. Females first lamb at 2 years; males are sexually mature at 13 months, but do not breed until 4–5 years old, when they establish territories. Lifespan 12 years. Impala are a very important component in the diet of large and medium-sized predators; in Kruger NP they provide 29% of lion kills, 28% leopard, 44% cheetah, 75% wild dog, and 15% spotted hyaena kills. Pythons take lambs and occasionally adults.

Behaviour Active mainly during the day. During the breeding season, territorial rams are continually active. Lives in herds, usually of about 6–20, aggregating to large groups of 50–100, exceptionally 200, in the winter as the distribution of food and water becomes restricted.

Females and young live in breeding herds, which often include a few adult males.

Between July and January adult males live in bachelor herds. In January bachelor herds fragment as males' testosterone levels rise in response to short day length. Fighting becomes more frequent and intense and males thrash bushes with their horns. Prime males, usually 4,5–8,5 years old, leave bachelor herds to establish territories of 5–8 ha by the beginning of April, driving other males out of the area. Territory holders advertise their status by 'roaring', which sounds like a mixture of cough and belch, with the neck stretched forward and the head tipped upwards, and parading with the penis extended. They urinate and defecate in large middens and scent mark by rubbing their foreheads on twigs and grass. Intruders are deterred by snorting, chasing and threats with the horns. Persistent intruders are attacked: fights involve charges and wrestling with locked horns, and are short but serious; injuries and deaths are not uncommon. Losers are pursued and gored in the flanks if overtaken. Territory advertisement, defence, and mating occupy so much time that territory holders have no time to feed, they lose body condition, and are replaced by fresher challengers. At the peak of the rut territories are held for only eight days.

As breeding herds move through male territories, residents check the females' reproductive condition by smelling and flehmen of their urine and genitals, and try to prevent oestrous females from leaving the territory by herding them with horn threats, running in front of them with neck stretched forward, and roaring. Mounting for about 10 seconds is repeated until mating is achieved. Once a female has been mated the male no longer herds her.

Lambs lie hidden for a day or two. Females stay in the herd they were born in; males leave and join bachelor herds, often after being driven out of a breeding herd by a territorial ram.

Herd vigilance is important for detecting predators. Within each herd there will nearly always be at least one animal not feeding or drinking at any particular time. Sudden alarms cause herds to scatter explosively in all directions, with graceful leaps up to 3 m high and 12 m long. They jump through narrow gaps in undergrowth and fences. The black patches on the back legs surround a gland whose scent may be released to mark an airborne trail for impala fleeing behind.

The incisor teeth are loose in their sockets so that they can be used to comb ticks out of the coat, and impala spend more time grooming than other antelope. They are also the only one of the medium and small antelope that usually have oxpeckers on them. Reciprocal grooming between herd members is an important means of removing ticks from areas that each animal cannot groom for itself. Territorial rams do not have time to groom, and they carry six times more ticks.

Field sign During the rut, horned bushes, middens. The dung pellets are 1,5 cm long, tapered at one end, blunt or hollow at the other.

Conservation The influence of impala on other species needs to be kept in mind, as mismanaged impala populations can degrade habitats.

There is only one species in this subfamily.

GREY RHEBOK

Vaalribbok

Pelea capreolus

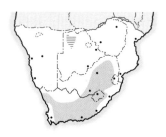 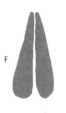 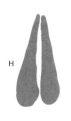 

Description Uniform greyish brown with white underparts, darker on the front of the legs. There is a conspicuous white ring around the eyes, and some white on the sides of the muzzle and chin. The tail is short and bushy, white at the tip and underneath. The neck is long and slender, the ears tall, narrow and pointed (wider in mountain reedbuck). The muzzle tapers only slightly towards the slightly bulbous nose (muzzle more tapered in mountain reedbuck). There are no preorbital glands in front of the eyes (present in mountain reedbuck). The coat is thick and woolly. Only males

have horns, which grow from above the eyes almost straight upwards with a slight forward curve, ringed on the bottom half, tapering gently to sharp points. Females have two pairs of mammae between their hind legs. Shoulder height 70–80 cm; weight 20 kg (19–30 kg); males are larger than females. *See scale drawing on p. 192.*

Habitat Rocky hills, mountain slopes and plateaux with good grass cover. In the Drakensberg it occurs at 1 400–3 300 m, higher than mountain reedbuck. Prefers slopes of 20° and less, north-facing slopes, and areas burnt within the past 4 years. Needs patches of longer grass for cover, and short grass for feeding. Independent of water.

Diet Browses on forbs growing in grassland: 90–97% of the diet is broad-leaved plants, with flowers selected if available; preferred feeding height is below 25 cm.

Life history Mating January–April in former Transvaal, March–May in KwaZulu-Natal; births in November–January and September–December respectively. Single lambs (rarely twins) are born after 261 days' gestation and weaned at 6–8 months. Most deaths are probably due to poor nutrition at the end of the winter. Important prey for caracals: 23% of caracal scats from Karoo NP contained grey rhebuck remains. Feral and free ranging dogs are a problem. Eagles take lambs.

Behaviour Active in spells throughout the day. Spends longer feeding in winter than in summer.

The social unit is a group of up to about a dozen, usually 3–5 females and young with a single adult ram, living on territories established by the ram: 30–75 ha in former Transvaal, up to 135 ha in the Drakensberg. Rams defecate and urinate on territory boundaries; the urine is mixed with dark secretion from the preputial gland. Both sexes have glands between the hooves of all four feet which produce an evil-smelling secretion. Territorial status is advertised by standing or walking with a very erect posture. Intruding males are challenged by approaching in an exaggerated slow walk, lateral and frontal displays, stamping the forefeet, and snorting. Territorial neighbours display on their common border by stotting, running parallel with one another along the border, stamping and snorting and mock fighting. Because the horns are such effective weapons, serious fights are rare. When they do occur they can be fatal.

A male does not breed until he has established a territory and recruited females. A ram checks female's reproductive condition by sniffing their genitals and urine, over-marks their urine with his own urine and faeces, and courts them by following close behind, sniffing and licking and raising a foreleg between the female's hind legs. Females leave the herd to give birth, and stay away for 1–2 weeks. Lambs lie hidden for 6 weeks.

Detection of predators is mainly by sight and sound. The alarm call is a snort. When alarmed herds bunch more closely. When fleeing they may stot with an exaggerated rocking horse action, displaying the white underside of the tail. Top speed is 65 km/h. Rams may defend their groups from predators.

Field sign Droppings are 1 cm long, tapered at one end, blunt at the other.

Three species in the subregion. The bluebuck (*Hippotragus leucophaeus*), which has become extinct in historical times, was also a member of this subfamily.

ROAN

Bastergemsbok
Hippotragus equinus

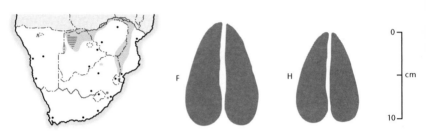

Description The second largest antelope; greyish brown with a tinge of strawberry, darker on the legs. Calves are much lighter rufous. Dark brown or black on the head, with white around the mouth and nose, large white patches in front of the eyes and pale patches behind them. The ears are very long and narrow, with tassels of dark brown hair at the tips. Along the back of the neck there is a mane of short, stiff hair with black tips. The tail has a brush of black hair at the end. Horns in both sexes rise from the top of the head and sweep backwards in an even curve, ridged almost to the tips. Females have two pairs of mammae between their hind legs. Shoulder height males 1,4 m, females 1,3 m; weight males 270 kg, females 250 kg. *See scale drawing on p. 213.* Males are larger and more heavily built than females, with longer, thicker horns; the penis sheath is clearly visible.

Habitat Roan have very strict requirements for lightly wooded savanna with open areas of medium to tall grass (e.g. in vleis) and access to water. Bush encroachment or removal of tall grass by other grazers degrades roan habitat. In northeastern Kruger NP maximum roan densities are 3 km from water.

Diet A grazer, selecting for leaf over stem in tall grasslands; will browse if the grazing is very poor. Preferred feeding height is 15–150 cm; will crop green shoots to 2 cm.

Life history Gestation 267–287 days. Single calves are born at any time of year and weaned at six months. Mean calving interval 317 days (Kruger NP); females first calve at 32–34 months. Lifespan 10–12 years. Selected prey of lions in northeastern Kruger NP: in relation to numbers they are taken five times more frequently than zebra and three times more than wildebeest; also taken by leopard, cheetah and wild dog. Mortality of calves in sub-optimal habitat in South Africa is up to 80% before 6 weeks old.

Behaviour Most active in the morning and late afternoon; spends the hottest part of the day in shade.

Females and their young live in nursery herds of up to about 12 adults, with home ranges of 60 km² overlapping other home ranges by up to 70%. Females have a dominance hierarchy, older cows tending to be dominant. Status is maintained by horn clashing. Young males up to 5–6 years old live in small bachelor herds of up to 9. Adult bulls who do not associate with nursery herds live alone.

Mature breeding bulls associate with nursery herds and maintain an exclusion zone about 300–500 m wide around their herd. They challenge males entering the exclusion zone by standing in a dominant pose with neck arched, chin tucked in, and ears out sideways. Submission is signalled by lowered head, upright ears and the tail being swished or tucked between the legs. Intruders who do not submit may be tackled with horn clashing and head pushing. Serious fights for take-over of a herd are lengthy contests of horn hooking and wrestling, both animals going down onto their knees; usually, one contestant breaks and runs before he is seriously injured. Young males are chased out of nursery herds at about two years old.

Both males and females thrash the leaves and bark off bushes with their horns, and horn the ground. Secretion from glands between the hooves of all four feet marks areas used by the roan.

A herd bull checks females' reproductive condition by sniffing their genitals, and sniffing and flehmen of their urine. He courts a female on heat by following closely behind and tapping between her hind legs with his foreleg.

Females leave the herd for 5–6 days to give birth. Calves lie hidden for 6 weeks; they rely on concealment to avoid predators and do not flee even if closely approached. Mothers visit twice a day to suckle and clean the young. When they join the herd youngsters stay with each other rather than with their mothers.

Old females act as sentinels against predators, standing on the periphery of the herd while the others feed. Herds scatter when alarmed.

Field sign Dung pellets are 2 cm long, tapered at one end, hollow at the other, similar in size to sable's, but roan do not leave scrape marks. Thrashed bushes.

Conservation In conservation areas where the ranges of zebra and wildebeest have been extended by provision of permanent water these two species graze down the long grass that roan depend on, and attract predators that also prey on roan. Roan are susceptible to anthrax: in the Kruger NP a vaccination programme was started in 1972 but stopped in 1992 after suspicions that herd disruption and stress killed more animals than the vaccinations saved. Scarcity raises prices, and translocations too often involve very small groups. Red Data Book: Endangered (widespread further north; populations south of the Limpopo are at the fringe of the species' range).

SABLE
Swartwitpens
Hippotragus niger

S326 V

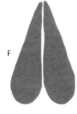
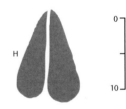

Description Adult bulls are black on the upper parts, cows and young bulls are browner; some old cows become very dark. White on the belly and inner thighs. Bright russet on the back of the ears, russet on the forehead. Contrasting black and white on the face, with a black band down the top of the muzzle, and a black stripe running through each eye to just above the mouth. Calves are reddish brown with indistinct markings. There is an upright mane from the top of the head to the shoulders. Horns in both sexes, rising from above the eyes, sweeping backwards in a long, even curve, flattened from side to side, heavily ridged. Females have two pairs of mammae between their hind legs. Shoulder height males 1,35 m, females 1,25 m; weight males 230 kg, females 210 kg. *See scale drawings on pp. 213 and 221.*

Males are larger and more robustly built than females, with longer, much heavier

horns. The penis sheath is prominent and has a dark tip.

Habitat Savanna woodland; avoids dense woodland and short grass. Dependent on water and rarely found more than 3 km from it. Very widely translocated.

Diet A selective grazer, preferred feeding height 4–14 cm; browses in late winter if the grass is very poor. Eats soil and chews bones to obtain minerals.

Life history Gestation 8–9 months. Single calves are born January–March with a peak in February in northern South Africa; births peak in March in Zimbabwe, January–early February in northern Botswana. Birth weight 13–18 kg; weaned at 6–8 months. Females are sexually mature at two years, first calve at three years. Lifespan at least 10 years. Leopards take calves.

Behaviour Most active in the morning, late afternoon and again from 2–3 hours after dark to midnight. Rests in shade during the middle of the day. Drinks at least once a day; prefers to wade into the water.

Females with males up to 3–4 years old form herds of 15–30, sometimes joining up into loose groups of up to 200 at the end of the dry season. Female herds have dominance hierarchies among the adult cows; older animals are higher ranking. Rank is advertised by rubbing the head and horns on the other animal, tipping the horns towards it, or short chases and charges ending in a blow or jab from the horns.

Submission is signalled by lowered head and tail. Both bulls and cows of similar rank display by standing sideways on, heads high and chins tucked in, and tails lifted; they may slowly circle one another. The lower ranking animal slowly lowers its tail and head, and breaks away.

Where food is available throughout the year, herds have home ranges. They may make seasonal movements where food availability drops too low in winter. Herd home ranges overlap the territories of bulls, and the herds move from territory to territory.

Young males are driven out of herds by territorial bulls at 3–4 years old, and join bachelor herds of less than 10 animals until they are 5–6 years old, when they begin to establish territories.

Mature bulls are territorial, patrolling along roads and paths, and sniffing droppings and urine of other sable. They scent-mark with faeces, scratching the ground with the forefeet before or afterwards, and thrash bushes with their horns, breaking off leaves, bark and branches. Status is advertised by a lateral display with neck arched, chin tucked in, and tail lifted. While a female herd is in his territory a bull follows them around, herding them vigorously if they try to leave by running in front of them with head stretched forward, snorting and sweeping his horns, escalating to chases and charges. Herds that persistently try to leave are successful sooner or later.

Bulls fight over territory by horn clashing, horn wrestling in which both combatants go down onto their knees, and attempts to stab by sideways slashing. Fatalities are not uncommon.

Aggressive interactions are frequent where sable have to leave their home ranges and territories to reach water. At waterholes, sable are aggressive to other species and are able to displace other antelope, zebra and even buffalo cows.

A territorial bull tests a female's reproductive condition by sniffing her genitals, putting his nose into the stream of urine she produces in response, and flehmen. Cows coming into oestrous are courted by herding, following, and tapping between the hind legs with one foreleg. Mounting is brief and repeated.

Females leave the herd to give birth, and stay away for about a week. Calves lie hidden for three weeks, and do not try to flee even when approached closely. Mothers visit twice a day to suckle and clean them. When they join the herd, calves form groups with other calves, and associate with their mothers only to suckle.

Old females act as sentinels, staying alert on the periphery of the herd while the others feed or rest. Sable defend themselves against predators by backing into a bush and slashing sideways with their horns.

Field sign Faeces 2 cm long, tapered at one end, hollow at the other, with scratch marks in the soil produced by territorial bulls. Thrashed bushes.

Conservation Sable are very popular game ranch animals. Unfortunately demand drives up prices and many translocated groups are perilously small. Red Data Book: Vulnerable.

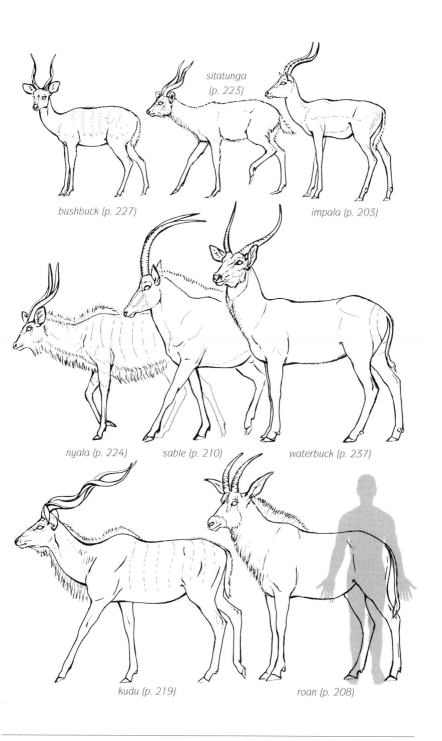

sitatunga
(p. 223)

bushbuck (p. 227)

impala (p. 203)

nyala (p. 224)   sable (p. 210)   waterbuck (p. 237)

kudu (p. 219)   roan (p. 208)

GEMSBOK

Gemsbok
Oryx gazella

S327

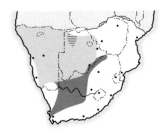

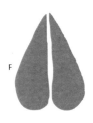

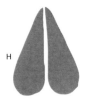

Description Pale fawn-grey; appears pale grey against a background of red sand. White on the underparts and insides of the legs. There is a black stripe down the spine, a black patch on top of the rump, and black bands between the grey flanks and the white underparts. All four legs are black on their top halves, white below the knees or hocks with black patches on the shins. The tail is black with a brush of long hair at the end. Distinctive black and white markings on the face: white around the nose and mouth, black on top of the muzzle, joining a black band running from in front of the ear through the eye to the middle of the lower jaw. Up to an age of 4–6 months calves are fawn or reddish brown. Both sexes have horns, rising backwards from the top of the head, long and nearly straight, ridged for about half their length. Females have two pairs of mammae between their hind legs. Shoulder height males 1,26 m (1,25–1,28 m), females 1,25 m (1,19–1,29 m); weight males 240 kg, exceptionally to 260 kg, females 210 kg. *See scale drawing on p. 235.*

Males and females are difficult to tell apart unless the udder or scrotum is visible. Males are slightly larger and more heavily built than females; their horns are thicker, but shorter and blunter. The record trophy is from a female: 122,9 cm.

Habitat Arid and semi-arid open grassland, scrub, light open woodland, penetrating into savanna woodland. Truly desert adapted, survives in the Kalahari and Namib without surface water. Widely translocated, sometimes into unsuitable habitat where it suffers seasonal nutritional stress and heavy infestations of ticks.

Diet Primarily a grazer, but will browse if grass is not available, and dig for roots, bulbs and tubers. Eats tsama melons (*Citrullus lanatus*) and gemsbok cucumbers (*Acanthosicyos naudianus*) for their water content. Obtains minerals by eating soil and salt encrustations at water holes.

Life history Gestation 264 days. Single calves are born at any time of year. In Northwest Province births peak in August–September, in Botswana in December–March, and in the southern Kalahari in August–September. Females are sexually mature at two years, males at two years but do not breed until five years old. Gemsbok are important prey for large carnivores: in the southern Kalahari they are 32% of lion kills and 52% of spotted hyaena kills. Calves are much more vulnerable than adults: 80% of spotted hyaena kills are calves.

Behaviour Spends up to 60% of the day inactive, in shade if possible, to save energy and water and to avoid overheating. Body temperature is allowed to rise to 45 °C during the day, then excess heat is lost at night. Grazes for long periods at night when the moisture content of the vegetation is higher. Blood flowing to the brain is cooled by heat exchange with blood flowing from the nasal membranes in a network of vessels called the carotid rete. This cools the hypothalamus, which controls the body's heat balance.

Breeding herds, with an average of eight members in the southern Kalahari, contain both males and females. Groups are smaller in the dry season. Bachelor herds are rare and usually contain fewer than five animals.

Both males and females are aggressive and there is a dominance hierarchy in each sex in a herd. Dominant animals signal their status by holding their heads high, threaten by tipping the horn tips towards the subordinate, and by ducking the head. Submission is signalled by lowering the head, keeping the horns back close to the neck, walking with a cringing posture and swishing the tail.

Blows with the length of the horn and jabs with the tips are common, and gemsbok usually stay more than a horn's length apart. In skirmishes the two animals cross horns near their bases and push and twist against each other. In serious fights between bulls the combatants stand alongside one another and stab backwards and sideways over their shoulders.

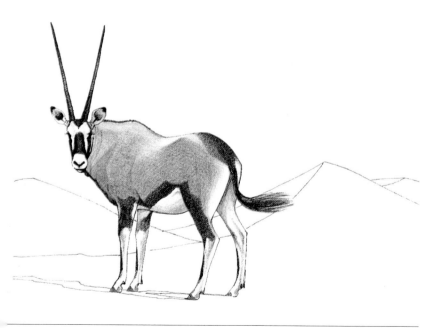

Mature bulls hold territories of 14–45 km^2 in the southern Kalahari and 4–10 km^2 in Namaqualand, and move with breeding herds in the Namib where food is scarce and unreliable. Territorial and herd alpha bulls dominate females and other males, and are recognisable by their head-high stance and larger scrotum. Territories are marked with small, neat dung piles, deposited in a very low crouch so that the pellets do not scatter, secretion from glands between the hooves of all four feet deposited by pawing the ground or while walking around, and by thrashing the leaves, bark and branches off bushes. In the southern Kalahari, female ranges average 248 km^2 in wet years, 1 002–2 750 km^2 in droughts. Home ranges are smaller if permanent water is available.

Only territorial or alpha bulls are sexually active. While breeding herds are on their territories bulls check the females' reproductive condition by sniffing and flehmen of their genitals and urine. Females also smell each other and show flehmen. Bulls court females in oestrus by tapping their hind legs with a foreleg.

Females leave their herd to give birth. Calves lie hidden for 3–6 weeks; by the time they emerge their horns have started to grow, hence the myth that they are born with horns. Mothers visit in the morning and evening to suckle and clean the calf, and may spend the night with it.

Herds bunch around calves if spotted hyaenas are detected, and the adults use their horns in defence. Even groups of hyaenas are usually unsuccessful in hunting adult gemsbok, which defend themselves against predators by slashing with their horns while covering their rear by backing into a thorny bush.

Field sign Pellets are 1,5 cm long, 1 cm across, tapered at one end and hollow at the other. Small, neat piles of droppings are deposited by territorial bulls. Thrashed bushes.

Conservation Gemsbok should be investigated as a sustainable way of producing meat in arid and semi-arid areas where sheep and goats cause serious environmental damage.

BUFFALO AND SPIRAL-HORNED ANTELOPE

Six species in the subregion: buffalo, kudu, sitatunga, nyala, eland and bushbuck.

AFRICAN BUFFALO
Buffel
Syncerus caffer

S328 ( ) ☼

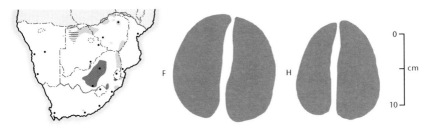

Description Except for their horns, buffalo look like heavily built cattle. Adult males are black or charcoal grey, females and youngsters have a reddish tinge. The hair is short and coarse, and becomes sparse with age. They have large heads and thick necks, massive bodies and short limbs. The horns of adults grow from thick, wrinkled bosses on the forehead, flare sideways and downwards and then curve upwards to the tips, which usually point slightly backwards. Females have two pairs of mammae between their hind legs. Total length males 3,2 m (2,9–3,4 m), females 3 m; tail 60 cm (50–70 cm); shoulder height males 1,45 m, females 1,4 m; weight males 625 kg, females 530 kg. Trophy bulls from Willem Pretorius GR weighed 800 kg (686–900 kg); heaviest bull from Kruger NP 802 kg. *See scale drawing on p. 221.*

Males have larger heads, thicker necks and heavier horns than females, and in old bulls the bosses join across the head.

Habitat Needs plentiful grass, preferably 5–80 cm tall, shade and water. Does not occur where there is less than 250 mm rain per year.

Diet An unselective grazer; browses very little. Prefers leaves to stems, and grass species high in crude protein. A 500 kg cow eats 15–17,5 kg dry matter a day.

Life history Gestation 330–346 days. Single young are born at any time of the year, nearly all in summer: October–April in northern Botswana; January–April in Kruger NP; November–April in Matusadona NP, Zimbabwe. Birth weight 36 kg. Calves are weaned at 5–15 months or just before the next calf is born, and associate with their mother for at least 2 years. Cows calve in alternate years or twice in three years. Cows first breed at 4–5 years old, bulls at 7–8 years when they have risen in the dominance hierarchy. Lifespan 15 years. Lions are the most important predators, then spotted hyaenas, though calves are taken by other large carnivores.

Buffalo are 41% of kills by Savuti lions in the dry season. Living in herds offers protection against predators; in Kruger NP lions kill twice as many males as females.

Behaviour Grazes for 8–10 hours a day; more able than other grazers to push in amongst bushes to reach grass. Sensitive to heat, and tends to feed in the evening, at night and in the morning when it is cool. Drinks at least once, and typically twice, a day, morning and afternoon, and spends the hottest part of the day in shade, ruminating. Wallowing in mud and water relieves heat stress and has social significance; bulls wallow more than females and subadults. Buffalo rest and ruminate very close together, even touching.

Very gregarious: the largest herds contain 1 000–2 000 animals; herds of a few hundred are more common. Large herds form in winter and split up in summer; individuals and social groups may move between herds. Some adult bulls form small bachelor groups of 2–6, exceptionally 20–30, and old bulls may be solitary. 'Bachelor' bulls return to the herds for mating; while in a herd they lose body condition and dominance rank, which they build up again when they go back to a bachelor group. The basic social units are family groups of related cows with their calves. There are separate dominance hierarchies among bulls and cows. Bigger, older animals tend to be high ranking, but cows rise in status when they have a calf at foot. High-ranking animals tend to be in the front centre of the herd where predation risks are smaller and food is more readily available. The dominance display is a head high pose with the nose pointing at the ground, standing sideways on to the opponent, or head-tossing and horn-hooking. Submission is signalled by lowering the head, approaching the opponent and putting the nose under its belly. Fights are most com-

monly over access to females on heat; opponents charge and clash heads, and horn wrestle.

Herd home ranges of 60–1 000 km² do not overlap, but are not defended as territories. Buffalo are not migratory but move in response to seasonal changes in food availability. Routes between grazing, water and cover are used repeatedly. Herds travel in column formation when not feeding, on a broad front when both grazing and moving.

Placid if undisturbed, but becomes extremely dangerous when molested. Investigates disturbances by raising the head with the nose held high, and may walk towards the source. If threatened, herds bunch more closely, with adults on the outside and cows with calves in the middle. Approaching predators and humans are threatened by head tossing. Attacking predators may be driven off by the victim's companions, and predators may be attacked on sight. Maximum speed is 56 km/h; 44 km/h is probably more typical.

Field sign Droppings are flattened cowpats.

Conservation Buffalo are susceptible to diseases such as bovine tuberculosis, carried by cattle, which is now spreading through the Kruger NP. There was an epidemic of anthrax in buffalo in Kruger NP in 1991. Their management is severely constrained by veterinary regulations designed to protect commercial stock farming from foot-and-mouth disease and corridor disease. As one of the hunter's big five and the ecotourist's big seven they have a high commercial value. Their potential for sustainable meat production needs to be properly investigated.

KUDU

S239

Koedoe
Tragelaphus strepsiceros

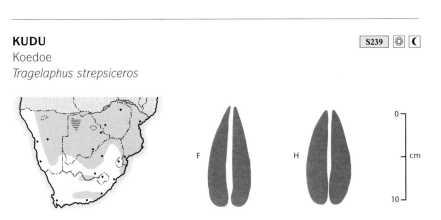

Description Tall and majestic. Males are fawn grey, females tinged cinnamon; old bulls become greyer and their necks become darker in the breeding season. There is a single narrow, white stripe down the middle of the back and 6–10 narrow white stripes across the back and down the flanks. Both sexes have a short upright mane from the top of the head to the shoulders, where it forms a crest. Adult bulls have a

long fringe underneath the neck. The ears are very large. There is a narrow white bar across the face just in front of the eyes, narrowly broken in the middle, variable white patches on the sides of the face, and white on the top lip and chin. The tail is white underneath. Only males have horns, rising from the top of the head in wide spirals with a distinct ridge along their length. Females have two pairs of mammae between their hind legs. Total length males 2,85 m (2,47–2,67 m), females 2,5 m (2,3–2,6 m); tail 43 cm (37–48 cm); shoulder height males 1,4 m, females 1,25 m; weight males 230 kg (190–260 kg) and up to 305 kg, females 157 kg (120–210 kg). *See scale drawings opposite and p. 213.*

Habitat Savanna woodland, including rocky areas and slopes. Does not occur in forest or desert, or in grassland or short scrub unless there is woodland nearby to provide cover. Valley bushveld in the Eastern Cape Province supports high densities of kudu. Can survive on farms, provided sufficient cover remains. Independent of water as long as green food is available.

Diet Browses on a very wide range of plants: 148 species are eaten in Kruger NP, including aloes and euphorbias. Acacia and *Combretum* species are favoured. Will eat freshly flushed green grass. Can become a serious crop and garden raider. Forbs

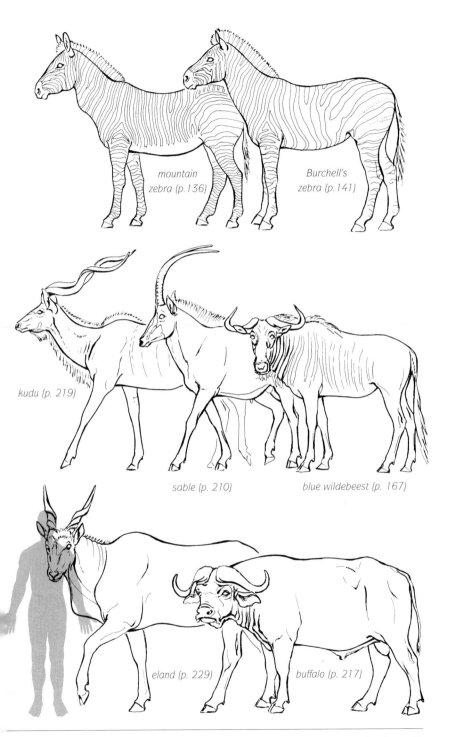

mountain zebra (p.136)

Burchell's zebra (p.141)

kudu (p. 219)

sable (p. 210)

blue wildebeest (p. 167)

eland (p. 229)

buffalo (p. 217)

are preferred over woody plants, making up 65% of the diet in Kruger NP for most of the year, but only 20% when trees flush new leaves.

Life history Gestation 210–225 days. Single calves are born throughout the year; no record of twins. In the lowveld most births in January–March with a peak in February, tailing off until June. In KwaZulu-Natal most births in December–January. Birth weight 16 kg. Weans at six months; horns start growing at five months. Males are sexually mature at three years and first breed at six years; females first calve at two or three years. Lifespan 15 years. Important prey for wild dogs in Hwange NP (23% of kills) and Kruger NP (8% of kills), 15% of spotted hyaena kills in Kruger NP. Males suffer more predation than females and adult sex ratios are one male to two females.

Behaviour Most active in the morning and late afternoon, sleeping before dawn; becomes more nocturnal where it is hunted. Feeds below 1,8 m; bulls are more likely than cows to feed at full stretch. Browses for only about a minute on each tree. If leaves are out of reach bulls break down branches with their horns.

Not territorial; herds have home ranges of 360–520 ha in Kruger NP, probably much larger in drier areas. Bulls wander more widely than cows, but return to a fixed core area. Cows, calves and subadults form small family herds, usually with 6–7 and up to 12 members; groups are smaller on farm land. Social grooming occurs in both family and bachelor herds. Temporary aggregations may form at water holes in the dry season. Males leave herds at 3 years old; adult bulls live alone or in bachelor groups of 2–6, joining female herds in May–August.

Dominance among bulls is based on size and displays of fighting ability. During the mating season prime bulls develop massive neck muscles, thrash bushes with their horns and dig up soil. Fights are rare and involve lunging, horn clashing, and wrestling with locked horns. Deaths occur from stab wounds and when horns become inextricably tangled.

A dominant bull checks a female's reproductive condition by sniffing and flehmen of her urine and genitals. He courts by approaching with head stretched forward, puts his neck over the female's and presses down. Male and female may lick each other. Before mounting the male rests his chin on the female's rump. Cows leave their herd to give birth. Calves lie hidden for up to a month, perhaps as long as three months.

Alert and nervous when on open ground; in cover stands motionless to avoid detection. The alarm call is a loud bark. Runs with tail curled upwards, exposing the white underside as an alarm signal. Bulls run with their horns laid back close to their shoulders. A strong jumper; clears 2 m high fences with ease, and 3 m under stress.

Field sign Thrashed bushes, horned up soil, broken down branches. Droppings are 2 cm long, slightly longer than wide, with a short point at one end and a hollow at the other.

Conservation Kudu are very vulnerable to anthrax, and are the reservoir of anthrax infection in Kruger NP.

SITATUNGA
Waterkoedoe
Tragelaphus spekei

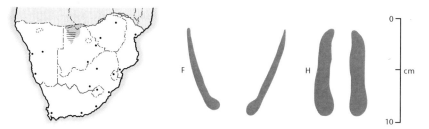

Description Dark brown; some females are redder, with a distinct black band down the middle of the back. There are a few indistinct blotches of yellowish brown and indistinct white stripes across the back and down the flanks, and a white band and white spots on the haunches. The coat is long and uneven. There are white patches above all four hooves, two white patches on the underside of the neck, white eyebrows and white bars running forward from the corner of each eye to almost meet on top of the muzzle. The top lip and chin are white. The hooves are unique, very long (up to 18 cm in adult rams), and able to splay widely for support on soft ground. Horns in males only, rising from the top of the head in shallow corkscrews, with a

prominent ridge running along them to near the white tips. Females have two pairs of mammae between the hind legs. Shoulder height males 90 cm, females 80 cm; weight males 115 kg, females 80 kg. *See scale drawing on p. 213.*

Habitat Restricted to dense reedbeds and adjacent grasslands in the wetlands of the Okavango and Chobe. Makes short seasonal movements out of reedbeds during the annual flood. Widely distributed in the same sort of habitat further north.

Diet Freshly sprouting reeds and rushes, especially papyrus, and papyrus flowers. Also grazes sedges and browses on trees, bushes, ferns and forbs.

Life history Single young are born in January–February in the western Okavango, June–July in eastern Caprivi. Weans at 4–5 months. Leopards, lions and wild dogs take sitatunga while they are on dry land, crocodiles catch them in the water.

Behaviour Active at any time of the day or night except the hotter midday period, when it lies up in shade. Moves out of reedbeds into woodland at night. Rests on platforms of broken down reeds and makes narrow pathways through the reeds. A strong swimmer, readily feeding in shoulder deep water.

Solitary or in herds of up to six females with a mature ram. Not territorial. Rams display to each other by standing tall, threatening with the horns, and horning the soil and vegetation. Fights are rarely observed (like the rest of sitatunga behaviour). A loud bark, given more often at night, may be a contact or spacing signal.

A ram tests a female's reproductive condition by sniffing and flehmen of her genitals and urine. He courts by following close behind her, resting his chin on her rump and back.

Calves are born on reed platforms prepared by their mothers. They lie hidden, and are too clumsy to escape by running away. Mothers visit 2–4 times a day to suckle. Calves can swim before they can walk properly.

As is appropriate in such dense habitat, danger is detected by sound. Sitatunga flee for only 50–100 m then stop and listen for pursuit. If hard pressed or wounded they take to the water and swim away, and may hide by submerging with only the nostrils above the surface.

Field sign Platforms of broken down reeds. Broken papyrus stems with the flowers bitten off.

Conservation Anything that threatens the Okavango and Chobe wetlands threatens the southern African populations of sitatunga.

NYALA

Njala

Tragelaphus angasii

S331

Description Adult males and females look completely different. Males of 2 years and older are slate grey to dark brown with up to 14 distinct white stripes across the

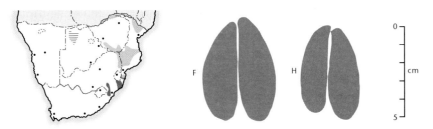

back and down the flanks, and white spots on the thighs and belly. The bottom half of each leg is bright yellow, with a dark brown or black band separating this from the colour of the body. There is a mane of long hair running from the top of the head to the root of the tail, the hair is white at the tips, producing a white stripe down the middle of the back when the mane lies flat. From below the jaw, down the underside of the neck, chest and belly and onto the undersides of the hind legs is a long, shaggy fringe of dark hair. The ears are long with a reddish tinge on the back. The tail is dark and bushy. Females and young are bright chestnut with up to 18 distinct white stripes across the back and down the flanks. They do not have manes or fringes of long hair. Males begin developing adult colour at 14 months. Both sexes have a white spot below the eyes, another spot lower down and further forward on the side of the face, and short white bars in front of the eyes that almost meet on top of the muzzle. Only males have horns, shallow corkscrews with a ridge up the outside of the curve, and short yellowish tips. Females have two pairs of mammae between their hind legs. Total length males 2,1 m (2–2,5 m), females 1,8 m (1,7–1,9 m); tail males 43 cm (37–47 cm), females 36 cm (34–40 cm); shoulder height males 1,12 m (1–1,2 m), females 97 cm (87–106 cm); weight males 107 kg (92–127 kg), females 62 kg (55–68 kg). *See scale drawing on p. 213.*

Habitat Thickets in savanna woodland, including forest patches on old termite hills, and dense riverine bush. Nyala benefit from shifting agriculture where abandoned fields and overgrazing cause bush encroachment and the growth of broad-leaved food plants. Not dependent on water as long as there is green food. Sensitive to cold; hot moist summers and warm dry winters are the preferred climate. High densities of nyala can degrade habitat for bushbuck, suni, and blue and red duiker. Widely translocated outside their natural distribution range.

Diet Browses and grazes according to seasonal and local availability of grass and broad-leaved plants. In Mozambique grass is 65% of the diet in the wet season, only a trace in the dry. Takes a wide range of species (108 species are browsed in Mozambique) and will eat both fresh and fallen leaves, shoots, fruit, flowers and bark. Males eat almost twice as much as females.

Life history Breeds throughout the year. Oestrous cycle 19 days; gestation 220 days. Single young, with a birth weight of 4,2–5,5 kg. Females first lamb at 2–3 years. Important prey for wild dogs in Hluhluwe-Umfolozi NP; baboons take lambs.

Behaviour Active in the morning and afternoon, and into the night; rests in the middle of the day and after midnight. Moves onto grassland to graze, only at night in areas where it is disturbed. Often associates with monkeys or baboons to feed on the fruit and leaves that they drop from trees.

Solitary or in herds of up to 30, usually up to 6. Herds are unstable with no permanent social bonds beyond a mother and her two youngest offspring. A young male leaves his mother's herd at two years old and joins a bachelor herd. Not territorial; home ranges in Hluhluwe are 65 ha for males, 83 ha for females, in Mozambique 3,9 km² for males, 3,6 km² for females.

Males dig up soil and thrash bushes with their horns. At highest intensity their status display involves raising the mane and parading slowly past the opponent with very slow, high steps of the bright yellow legs, with the head down and the horns pointed forward, and the tail curled up over the back to show its white underside. Sparring involves head pushing and horn clashing. Serious fights are rare, but fierce and sometimes fatal.

Males test any females they meet by sniffing the base of their tails, and sniffing and flehmen of their urine. Females are attractive for two days before they become receptive. A male courts by approaching with head stretched forward, puts his nose between the female's hind legs and butts her, sometimes hard enough to lift her hindquarters off the ground. A courting male may be displaced by a higher ranking challenger. When the female becomes receptive the male puts his neck across hers and presses her head down, then moves back until his head rests on her rump, and mounts. A female's lowering her head to drink may stimulate a male to mount.

Females give birth in thickets. Lambs lie hidden for 18 days.

The alarm call is a deep bark; lost lambs bleat to attract their mothers. Nyala react to the alarm calls of baboons, impala and kudu. Flee into heavy cover.

Field sign Horned up soil and thrashed bushes. Droppings are 1,5 cm long with a small bump at one end and a hollow at the other.

Conservation Nyala thrive in protected habitat, and can out-compete other species.

BUSHBUCK

S332

Bosbok
Tragelaphus scriptus

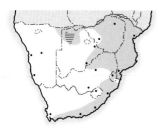
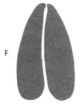
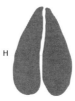

F   H

0
cm
3

Description Stockily built, with short neck and legs. Colour and markings vary with sex and locality, and between individuals. In southern South Africa males are dark brown with a few white spots on the flanks and thighs, and a crest of yellowish hair down the middle of the back. In northern Botswana and Caprivi the ground colour is

dark red with distinct white stripes and spots. In northern South Africa, southern Botswana, Zimbabwe and Mozambique the ground colour is reddish brown and the markings are intermediate. In all forms there is a white patch high on the throat and a white band at the base of the neck. Females are paler than males from the same area, with the same markings. Only males have horns, twisted and very shallowly corkscrewed, triangular in cross-section with a prominent ridge, rising from just behind the eyes, almost in the plane of the face. Females have two pairs of mammae between their hind legs. Measurements and weight vary with locality: total length males 1,5 m (1,3–1,7 m), females 1,4 m (1,3–1,6 m); tail 21 cm (19–24 cm); shoulder height males 79 cm (73–86 cm), females 69 cm (63–74 cm); weight males 42 kg (29–54 kg, exceptionally to 83 kg), females 28 kg (24–34 kg). *See scale drawing on p. 213.*

Habitat Dense cover in the underbrush of woodland and forest, near permanent water. May make short seasonal movements away from permanent water when surface water is temporarily available. Forest edges are important sources of food. Able to persist in farming areas and even close to large cities as long as dense cover and water are available.

Diet A browser, selecting for plant part and species. Most of the diet is leaves and shoots; buds, flowers, fruit and newly sprouted grass are taken seasonally. Will take dry fallen leaves in winter. In Knysna forest browse makes up 93% of the diet, grass 10%, fungi 5%, ferns 1%. In Botswana grass occurred in 55% of stomachs. Can be a problem in forestry plantations and crops.

Life history Gestation 180 days. Single young are born at any time of year. Birth weight 3,5–4,5 kg. Males are sexually mature at 10–11 months, females at 14 months; males first breed at 4 years when they have risen in the dominance hierarchy. Lifespan 13 years. Taken by large and medium-sized carnivores, and pythons. Suffers from heavy poaching with dogs and snares, and is a popular quarry with hunters.

Behaviour Active in the evenings, at night and in the early mornings. Rests during the day in the densest cover. Associates with baboons and monkeys to feed on fruit and leaves dropped from the trees.

Social organisation probably varies with locality and details of habitat; usually both sexes are solitary and live in overlapping home ranges, with a dominance hierarchy among an area's residents. Small groups of either or both sexes may form. Lambs stay with their mothers until eight months old. In Chobe home ranges are about 0,5 ha in winter, 6 ha in summer; in KwaZulu-Natal 120 ha for males, 60 ha for females; in the Western Cape, 55–174 ha for males, 15–113 ha for females.

Males horn the soil and bushes, and rub the head and neck on bushes and trees. The hair low on the neck gets worn thin by this rubbing. The dominance display between two males is a slow circling with the crest along the back erected, the tail curled up and the head turned towards the opponent. Chasing and horn clashing may follow. In serious fights opponents engage horns and try to push and twist each other off balance; at the highest intensity they lunge and stab. Fights can be fatal.

Males detect when a female is on heat from the smell of her urine and genitals; dominant males monopolise access to females in oestrous. Young lie hidden for four months. Social bonds between ewe and lamb are strengthened by mutual licking.

Not a very fast runner; avoids predators by hiding. Takes readily to water and swims strongly. The alarm call is a loud, very dog-like bark. Very aggressive against predators and human hunters.

Field sign Droppings are distinctive tubular clusters of pellets, sometimes looking like miniature black maize cobs. Clusters are 2–3 cm across.

Conservation Susceptible to habitat loss when dense bush along waterways is cleared for agriculture and horticulture, degraded by overgrazing and badly managed fires, or surrounded by forestry plantations. Over-utilisation of bush by both domestic and wild animals (e.g. nyala and elephants) degrades bushbuck habitat. Selective hunting of males reduces population reproductive rates.

ELAND

S333

Eland

Taurotragus oryx

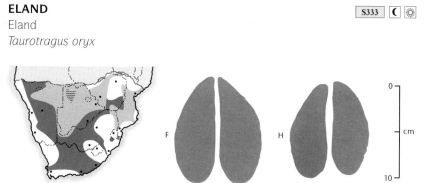

Description Largest of the African antelope. Dull fawn, sometimes with up to five vertical white stripes on the flanks; mature bulls become progressively blue-grey, especially on the neck. Calves are reddish fawn. There is a brown patch on the back of the forelegs, just above the knee. Males have a patch of stiff, dark brown hair on the forehead overlying glandular skin. This hair is often mud-caked. The ears are relatively small. Both sexes have a dewlap with a tuft of dark hair on its lower edge, much deeper and more developed in males. Both sexes have horns, rising from the top of the head and lying back in the plane of the face, nearly straight, with a spiral ridge; longer, much thicker and much more prominently ridged in males than in females. Females have two pairs of mammae between their hind legs. Shoulder height males 1,7 m, females 1,5 m; weight males 700 kg (up to 840 kg and probably even heavier), females 460 kg. In KwaZulu-Natal shoulder height males 1,55 m, females 1,35 m; weight males 575 kg, females 316 kg. *See scale drawing on p.221.*

Habitat Arid scrub and grassland, savanna woodland, Cape macchia and montane grassland up to 2 400–2 700 m in the Drakensberg. Independent of water. May make local seasonal movements or migrate long distances to reach food. In the southern Kalahari, moves east in the summer and west in the winter, probably to reach artificial water points in Kalahari Gemsbok NP. In the Drakensberg, moves to higher ground in summer. Migrations in the central Kalahari are blocked by veterinary cordon fences. Widely translocated; can survive on cattle farms.

Diet Predominantly a browser, but will eat green grass, which is the bulk of the diet in summer. Prefers grass burned within the past year. Browses on both leaves and twigs, and also takes fruit and berries. Will eat dry fallen leaves. Can be a problem in crops and is very difficult to fence out.

Life history Single calves are born after a gestation of nine months. In KwaZulu-Natal mating December–January, most births September–October. In western Mpumalanga births August–October. Birth weight 32–36 kg, male calves are heavier than females; weaned at 6–8 months. Females first calve at 2–4 years; males mature at 18 months but do not mate until they reach high dominance rank. Lifespan 12–20 years. Females are infertile after 15 years. Adults are too large for anything except lions and spotted hyaenas to tackle; leopards and spotted hyaenas take calves (7% of spotted hyaena kills in the southern Kalahari).

Behaviour Feeds at night when vegetation contains more water, pulling leaves into the mouth with the lips, not the tongue. Breaks down branches by twisting them between the horns, or hooking the horns over them.

Rather than sweating to stay cool, allows body temperature to rise during the day, then unloads excess heat at night.

Ranges over huge areas: 8 000–14 000 km^2 in the southern Kalahari. Nomadic movements lead to dramatic fluctuations in numbers in some areas: one area held 13 000 eland in September 1981 and only 12 of them in March 1982.

Forms small mixed herds of 4–10 in winter, large mixed herds of up to a few hundred in summer, exceptionally over 1 000. Herd members groom one another. Not territorial. Males and females have separate dominance hierarchies; larger, older animals are high ranking and bulls dominate cows. Threat is signalled by head shaking with the head up, jabbing with the horns, and charging. Head shaking with the head lowered, and moving away, signal submission. Blows with the sides of the horns are used against subordinates that do not move away quickly enough. Bulls fight by clashing and locking horns and pushing and twisting. Losers break and run, but may be fatally gored.

Bulls horn the soil and bushes, and rub the tuft of hair on the forehead in soil where they or an oestrous female have just urinated, caking it with mud. Dominant bulls bellow, and grunt when displacing subordinates. Cows bark when disturbed, moo, click and grunt to attract their calves. Calves bleat to attract their mothers. As they walk, eland, especially large bulls, make a clicking noise whose origin has not finally been settled.

Eland are slow runners, and trot rather than galloping. When threatened by predators, herds bunch with calves in the middle, and counterattack with horns and hooves. Adult bulls can jump 2 m fences, younger animals 3 m.

Both males and females investigate each other's urine by sniffing and flehmen. Cows in heat are shadowed by dominant bulls, who drive other bulls away. A bull courts a cow by rubbing his head on her flanks, licking her, resting his chin on her back, sniffing and licking her genitals, and pawing and horning the ground.

Calves can stand soon after birth, and can follow the mother after 3–4 hours, but lie hidden for up to 2 weeks. Calves will follow any adult, and try to suckle from any female. Females aggressively repel suckling attempts by calves other than their own. Calves are more closely bonded to other calves than to their mothers, and form crèche groups within the herd.

Field sign Broken down branches, horned mud patches. Droppings are 2–3 cm long, tapered or rounded at one end, blunt at the other, sometimes in cylindrical clumps.

Conservation Eland have important potential for sustainable meat production.

Five species in the subregion: waterbuck, reedbuck, mountain reedbuck, red lechwe and puku.

REEDBUCK

S334 **(**

Rietbok

Redunca arundinum

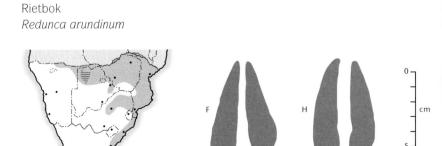

Description Greyish brown to buffy yellow upper parts, often slightly darker on the back. White underparts, greyish white underneath the neck and chest. There is a paler crescent high on the throat which is more obvious in males. The lips and chin are white. The ears have triangular tips (more rounded in mountain reedbuck). In some populations (e.g. Kruger NP) there is a bare glandular patch on the side of the

neck below the ear; in others this is absent (always present in mountain reedbuck). There is a dark band down the front of each foreleg, and less distinctly down the front of the lower part of each hind leg (absent in mountain reedbuck and the best feature to separate females of the two species). The tail is very bushy, white underneath. Horns only in males, rising from the top of the head with an even forward curve (sharply hooked at the tip in mountain reedbuck), ridged for about two thirds of their length. At the base of each horn is a distinctive band of pale, soft, rubbery tissue. Females have two pairs of mammae between their hind legs. Total length males 1,6 m (1,5–1,8 m), females 1,6 m (1,4–1,7 m); tail 25 cm (20–30 cm); shoulder height males 90 cm (84–97 cm), females 80 cm; weight males 52 kg (43–68 kg), females 38 kg (32–51 kg). *See scale drawing on p. 235.*

Habitat Wet vleis; grassland near permanent water courses. Dependent on tall grass or scrub for cover, and free access to water, therefore confined naturally to the eastern and northern parts of the subregion and patchily distributed. Prefers burnt areas for feeding. Occurs up to 1 800–2 000 m in the Drakensberg.

Diet A grazer; browses if the nutritional quality of the grass falls too low. A pest in planted pastures in KwaZulu-Natal during winter.

Life history Gestation 24 weeks. Single young are born throughout the year, with peaks in December–May in Kruger NP, September onwards in Kyle NP, December–January in KwaZulu-Natal highlands. Females first give birth at 2–3 years; males mature at 9 months but must hold territory to mate. Average lifespan 4–5 years, maximum 10 years. Occasional prey of large and medium sized carnivores. Lambs are probably taken by pythons.

Behaviour Most active at night; feeding extends into daylight when food supplies decline during winter. Drinks several times a day, especially during dry weather. Usually rests in patches of bushes or tall grass trampled down to make a bed.

Lives singly, in pairs or threes; occasionally about a dozen congregate on good grazing. Territorial in Kruger NP, overlapping ranges of 5–6 ha in St Lucia, overlapping ranges of 74–123 ha in KwaZulu-Natal highlands, with males territorial during the mating season. Territories are maintained by the ram. Occupation is advertised by a proud posture with the neck erect and head held high to show the white throat band, by running with an exaggerated rocking canter, ritual urination and defecation, and loud whistling. Intruders are challenged with the same displays. Fights are ritualised horn clashing, escalating to forward, downward jabs. Deaths can be common. Submission is signalled by lowering the head.

The alarm call is a loud high-pitched whistle, which may also tell the predator that it has lost the element of surprise. Flees at a gallop with occasional long jumps. Two styles of stotting: jerking the hind legs backwards and outwards, which produces a 'pop', probably from the sudden opening of glands in the groin; or jumping with the hind legs tucked up, hindquarters high and head back, snorting at each jump.

Males court by approaching with head low and stretched forward, nuzzling and sniffing the female's genitals. Females give birth in cover, and lambs lie hidden for two months; mothers visit once a day and once or twice at night to suckle and clean them. Mother and young rejoin the male after 3–4 months.

Field sign Flattened beds of grass in patches of tall grass. Droppings are 1,5 cm long, tapered at one end, blunt at the other.

Conservation Susceptible to habitat loss from destruction of wetlands, badly managed burning of grassland and vleis, and overgrazing. Its status is secured by its popularity with hunters for trophies and meat.

MOUNTAIN REEDBUCK
Rooiribbok
Redunca fulvorufula

S335 🌙 ☼

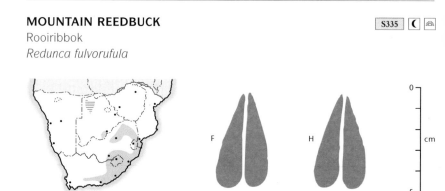

Description Greyish upper parts, yellower on the neck; white underparts. No dark line down the front of the legs (dark line in reedbuck). Ears narrow with rounded tips (broader triangular tips in reedbuck, very tall and narrow in grey rhebok). Dark glandular patches on the sides of the neck below the ears are always present (sometimes

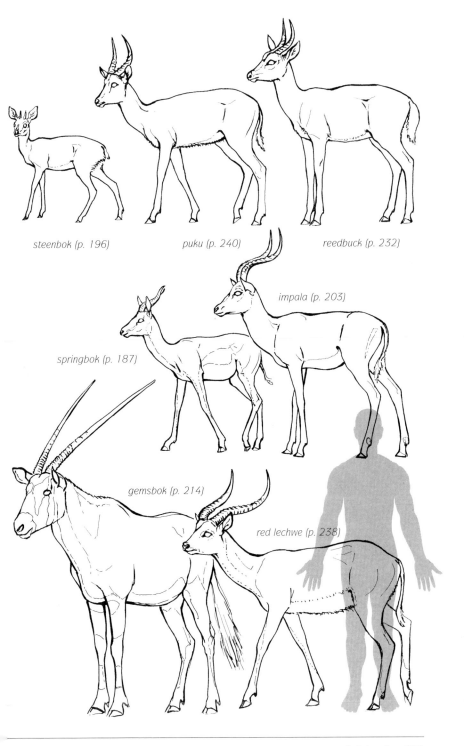

steenbok (p. 196)

puku (p. 240)

reedbuck (p. 232)

springbok (p. 187)

impala (p. 203)

gemsbok (p. 214)

red lechwe (p. 238)

absent in reedbuck, absent in grey rhebok). The neck is noticeably thin in females. The muzzle is pointed (rounded thick muzzle in grey rhebok). The tail is bushy; grey on top, white underneath. The coat is thick and woolly. Only males have horns, rising from the top of the head, almost straight back with tips hooked sharply forward (even forward curve in reedbuck, straight spikes in grey rhebok), ridged to the hook. Females have two pairs of mammae between their hind legs. Total length 1,3 m (1,2–1,4 m); head and body 1,15 m (1–1,25 m); shoulder height males 75 cm, females 70 cm; weight males 30 kg (22–38 kg), females 28 kg (14,5–35 kg). The weight of males varies by 25% from season to season. *See scale drawing on p. 192.*

Habitat Dry, stony 20–30° slopes of hills and mountains, with grass cover and scattered bushes and trees. Up to 2 200 m in Drakensberg. Dependent on water. May make seasonal movements.

Diet A grazer: 99% of diet is grass; selects for species and leaf. Prefers short grass burned within the past year.

Life history Single lambs are born after a gestation of 236–251 days. Peak of mating April–May; peak in births October–January, some births at other times. Birth weight 3 kg. Females mature at 12–14 months, 9 months if very well fed; males mature at 27 months, but do not mate until they hold territory. Horns begin growing at 15 months, curve forward at 2 years, develop ridges at 3 years. Lifespan 12 years. Harsh winter weather is an important cause of death. Important prey of caracals; in the Mountain Zebra NP 20% of caracal scats contained mountain reedbuck remains.

Behaviour Most active in the early morning, late afternoon and at night. Rests during the day in the cover of bushes and trees; herd members lie close together. Moves down from slopes to feed and reach water at night. Spends longer feeding in winter to compensate for the poorer quality of the grass.

Lives singly or in small herds of 3–6, exceptionally in aggregations of up to 30. Mature rams hold territories of about 30 ha. Males without territories live alone or in bachelor groups. Female herds have unstable membership and home ranges that overlap several male territories. Territorial rams chase young males out of breeding herds at 9–15 months.

The alarm call is a loud, shrill whistle; may flee with an exaggerated rocking-horse action with the tail curled up to show the white underside.

Males court by approaching with the head stretched forward. Females give birth in cover. Lambs lie hidden for 2–3 months; females visit once or twice a day, and presumably also at night, to suckle and clean them.

Field sign Droppings are clusters of squashed, round pellets.

WATERBUCK
Waterbok / Kringgat
Kobus ellipsiprymnus

F H

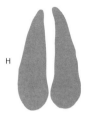

0

cm

5

Description Stockily built, with short legs. Greyish brown, with a white collar high on the throat, white eyebrow stripes, and a distinctive white 'lavatory seat' ring on the rump. The coat is very often rough and shaggy and there is a shaggy ruff on the underside of the neck. Horns in males only, long and spreading sideways then slightly inwards with a smooth forward curve. Strongly ridged to close to the sharp tips. Mature bulls have a strong, goaty odour. Females have two pairs of mammae between their hind legs. Shoulder height males 1,3–1,7 m, females 1,1 m; weight males 270 kg, females 180 kg. *See scale drawing on p. 213.*

Habitat Floodplain, reedbeds, grassland, woodland and rocky areas within 2 km of water. Habitat can be degraded by overgrazing by nyala and impala. Translocated.

Diet Mainly a grazer, with a preference for long grass; some browsing when grass is low in protein. Prefers long grass. Favoured species vary with locality; also eats maru-

las, and in Hwange NP in winter eats baboon droppings.

Life history Gestation 280 days. Single young (rarely twins) are born throughout the year, possibly with peaks in summer; in KwaZulu-Natal births December–July with a peak in February–March. Weans at 6–9 months. Females first calve at two years. Lifespan 11 years. Readily taken by large carnivores. The belief that predators avoid waterbuck because of their odour is not supported by data.

Behaviour Most active in the early morning and late afternoon; also feeds at night. At Lake McIlwaine, Zimbabwe, feeding time decreases in winter.

Usually in herds of 6–12, sometimes up to 30; herds tend to be bigger in summer. Females and young form nursery herds, mature bulls are territorial, males without territories form bachelor herds.

Bulls first hold territories at 5–6 years old. Territorial bulls have a very strong goaty body odour which taints the meat if the skin is allowed to touch it. Occupation and status are advertised by standing in a proud posture with the neck erect and head up, showing the white band on the throat. Lowering the horns towards an intruder and shaking the head is a stronger threat. Serious fights are fierce and more commonly fatal than in other antelope. Lowering the head with the horns back against the neck is a submissive display. Some territorial bulls tolerate the presence of a subordinate male. Sizes of territory differ markedly with habitat, probably according to richness and dispersion of food supply; 660 ha in KwaZulu-Natal, 90 ha at Lake McIlwaine, Zimbabwe. Bachelor herds tend to stay in sub-optimal habitat outside bulls' territories. They are allowed to move through territories as long as they behave submissively.

Nursery herds have home ranges overlapping male territories. As females move through territories, bulls test their reproductive condition by sniffing and flehmen of their genitals and urine. Females in oestrous are herded into a bull's territory and he courts them by rubbing his face and the bases of his horns on their flanks and rumps, resting his chin on their backs and tapping between their hind legs with a foreleg.

Cows leave the herd to give birth. Calves lie hidden for 3–4 weeks, but if approached they run rather than freezing. Young males transfer to bachelor herds at 9–12 months when horns start to grow. Females stay in the herd they were born in.

Field sign Droppings are rounded clumps of flattened pellets, or separate pellets 2 cm long, tapered at one end and blunt at the other.

RED LECHWE

S337 ⬡

Rooi-lechwe

Kobus leche

Description The rump is distinctly higher than the shoulders. Reddish yellow upper parts, darker on the back than on the flanks and legs. White on the underparts, with

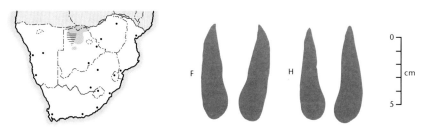

a white band up the front of the neck and onto the lower jaw (no such band in puku or impala). Dark brown or black down the front of the legs (not in puku or impala). The tail hangs almost to the hocks, with a black brush at the end. Only the males have horns: long (shorter in puku), spreading back and outwards, then curving smoothly inwards and forwards, strongly ridged except at the tips. Females have two pairs of mammae between their hind legs. Head and body length males 1,6 m (1,5–1,75 m), females 1,5 m (1,3–1,6 m); shoulder height males 1 m (0,9–1,1 m), females 95 cm (90–100 cm); weight males 113 kg (88–135 kg), females 71 kg (52–89 kg). *See scale drawing on p. 235.*

Habitat Seasonally and permanently wet grasslands in northern Botswana. Always near water.

Diet An almost pure grazer; more than 99% of the diet is grasses and sedges.

Life history Gestation 7–8 months; the single lambs have a birth weight of 5 kg and wean at 7 months. In Linyanti swamp 80% of breeding is in December–March and births peak in August–October. In the Okavango swamp births peak in October–December. Timing is possibly dependent on the progress of the flood. Females mature at 2 years; males are sexually mature at 2 years but do not mate

until they hold territory at 3–4 years. Preyed on by lions and leopards.

Behaviour Most active in the early morning. Feeds up to 1 km from water; drinks up to 3 times a day in hot weather, and moves closer to water at night. Tends to rest on termite heaps for better visibility. Always flees towards water, where its high rump allows it to run at high speed with the back legs tucked high under the body.

Usually in small groups of 1–5, sometimes in herds of up to 120. Breeding rams hold territories of 2–6 ha (exceptionally as small as 0,5 ha) in areas of rich grazing, occupied throughout the year. They advertise their status with a broadside display to intruders. Subordinate males hold their heads low with their horns back along the neck. Fights involve pushing contests and escalate to attempts to gore the opponent with sweeps of the horns. Losers break and run and may be pursued over considerable distances.

Female herds move through male territories. A ram checks a female's reproductive status by sniffing and flehmen of her genitals and urine, and courts by tapping her between the hind legs with a foreleg, putting his muzzle under her belly, and resting his chin on her rump. Several mounting attempts may be necessary before mating is achieved.

Lambs lie hidden for up to two months. Once they are mobile they spend more time with other lambs than with their mothers.

Field sign Dung pellets are 1–2 cm long, rounded at one end, blunt at the other.

Conservation Red lechwe are dependent on wetland habitat. Anything which threatens the wetlands in northern Botswana also threatens the lechwe populations.

PUKU

Poekoe
Kobus vardonii

S338

Description Golden yellow upper parts; white underparts, throat, muzzle and stripes above the eyes (whole of front of neck is white in red lechwe). No dark bands down the front of the legs (dark bands in red lechwe). Tail slightly shorter than in red lechwe, same colour as the body with a tuft of long hair at the tip. Only males have horns, much shorter than in red lechwe, spreading up and back then curving for-

---

wards, heavily ridged for two thirds of their length. Females have two pairs of mammae between their hind legs. Total length males 1,7 m (1,6–1,7 m), females 1,6 m (1,5–1,7 m); head and body length males 1,4 m (1,3–1,46 m), females 1,3 m (1,26–1,42 m); shoulder height males 81 cm, females 78 cm (73–83 cm); weight males 74 kg (67–78 kg), females 61 kg (47–80 kg) (measurements from Zambia). *See scale drawing on p. 235.*

Habitat Within the subregion puku are restricted to a small patch of floodplain on the southern bank of the Chobe River in northern Botswana. More widely distributed further north.

Diet Grazers.

Life history Breeds throughout the year. Single young are born after a gestation of eight months. Females mature at two years, males at three.

Behaviour Lives in small herds of up to about 30 (usually up to 6) with unstable membership of either females with their young or bachelor males.

Mature rams are territorial. Territory holders horn up grass, challenge intruders by standing tall while wagging the tail, and horn clash with challengers.

Female herds move through male territories; males try to keep females within their territories by herding them. Males check females' reproductive condition by sniffing and flehmen of their genitals and urine.

Calves lie hidden for a month.

Field sign Dung pellets are rounded and squashed together in small clumps.

Conservation The southern African puku population is on the fringe of the species' range, and is teetering on the brink of extinction.

ORDER
CARNIVORA
CARNIVORES

When this order was named it was thought that all its members were flesh eaters. We know now that, although they are all predatory to some extent, many of the smaller species live mainly on insects, aardwolves are exclusively insectivorous, and the African civet also eats large amounts of fruit.

FAMILY PROTELIDAE

AARDWOLF

The aardwolf is the only species in this family. It is so closely related to the hyaenas that it is sometimes included in the family Hyaenidae as the subfamily Protelinae.

AARDWOLF S244 R C
Aardwolf
Proteles cristatus

Description An aardwolf gives the impression of being a lightly built, jackal-sized hyaena. Its head is dog-like, with a broad, naked black muzzle, its ears are upright and pointed, and black on the back. The ground colour is pale buff to yellowish, with 4–5 narrow, vertical black stripes on the body, and irregular black stripes on the upper limbs. The hair is long, and forms a mane along the top of the neck and back. The tail is bushy and has a broad black tip. The legs are lightly built, and the feet are small and black with five toes on the forefeet and four on the hind. Except for the canines its teeth are small. Total length 91 cm (84–99 cm); tail 23 cm (16–28 cm); shoulder height 50 cm; weight 7,5 kg (5,2–10,7 kg) (varies seasonally by up to 25%). Females and males are the same size. *See scale drawing on p. 246.*
Habitat Occurs in most habitats except true desert and forest, as long as harvester

---

termites are available. Favours open grassland or scrub, with rainfall of 100–600 mm per year.

Diet Almost exclusively harvester termites, mainly *Trinervitermes*. In the Northern Cape large *Hodotermes* are taken in winter when cold nights keep *Trinervitermes* underground; in the former Transvaal *Hodotermes* are taken in summer when they forage on warm humid nights. Intake 300 000 termites a night. Other insects are occasionally eaten. Shortage of food in winter leads to losses of up to 25% in weight. Aardwolves do not prey on mammals and their teeth are too small to chew meat.

Life history Mates in midwinter, July in the Northern Cape. Gestation 90 days. Litters of 2–4 are born in October. Cubs first emerge from dens at three weeks old, stay near the den until three months old, and forage with the parents for a month; they are weaned and starting to forage independently at four months. They share their parents' territory until they are a year old. Black-backed jackals kill unguarded cubs.

Behaviour Nocturnal in summer when *Trinervitermes* termites are active at night; in the winter, active from the late afternoon onwards in order to feed on *Hodotermes* termites which come out during the day. Termites are detected by scent and sound, and are licked off the soil surface. Shelters in burrows which may be adapted from springhare or aardvark holes. To conserve energy in winter, stays in the warm (above

12 °C) burrow during cold spells, and allows its body temperature to drop to 31 °C while it is inactive.

Pairs share a territory of 1–4 km², but forage and sleep alone. Trespassers are chased and attacked by residents. Territories are demarcated by scent-marks of anal gland secretion deposited on grass stems at a rate of 10–20 marks per km of the 8–12 km covered in a night's foraging. Scent marking is easily recognised as the aardwolf lifts its tail, crouches, and wipes its extruded anal gland sideways across a grass stem.

Faeces and urine are buried in middens; an aardwolf begins its activity cycle by making a beeline for the nearest midden and depositing up to 10% of its body weight in faeces.

Pairs are nominally monogamous, but both sexes will mate with others if the chance arises. Males help to raise cubs by guarding them from jackals while the female forages.

Communication is mainly by odour via scent marks. Also gives quiet short-range contact calls, and under stress a clucking noise, an explosive bark or a loud, deep roar. An aardwolf can make itself look nearly twice as big by erecting its mane.

Field sign Middens are areas of bare soil 2–3 m across containing the remains of buried faeces. The faeces are very large (5 cm diameter) and consist mainly of sand mixed with termite heads. They have the pine needle-eucalyptus odour of the termites' defensive secretions.

Conservation Rare, but the population is stable. Extensive cattle and small-stock agriculture produces good aardwolf habitat, and aardwolves do some good by eating termites. Locust control with insecticides kills aardwolves by secondary poisoning, and can cause serious local losses. Red Data Book: Rare.

FAMILY HYAENIDAE

HYAENAS

Two species in the subregion. Both are scavengers with enormously powerful jaws and large teeth for crushing bones and cutting hide, and in addition spotted hyaenas are very efficient hunters.

BROWN HYAENA

S245 R (

Strandjut / bruin hiëna (strandwolf)
Hyaena brunnea

Description Looks superficially like a large shaggy dog. Dark to very dark brown or black, with off-white or tawny white on the neck and shoulders, black on the muzzle and face. The ears are large, high and pointed (more rounded in spotted hyaena). The lower limbs are striped, and the tail is bushy. The hair is long (short in spotted hyaena). Sturdily built, especially the forequarters, neck and head; the head is large, with a heavy muzzle. The heavy forequarters and longer front legs give a sloping outline to the back. Females have two pairs of mammae between their hind legs. Total length 1,4 m (up to 1,6 m); shoulder height 80 cm (up to 88 cm); tail 20 cm (up to 30 cm); weight 40 kg (up to 47 kg) in the Kalahari, males 47 kg (up to 50 kg), females 42 kg (up to 45 kg) in former Transvaal. *See scale drawing on p. 246.*

Habitat Occupies a wide range of habitats from savanna woodland to desert,

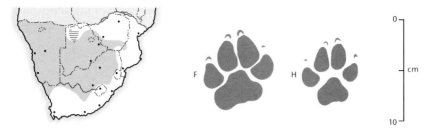

including the Namib coast. More common towards the drier west than in the east. Avoids areas with large numbers of spotted hyaenas. Because it is shy and secretive its presence in an area is not always recognised; lives unobtrusively in areas like the Magaliesberg just north of Pretoria.

Diet Mainly scavenged vertebrate remains, also insects, eggs (especially ostrich eggs), reptiles, fruit, Kalahari truffles and tsama melons (*Citrullus lanatus*), which also provide water. On the Namib coast the staple diet is seals. Also scavenges in rubbish dumps. Daily intake in the southern Kalahari is 2,8 kg.

Life history Usually only one female in a group breeds. Mating is usually with nomadic or immigrant males from outside the social group. Gestation 90 days. Litters of 1–4 are born at any time of year. Weaning starts at 3 months but is not complete until 12–16 months. Adults bring food to the den. After 10 months cubs begin foraging for themselves. Permanent teeth erupt by 15 months; full grown at 30 months. Lifespan up to at least 16 years. Brown hyaenas are sometimes killed by lions and spotted hyaenas but the carcass is not usually eaten. Trapping and poisoning are important causes of mortality.

Behaviour Active for most of the night; sometimes seen at dawn and dusk. Usually shelters in thick vegetation, sometimes sleeps in caves. Clan dens are refuges for cubs, with narrow tunnels that adults and other large carnivores cannot enter.

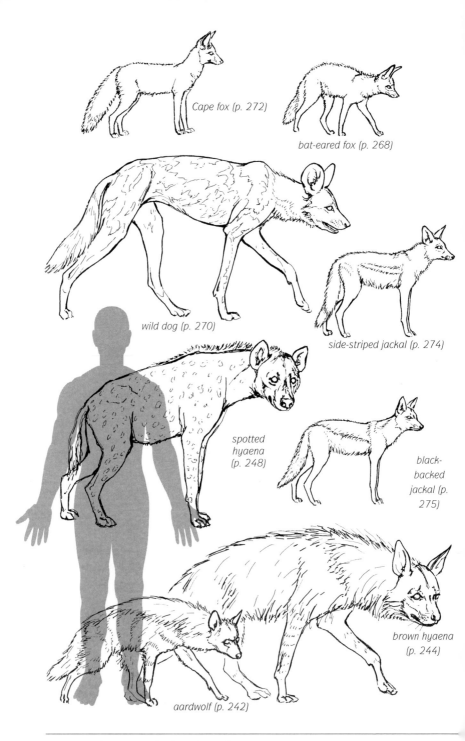

Cape fox (p. 272)

bat-eared fox (p. 268)

wild dog (p. 270)

side-striped jackal (p. 274)

spotted hyaena (p. 248)

black-backed jackal (p. 275)

brown hyaena (p. 244)

aardwolf (p. 242)

Lives in social clans with up to 12 members which defend large territories, or as solitary nomadic males. Territories are marked with anal-gland secretion by an elaborate behaviour known as pasting. The hyaena walks over a tall grass stem, bending it down under its body; it crouches over the bent stem, lifts its tail and extrudes its large anal-gland, touches the gland onto the stem to leave a blob of white secretion, and retracts the gland as it steps forward, leaving a smear of black secretion just above the white. On average 2,6 marks are deposited for each 1 km of foraging. A mark's odour signals the identity of its producer and the time since it was deposited. The odour lasts for at least a month, and a territory may contain 20 000 active marks. Within a territory a brown hyaena will usually be within 500 m of an active scent mark. Faeces are deposited in latrines which are concentrated near territory borders and along regular routes, and probably have a scent-marking function.

Territory size and group size vary with food supply: 500 km² for a single female and her cubs, where food is scarce; 235 km² for a group of 12, where food is abundant; up to 50 km² in Northwest Province; 32–220 km² in the Namib. May make long journeys of up to 650 km.

Forages alone, although several may congregate at a rich food source such as a large carcass; covers about 30 km per night. Food is detected by smell: carrion can be detected from at least 14 km downwind. Very powerful jaws and crushing teeth allow bones to be broken open for their nutritious marrow; hyaenas can digest bone and hide. An inefficient hunter; in the Kalahari only about 5% of its food intake is its own kills, but occasional individuals become pests by killing domestic stock. Surplus food is stored in scattered caches. Brown hyaenas are displaced from carcasses by lions and spotted hyaenas.

Cubs whine when begging for food. When they meet, group members sniff each other's face, head, neck and anal region; the animal being sniffed may extrude its anal gland. Muzzle wrestling in which two animals bite at each other's noses and faces is a restrained, friendly interaction between group companions. More serious fights, including those between brown hyaenas from different groups, involve neck biting, growls and yells. There is no long-range contact call.

All clan members help to raise cubs by bringing food back to the den. Females sometimes suckle one another's cubs.

Field sign Middens containing white faeces (dark when very fresh), folded cylinders with tapered ends. Scent marks on grass stems; the white secretion turns brown in a few days. Accumulations of bones and other food remains at dens (spotted hyaenas do not bring food back to their cubs and so their dens do not have as many bones lying around).

Conservation Brown hyaenas are widespread, but rare over most of their range (e.g. about two animals per 100 km² in the southern Kalahari). They do not thrive in conservation areas if there are large numbers of spotted hyaenas. A more enlightened attitude towards predators on stock farms would improve their status. Red Data Book: Rare. CITES Appendix II.

SPOTTED HYAENA

E | S246 | **(**

Gevlekte hiëna

Crocuta crocuta

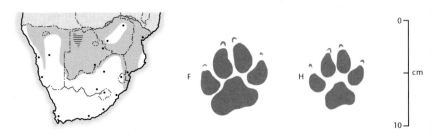

F   H   0 ⌐

cm

10 ⌐

Description Somewhat like a large, heavily built dog. Off-white to light brown with irregular dark spots that tend to fade with age. The muzzle is black, and the face is the same colour as the body. The head is massive, with a heavy muzzle. The ears are rounded (pointed in brown hyaena). The limbs are sturdily built, the front legs longer than the hind. The forequarters are more heavily built than the hindquarters, giving a sloping outline to the back. The hair is short and somewhat woolly (long and coarse in brown hyaenas), and becomes sparse with age. The tail has a bushy, black tip. Both males and females have prominent genitals, those of the females mimicking the males'. Females have a fat-filled pseudoscrotum and the clitoris is erectile, the same size and almost the same shape as a male's penis. Careful scrutiny is needed to tell the sexes apart: a female's pseudoscrotum is less deeply lobed than a male's scrotum, her clitoris has no 'neck' and the tip is blunt, while the male's penis has a narrow 'neck' and a pointed tip. Lactating females have one pair of prominent mammae between their hind legs, and a female's belly slopes less sharply upwards than a male's. Total length 1,6 m (up to 1,7 m); tail 25 cm (up to 28 cm); shoulder height 80 cm (up to 88 cm); weight males 60 kg, females 70 kg (up to 88 kg). *See scale drawing on p. 246.*

male  *female*

Habitat A wide range of habitats, excluding only dense forest and desert. Widely distributed in the past, now eliminated from nearly all of South Africa, southern Namibia, and central Zimbabwe. The main habitat requirement is a supply of medium-sized ungulate prey.

Diet The staple diet is medium-sized and large ungulates such as blue wildebeest, gemsbok, zebra and impala. Also takes smaller mammals, down to the size of mice, birds, reptiles, fruit, eggs, insects and garbage; 43 different foods are recorded. Spotted hyaenas both hunt and scavenge: in Kruger NP they kill 50% of their own food, in the Namib 50–93%, in the Kalahari, Etosha NP, and Chobe 70–80%. Food intake varies from 3,8 kg per day in Kruger NP and Hluhluwe-Umfolozi NP to 6,2 kg per day in the southern Kalahari. They can eat 18 kg at a sitting.

In Savuti in the dry season 80% of hyaena kills are Burchell's zebra. In Etosha the main prey are springbok. In Kruger NP kills are blue wildebeest 15%, kudu 15%, impala 15%, steenbok 22%. In the southern Kalahari kills are gemsbok 50%, blue wildebeest 18%, eland 9%, springbok 6%.

Life history Gestation 90 days. Litters of 1–2 are born at any time of year; in Chobe most births fall between May and November, with two thirds in June. Twins are usually of different sexes, occasionally both males but very rarely both females. Cubs are born with eyes open and teeth well developed, and they fight savagely, especially if both are the same sex and more especially if both are females. Commonly, one of a pair of female twins kills her sister. Weaning begins at 9 months, and is complete by 12–16 months. Cubs first accompany adults at 6–9 months. Adults bring very little food to the den. Permanent teeth are erupted by 15 months. Sexually mature at 3 years; males are full grown at 30 months, females at 36 months. Females may put on weight for 10 years. In the southern Kalahari they suffer sporadic outbreaks of rabies. Lions kill spotted hyaenas but rarely eat them.

Behaviour Mostly active at night, travelling as much as 70 km. Often seen during the day resting in shade or lying in shallow water; uses caves, aardvark holes and drain culverts as dens. Highly social, living in clans whose size is related to food supply: 4–8 in the Namib, 5–10 in the Kalahari, 10–30 in Kruger NP, up to 50 in Savuti. The stable core of a clan is its females, males disperse. There are separate domi-

nance hierarchies among males and females, and females dominate all males. High-ranking females have priority of access to food and to resting sites near the den entrance and they rear more cubs than low-rankers. High-ranking males have priority of access to females. Males integrate themselves into new clans by months of persistent submissiveness to the females.

Clan companions greet each other in a unique ceremony: the two stand alongside each other, nose to tail, each lifts the hind leg nearest its partner, and erects its penis or pseudopenis, and the two then sniff and lick each other's genitals.

Clans are territorial, and territory size varies with food supply: up to 1 800 km² in the Kalahari, 150 km² in Kruger NP. Neighbouring clans may fight pitched battles to defend their areas. Territories are patrolled by groups of residents and are demarcated by anal gland scent marks and middens containing large accumulations of white faeces. To scent mark, a spotted hyaena walks over a clump of tall grass, bending it down, lifts its tail and extrudes its anal gland, and wipes the gland onto the grass, leaving a smear of creamy white secretion on several stems at once. In the Kalahari they deposit a mark on average every 8 km. Most pastings are close to middens. Adult males scent mark the most.

Spotted hyaena hunt by running down their prey at speeds of up to 60 km/h over distances of up to 3 km. They kill by disembowelling the prey and biting major blood vessels. Foraging group size depends on intended prey: 55–62% of foraging is carried out alone in Etosha NP, Kruger NP and Timbavati, 30% in the Kalahari and Hluhluwe-Umfolozi NP. Generally springbok and springhares are hunted by single hyaenas, wildebeest by groups of three, eland and adult gemsbok by groups of four.

Carrion is detected by smell from as far as 4,2 km downwind. Live prey is detected by sight and sound. The sound of other predators feeding attracts spotted hyaenas from up to 10 km away. Usually, lions cannot be displaced from a carcass if an adult male lion is present; lionesses and subadults can be if they are outnumbered four to one. Lions will steal carcasses from spotted hyaenas. Excess food is occasionally cached, most often in shallow water.

All the females in a clan breed. Their cubs den together but each female suckles only her own; a female suckling another's cubs has been recorded only once. Cubs are not provided with meat.

The most distinctive call is a drawn out 'whooo-oop', which is a long-range contact call and assembly signal. They also low like cattle. Around carcasses, in fights and when mobbing lions they scream, giggle, whoop, laugh, low, growl and snarl. Cubs whine for food and milk.

Field sign Scent marks are brown smears (white when very fresh) on bunches of grass stems. Middens containing large numbers of white faeces (dark when very fresh), lumpy cylinders with tapered ends. Spotted hyaena dens are less likely than brown hyaena dens to have large accumulations of bones.

Conservation Spotted hyaenas thrive in large conservation areas where there is plenty of prey. They cannot coexist with agriculture.

CATS

Cats are the most specialised of the carnivores for the capture of live prey, and the most dependent on a diet of meat. There are seven indigenous species in the sub-region, in three genera, and feral cats (*Felis catus*), S254, are widespread.

CHEETAH

S247 ☼

Jagluiperd
Acinonyx jubatus

F   H   0 ┐
           │ cm
           10 ┘

Description Small-headed, long-legged and wasp-waisted. The head, body, legs and the first two thirds of the tail are covered with black spots (leopard has rosettes of spots) on a buffy background. 'King' cheetahs are genetic variants with stripes instead of spots. The tail is long (short in serval), its end third is banded with black, and it has a white tip. The underparts are white. There is a short ruff on the neck and a short mane from the back of the neck to the shoulders. Up to an age of 12 weeks, cubs have a mantle of long, grey hair on their backs. The head is small and rounded, the eyes are large and there is a distinctive tear stripe from the inner corner of each eye to the corner of the lips (absent in leopard; stripe does not reach to corner of

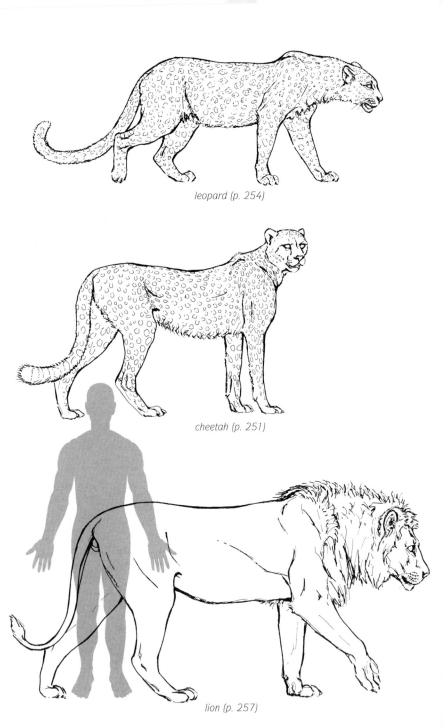

leopard (p. 254)

cheetah (p. 251)

lion (p. 257)

mouth in serval). The ears are small and rounded (large in serval). The legs are long. The claws are permanently exposed, not retracted into sheaths as in other cats, and blunt, except for the dew claw of the front feet which is a sharp hook. Total length 2 m (males up to 2,2 m); tail 70 cm; shoulder height 87 cm (up to 94 cm); weight males 54 kg (up to 60 kg), females 43 kg (up to 48 kg). *See scale drawing opposite*

Habitat Open grassland and savanna woodland, extending into arid areas. Avoids forest and woodland with thick undergrowth. Independent of water.

Diet Small to medium-sized antelope, e.g. impala, steenbok, springbok, common duiker; also takes smaller mammals such as hares and springhares, and ground birds. Male coalitions take larger species, e.g. yearling wildebeest, kudu, waterbuck, gemsbok. In the southern Kalahari 87% of cheetah kills are springbok, in Kruger NP 44% impala, 13% common duiker, 13% steenbok, in Etosha NP 97% springbok. Lactating females double their food intake.

Life history Gestation 90–95 days. Litters of 1–6 are born at any time of year. Eyes open at 10–12 days. Weaning starts at 8 weeks when cubs first accompany their mother away from the lair, but may not be complete for another 4 months; permanent teeth erupt at 8–9 months. Independent at 18 months; females are sexually mature at 2 years. Cheetah cubs are very vulnerable: in the Serengeti lions kill about 70% of them, and only 5% live to independence. They also fall prey to spotted hyaenas and leopards. Survival is higher in the thicker bush of the Kruger NP.

Behaviour Typically hunts during the day, but night-time hunting has been recorded in Etosha NP, and springhares must be hunted at night because they are strictly nocturnal. The classical cheetah hunting technique is a high-speed chase over distances of up to 600 m: it lacks the stamina for longer chases. Highest speed reliably measured is 90 km/h. The prey is tripped by grappling with one or both front feet, and strangled with a sustained bite to the throat. Cheetahs' canine teeth are too short for the stabbing killing bite used by other cats. If possible the prey is dragged into cover to avoid the attentions of other carnivores and vultures. Cheetahs feed quickly before their kills are stolen. They rarely scavenge. Their light build and small teeth make them very vulnerable to attacks by other predators, and their kills are stolen by lions, spotted hyaenas, brown hyaenas, leopards and even warthogs. In Kruger NP cheetahs lose 14% of their kills to spotted hyaenas. This may be one reason why they hunt during the day when other predators are inactive. Jackals avoid cheetahs, presumably because cheetahs are fast enough to catch them.

Females are solitary, or accompanied by their cubs of up to 18 months old. On stock farms in Namibia cheetahs form female and mixed-sex groups of up to 7, with circumstantial evidence of a group of 14. Females live in overlapping home ranges but avoid contact with other females. Home range size varies with food supply: in the Kalahari where prey is migratory, several hundred km²; in Kruger NP where prey is sedentary, 100–200 km². Some males form coalitions of up to four, which are usually brothers. Males hold territories of 100–200 km² in which they monopolise access to females, and which they defend savagely: intruders may be killed, and even eaten. Males scent mark with sprayed urine; territorial males use traditional sites on large rocks and trees. Females spray more frequently when they are in oestrous.

Females on heat attract males by the smell of their urine. Males fight for mating rights, but within coalitions matings are shared. Females respond aggressively to male courtship, which lasts up to two weeks. Females give birth and hide their cubs in dense cover. Cubs are moved frequently, presumably to avoid predators. The mother brings live prey for cubs to practise on when they are 4–5 months old. After independence litters of siblings roam together. Females leave sibling groups when they first breed.

In captivity cheetah breed well only if their natural social system is mimicked by keeping males and females apart until the females are on heat.

High pitched chirrups are short-range contact and greeting calls; they growl and snarl in agonistic interactions, and purr loudly when content.

Field sign Carcasses with most of the bones and skin intact. The only cat whose claws mark in the spoor. Droppings are short, segmented sausages with tapered ends, about 3 cm thick. Urine marks on trees and rocks.

Conservation Cheetah passed through a population bottleneck of less than a few hundred individuals 10–20 thousand years ago, which reduced their genetic variability to less than half the average for carnivores, but this has not led to the expected poor reproductive performance and increased susceptibility to disease. Nonetheless, cheetah are rare wherever they occur. There are only about 200 in Kruger NP, 60 in Kalahari Gemsbok NP, 50–75 in Etosha NP. Paradoxically, the largest cheetah populations are outside conservation areas, because they suffer significant competition and predation from the lions and spotted hyaenas that flourish in large conservation areas.

One of ecotourism's big seven. Enlightened management of cheetah on extensive stock farms will dramatically improve the species' status. The breakthrough in captive breeding by the De Wildt Cheetah Research and Breeding Station changed the cheetah's Red Data Book status to Out of Danger. Appendix I of CITES.

LEOPARD

 S248 R (

Luiperd
Panthera pardus

Description Stockier in build than cheetah and serval, which are the only other spotted cats of comparable size in the subregion. Ground colour is pale buff to golden yellow, with black spots forming rosettes on the flanks, hips and shoulders (single spots in cheetah, spots and stripes in serval). There are two stripes across the lower neck. Black and 'golden' leopards are genetic variants. The tail is long (short in serval), spotted for about half its length, banded with black towards the tip, which is

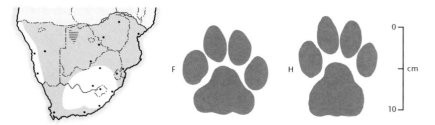

white underneath. The ears are small and rounded (large in serval). Females have two pairs of mammae on the belly. Size varies markedly with locality: in the southern Western Cape Province total length 1,75 m; head and body 1,06 m; tail 68 cm; weight males 31 kg (up to 45 kg), females 21 kg (up to 26 kg). In Zimbabwe, total length males 2,1 m (up to 2,36 m), females 1,85 m (up to 1,88 m); weight males 60 kg (up to 71,3 kg), females 32 kg (up to 35 kg). Record length 2,92 m, maximum weight 90 kg. *See scale drawing on p. 252.*

Habitat Wide habitat tolerance; usually associated with broken rocky country or forests, and dependent on good cover for shelter and hunting. Not dependent on water, and can live in arid areas, but not in true desert.

Diet Takes a very wide range of vertebrate prey from mice to large antelope and baby giraffe, including hares, dassies, primates, small carnivores, porcupines, birds, reptiles and fish. Also eats fruit, and readily scavenges. Very rarely kills people. Main prey are medium-sized antelope such as impala and springbok; may turn to stock killing. Subadults hunt smaller prey than adults. In Kruger NP more small prey is taken in the dry season. In Augrabies NP remains of rock dassies occur in just over half of scats. In the Kalahari Gemsbok NP remains of porcupines occur in 30% of scats, gemsbok in 25%, common duiker in 25%, springhare 15% and black-backed jackal 15%. Kills in the Kalahari Gemsbok NP are springbok 65%, hartebeest calves

6%, steenbok 6%, black-backed jackal 4%. Kills in Kruger NP are impala 28%, warthog 15%, duiker 15%, small carnivores 11% and primates 10%.

Life history Gestation 100 days. Litters of 1–6 cubs, usually 2 in Kruger NP, where cub mortality is more than 50%. Eyes open at 6 days; weaned from 6–12 weeks. Independent at 18 months; sexually mature at 2–4 years. In Kruger NP females breed every 2,5 years. Leopard cubs are killed by lions and spotted hyaenas.

Behaviour Most active at night, but may be seen during the day, especially in protected areas. In the Cedarberg it is active during the day. Rests in thick cover, in caves, or draped along the limb of a tree with a dense, shady canopy.

Hunting technique is classically feline: a stalk using cover to within 10 m of the prey, a rush and pounce on the prey which is grappled with the foreclaws, and a killing bite to the back of the skull, nape of the neck, or the throat. Guts of large prey are pulled out and discarded, sometimes covered with soil. Remains of carcasses may be covered with loose soil, litter or branches. Where there are many scavengers, carcasses are taken into trees. Leopards readily eat rotten meat, and a stored carcass may be fed on for up to four days. Furry mammals and birds are plucked before being eaten.

Both sexes are solitary and territorial. In Kruger NP male territories are 16–96 km^2, overlapping up to six female territories of 5,6–30 km^2; in the Cedarberg male territories are up to 69 km^2; in mountains near Stellenbosch 388 and 484 km^2; in Matopos NP 20–30 km^2. Territorial males have priority of access to females; territorial females have priority of access to food.

Both sexes spray urine, males especially also scrape the ground with their hind feet. Urine is probably a territorial marker.

Rasping is the most distinctive call, and sounds like a thin plank being cut with a coarse saw. It is probably a long-range contact call. Females give more strokes per call and more calls per calling period, and have longer pauses between calls, and longer calling periods. Most calling occurs in the early evening and in the dry season. Also growls and snarls in agonistic interactions.

Males detect females on heat from the smell of their urine. Mating pairs may stay together for a few days, and share kills, but males play no part in raising cubs. Cubs are born in heavy cover, caves or holes in the ground. They first accompany their mother on hunts at four months, and make their first kills at five months.

Field sign Carcasses in trees, feathers and fur plucked from kills. Scrapes on the ground. Claw marks on bark. Faeces are segmented sausages with tapered ends, 2–3,5 cm thick, nearly always with hair and bone fragments; they are left exposed, sometimes in prominent places.

Conservation Leopards are surprisingly adaptable and resilient in the face of human encroachment. In crop-farming areas they provide a valuable service by killing crop raiders such as bush pigs. They are one of the hunter's big five, and ecotourism's big seven. Red Data Book: Rare. CITES Appendix 1.

LION
Leeu
Panthera leo

Description A massive cat, biggest of the African carnivores. Pale tawny to sandy brown, with white underparts. Cubs are faintly spotted; some adults retain traces of the spots, especially low on the body. So-called 'white' lions are very pale buff genetic variants. The long tail is short-haired, with a distinctive black tuft at the tip. Adult males have manes varying in colour from tawny to black, and in size from a slight ruff around the neck to a luxuriant growth framing the face, covering the head between the ears, the neck, shoulders and chest and extending as a fringe below the belly. The head is large with a strong, heavy muzzle; the pattern of spots at the roots of the whiskers is unique to each individual. Head and body length 2,6–3,3 m; tail 60–100 cm; shoulder height males 1,2 m, females 90 cm; weight males 190 kg, females 130 kg (69–135 kg). Heaviest male 260 kg, from Etosha NP; heaviest male from Kruger NP 225 kg, heaviest female 152 kg. *See scale drawing on p. 252.*

Habitat Able to exploit a wide range of habitats except rain forest and true desert. It can penetrate into arid areas along drainage lines, and can go for long periods without drinking. Incompatible with stock farming and human settlement.

Diet Mainly medium-sized and large prey, e.g buffalo, wildebeest, zebra and gemsbok, but will take a very wide range down to the size of mice, and occasionally larger species such as giraffe, hippo and young elephants. Also eats birds, reptiles, fish, and even insects. Kills other carnivores but rarely eats them. Some cases of cannibalism have been recorded. Occasionally eats people. Scavenges frequently. In the Kruger NP lions eat more zebra and wildebeest in wet periods, buffalo and waterbuck in droughts. Kills in southern Kalahari: wildebeest 37%, gemsbok 32%, springbok 13%, hartebeest 7%, eland 4%, ostrich 4%, porcupine 2%. In Kruger NP, in years of normal rain: impala 29%, Burchell's zebra 16%, wildebeest 14%, warthog 13%, porcupine 13% (biased upwards by one specialist pride). Savuti wet season: buffalo 41%, zebra 29%. Mana Pools: impala 45%, buffalo 20%, waterbuck 15%, warthog 7%, zebra 7%. Average daily intake 7 kg for males, 4,5 kg for females; maximum at one meal up to 15% of body weight; 35 kg for males, 22 kg for females.

Life history Gestation 110 days. Litters of up to 6 cubs (usually 1–4) are born at any time of year, concealed in dense cover or in a cave, away from the pride. Birth weight 1,5 kg, only 1% of adult weight. Introduced to pride at 6–8 weeks, or later if there are older cubs in the pride. Weaning starts at 10 weeks, and is completed by 6 months. Females stay in the pride, males leave by three years of age. Competent hunters at two years, full-grown at 3–4 years, weight peaks at 7 years. Lifespan 13 years. Unguarded cubs may fall prey to other predators. Old or disabled lions may be killed by spotted hyaenas.

Behaviour Typically active for only 2–4 hours in 24; most active at night, resting during the day in shade.

The only conspicuously social species of wild cat. In the classical picture of lion social organisation the basic unit is the pride, consisting of a group of 2–12 (typically 3–6) closely related adult females with their young, attended by 1–6 adult males. If there is more than one male they are often, but not always, close relatives, often brothers. Only pride males have access to the pride's females. Males take over prides by driving out the current males in savage and sometimes fatal fights, and are in turn displaced by new challengers after tenure of 1–10 years. Larger coalitions have longer tenures. After a take-over the new males drive out any young males in the pride, and try to kill all the cubs in order to bring their mothers quickly back into breeding condition. Females prefer their pride to have a large male coalition because a longer tenure reduces the number of cubs lost to infanticide at take-overs. After a take-over females come into heat and mate, but do not conceive until the new males have established their status against possible challengers. Lionesses cooperate to defend their cubs from infanticide, which may be why they live in groups.

Pride companions groom and rub against each other. There is no dominance within a pride: males simply use size and strength to take food away from females. Pride members are not always together, separating into smaller sub-groups which move separately for days or weeks. Females whose cubs are the same age stay together.

Departures from the classical picture include nomadic males, groups of females with no resident males, and aggregations of up to 17 young nomadic lions. In Savuti 12% of lions are not pride members.

Prides hold territory, males defending against males, and females against females: in Savuti, from 42 km² to more than 450 km², in Kruger NP, 150 km²; ranges are larger where prey is scarcer or more scattered. Males scent mark by spraying urine.

The hunting technique of individual lions is typically feline, a stalk to within 20 m, using what cover is available, a rush and chase, not usually longer than 200 m, a pounce on the prey which is grappled with the claws, pulled down and killed with a suffocating throat bite, or by having its muzzle covered by the lion's mouth. Lions differ from other cats in regularly hunting in groups. The degree and type of cooperation depends on the difficulty of the hunt. If a herd of small prey such as impala are the target, each lion pursues its own; with larger, dangerous prey cooperation may be needed to split a herd or pull down and kill one animal. Cooperation includes stalking in line abreast, partly encircling the prey, or one lion flushing the prey towards its companions. Cooperative hunting increases success rates, e.g. when hunting blue wildebeest in Etosha single lionesses make 0,28 kills per hunt; groups of 7 make 0,75 kills per hunt.

Most of a pride's hunting is done by the females, which are less conspicuous than the larger, maned males, but unattached males have to hunt for themselves. In prides, the males take what food they want from the females. Cubs get what the adults leave, and in times of food shortage, starvation is their major cause of death.

Hunts are more successful on dark nights, in dense cover, for lone prey and when a close stalk is possible. Some prides specialise in particular prey: one pride in Kruger NP specialises in porcupines. In Kruger NP half the animals killed by predators fall to lions. Lions (and other predators) prosper during droughts as prey animals weaken: lion densities in northern Kruger NP increased from 1 per 30 km² in 1989, to 1 per 8–9 km² in 1993 after the 1991–1992 drought.

Unless heavily outnumbered (4:1 by spotted hyaenas) lionesses can defend their kills against other predators, or steal the others' kills. Adult males do not make way for other predators and their presence in a pride reduces losses of kills to spotted hyaenas. In Kruger NP hyaenas rarely displace lions from kills; in Savuti, with fewer males, lions lose 20% of their food to spotted hyaenas.

Roaring advertises a lion's location, shows that an area is occupied, and allows pride members to keep track of one another. A full roar begins with a series of grunts, building in volume and length, and then tails off again. Lions also grunt, cough and snarl. A series of explosive coughs is given as a threat to intruding humans. Small cubs 'meow' loudly.

Lions mate about 4 times an hour over 2–3 days. Males do not compete for matings; a female will mate with all of a pride's males in turn as each loses interest in her. Pride females suckle one another's cubs, with no bias towards their own.

Field sign Droppings are segmented sausages with tapered ends, 4 cm thick, usually with hair and bone fragments. Very dark faeces point to a diet of meat with little bone, light-coloured faeces indicate more bone in the diet.

Conservation Lions thrive in conservation areas where there are large numbers of big herbivores. They are one of the hunter's big five, and top of the list of ecotourism's big seven. Translocations of small numbers may call for special management. Outbreaks of infectious disease can threaten local lion populations.

CARACAL
Rooikat
Felis caracal

S250 · (

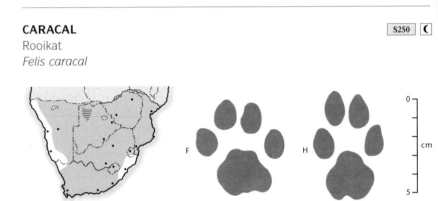

Description Largest of the African small cats, very robustly built, especially adult males. Uniform body colour varies with locality: silvery grey in the south, pinkish red in the west, sandy brown or brick red in the east. The underparts are white with indistinct spots. There are distinctive black markings on the face at the base of the whiskers, from the inside corners of the eyes to the nose, and above the eyes. The

backs of the ears are black with a heavy sprinkling of silvery white, and there are long tassels of black hair on the tips of the ears, which are unique among African cats. The tail is short, reaching only to the hocks. Total length males 1,1 m (up to 1,27 m), females 1 m (up to 1,22 m); head and body length males 87 cm (75–108 cm), females 82 cm (71–103 cm); shoulder height 40–45 cm; weight males 13 kg (7,2–20 kg), females 10 kg (8–16 kg). *See scale drawing on p. 263.*

Habitat A very wide habitat range; does not occur in true desert.

Diet Mainly mammals up to the size of medium-sized antelope weighing about 40 kg: springbok, grey rhebok, mountain reedbuck, klipspringer, dassies, hares and rabbits, springhares, rodents, small carnivores, birds up to the size of guineafowl, reptiles, amphibians, arthropods. Caracals rarely scavenge but will return to kills if they are not disturbed. Individuals may become serious pests on sheep and goat farms. Intake about 500 g per day. In the Mountain Zebra NP remains of dassies occurred in 53% of scats, mountain reedbuck in 20% and birds in 5%. In the eastern Karoo rodents occur in 50% and antelope in 11% of scats. In the Karoo NP rodents are found in 39% of scats, grey rhebok in 23%, dassies in 22%, hares and rabbits in 19%, invertebrates in 17%. On Eastern Cape farms 46–68% of stomachs from hunted caracal contain sheep and goat remains, and 6–31% contain dassies.

Life history Gestation 78–81 days. Litters of up to four are usually born in summer (October–February). Eyes open at 6–10 days. First eats solid food at 4 weeks, weaned at 4–6 months. Full grown at 10 months, when families split up. Sexually mature at 14 months (in captivity). Occasionally killed by larger predators. Kittens may be taken by large raptors. The role of black-backed jackals in keeping caracal numbers down by killing kittens is unconfirmed. In stock farming areas the major cause of death is blanket predator control.

Behaviour Nocturnal, but may be seen at dawn and dusk. Solitary and probably territorial, though this may vary with locality and habitat. Home ranges in Eastern Cape Province 15–65 km²; in West Coast NP, male 27 km², female 7,4 km²; in Kalahari 308 km²; in southern Western Cape, females 18,2 km². males 48 km². Young males disperse up to 180 km from where they were born.

Hunting behaviour is classically feline: prey is detected mainly by sight or sound, stalked, rushed at from close range, pounced on and grappled with the claws, and killed with a bite to the throat or the nape of the neck. Fur may be plucked from prey. With antelope and small stock, feeding begins at the soft skin inside the thighs: the hindquarters are eaten first, then the shoulder. The guts are not removed from the prey (contrast leopard). Prey may be dragged into cover, sometimes covered with soil or litter. Caracals return to kills if they are undisturbed.

Males detect that a female is in oestrus from the smell of her urine. Matings are repeated over up to three days.

Field sign Faeces are segmented sausages with tapered ends, up to 2 cm thick; may be buried or left exposed. Kills can be identified by tooth marks and bruising on the throat or nape of the neck, sometimes claw marks on the shoulders, marks of canine teeth 24–30 mm apart (same for black-backed jackal; dogs from fox terrier size upwards 35–60 mm apart). Hair or wool sometimes plucked. Feeding starts inside hind leg. Guts not removed (leopard removes guts).

Conservation Caracal are resilient pests in extensive small-stock farming areas but are displaced by intensive agriculture and urban development.

AFRICAN WILD CAT
Vaalboskat
Felis lybica

S251   V   ☾   ☸

African wild cats are so closely related to domestic cats that both can be considered to be subspecies of *Felis catus* (S254).

Description Very much like a domestic tabby. Cats in the drier western half of the subregion have a light sandy ground colour with brown or rufous markings; in the eastern half they are light grey with charcoal or black markings; there is a wide area with intermediate colouring. A dark stripe runs along the midline of the neck and back, 2 distinct stripes circle the neck, and there are 6–7 vertical stripes on the flanks (the small spotted cat has spots). The legs are banded; markings are more distinct on lower limbs. Some cats have markings on the back and flanks so diffuse that

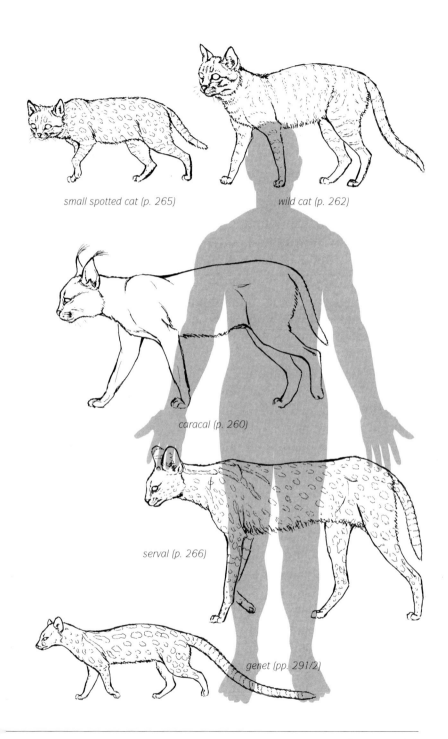

small spotted cat (p. 265)

wild cat (p. 262)

caracal (p. 260)

serval (p. 266)

genet (pp. 291/2)

the colour appears uniform. Chin, chest and throat are white, or tinged rufous or grey; the belly is pale rufous, grey or cream. The tail is long, darkly banded and black-tipped (serval and small spotted cat have shorter tails). The undersides of the feet are black (also in black-footed cat). The backs of the ears are bright rufous brown, chestnut or orange (black or brown in domestic cats, hybrids and small spotted cat). Total length males 91 cm (85–100 cm), females 86,5 cm (82–95 cm); tail males 32,5 cm (27,5–36 cm), females 21 cm (25–37 cm); weight males 5 kg (3,8–6,4 kg), females 3,7 kg (2,4–5,5 kg). Larger in Botswana than in the Cape. *See scale drawing on p. 263.*

Habitat   Found throughout the subregion in all habitats except desert. Depends on cover to hide in during the day, such as holes in the ground, caves, rock crevices, holes in trees, thickets and burrows dug by other animals.

Diet   Mammals up to the size of dassies, hares and the young of small antelopes, birds up to the size of guineafowl, invertebrates, reptiles. The larger species may be taken as carrion. Also jackal berries (*Diospyros mespiliformis*). Mice and rats are preferred but if these are scarce wild cats readily switch to arthropods and birds. Diet changes seasonally and depends on food availability. Sometimes raids domestic poultry, and is persecuted for killing lambs without there being strong evidence that it does so. Remains of rodents occur in 74–100% of stomachs and scats, other mammals in up to 10%, invertebrates in 30–80%, birds in 10–20%, reptiles in about 12% and plant material in 14%.

Life history   Mating July–January; no recorded observations of courtship or mating in the wild. Gestation 65 days. Up to three litters a year in captivity, only one in the wild. Nearly all births are September–March, when summer rains improve food supplies. Litters of 2–5 (average 3) are born in rock crevices, holes in the ground, or dense vegetation; their mother may carry them to a new refuge every few days, presumably to avoid predation. Eyes open at 10–14 days; families disperse at 5 months; no information on weaning.

Behaviour   Active at night and in the early mornings, and during the day in cool weather; usually solitary and probably territorial, depending on population density and food availability. Knowledge of African wild cat behaviour is seriously inadequate. Spends most of the time on the ground, but is an agile climber and readily flees into trees if pursued.

Detects prey by sight or sound, stalks in a crouch with head low, using cover, rushes forward and pounces, grappling prey with the claws of the forefeet. Doves are ambushed at water holes and snatched from the air as they fly in or out. Precise killing bites are used; where these are directed depends on the size of the prey.

Spitting with the ears flattened is a defensive threat, arching the back and tail and fluffing up the hair is a neutral threat, caterwauling precedes aggression. Droppings are buried, left exposed, or accumulated into middens. This may be connected to territoriality.

Field sign   Claws are sheathed while walking and do not mark in the spoor. Spoor and faeces are indistinguishable from those of domestic cats. Plucks feathers from prey (genets do not).

Conservation The integrity of *Felis lybica* as a species (or subspecies) is threatened by the influx of *Felis catus* genes from breeding with domestic cats. Red Data Book: Vulnerable. CITES: Appendix II.

SMALL SPOTTED CAT (BLACK-FOOTED CAT)   **E** S252 R C
Klein gekolde kat (miershooptier)
Felis nigripes

Description Colour varies: cinnamon buff, tawny or off-white. There are dark, rust-tinged bands on top of the shoulders and high on the legs, and distinct spots of the same colour on the body (diffuse stripes in African wild cat). There are two or three black or reddish stripes across the throat. Underparts are pale buff or white. The tail is short (long in African wild cat) and has a black tip, and the backs of the ears are the same colour as the body (russet in African wild cat). Among the smallest of the world's cats; total length males 53–63 cm, females 49–53 cm; tail males 16–20 cm, females 12–17 cm; shoulder height 20–25 cm; body weight males 1,5–2,4 kg, females 1,0–1,6 kg. *See scale drawing on p. 263.*

Habitat Dry, open grassland and scrub with 100–500 mm rain annually.

Diet Rodents, shrews, hares, Smith's red rock rabbits, birds up to the size of black korhaans (*Eupodotis afra*), elephant shrews, arthropods, reptiles and birds' eggs, an unusual item for a cat. Cape hares (1,5 kg) and black korhaans are large prey for such

a small predator. Also recorded scavenging at a springbok carcass. Can eat up to 450 g (approximately 35% of body weight) in a night, but usually takes 200–300 g and accounts for an average of eight rodents per night.

Life history Oestrus 1–2 days; gestation 63–68 days. Litters of up to 3 (usually 1–2) are born in summer; there may be 2 litters a year. Birth weight 60–90 g. Eyes open at 3–9 days, first takes solid food at 32–35 days, weaned by 2 months, independent at 3 months, but stays in the mother's home range.

Behaviour Nocturnal; becomes active only after sunset. Cats hunting while it is still light are mobbed by ant-eating chats (*Myrmecocichla formicivora*) and clapper larks (*Mirafra apiata*). Shelters during the day in disused springhare burrows, under rock slabs or in holes in termite mounds, from which it gets its Afrikaans name 'miershooptier'.

Hunting is the classical feline stalk, rush and pounce; prey is located by active search or by waiting at rodent burrows. Birds may be snatched from the air. Rodents and shrews are killed with a head or neck bite; the whole animal is eaten, including the guts, but the gut contents may be squeezed out by running the intestine between the incisor teeth. Excess food is cached. Small spotted cats may be shadowed by marsh owls (*Asio capensis*) which catch birds flushed by the cats.

Solitary, with home ranges of 700–900 ha, of which 70 ha is covered in 4–13 km travelling each night. Young males scent mark with sprayed urine; faeces are left exposed except by females near maternity dens. A repeated loud, deep 'raaow' is a contact call. Play has been observed between young adult litter-mates.

Conservation Red Data Book: Rare. CITES Appendix I.

SERVAL

S253 R ☾ ⛅

Tierboskat
Felis serval

Description An elegant, lightly built cat with long legs and neck, and a small head. Ground colour varies from white to light golden yellow, with distinct black bands and spots. The ears are very large (small in cheetah and leopard), black on the back with white patches, and the tail is short, only just reaching to the hocks of the hind legs

(long in cheetah and leopard). Females have three pairs of mammae. Total length 1,1 m (0,96–1,23 m); tail 30 cm (24–35 cm); shoulder height 54–62 cm; weight males 11 kg (9–13,5 kg), females 9,7 kg (8,6–11,8 kg). *See scale drawing on p.263.*

Habitat Dense, well-watered grassland, reedbeds, always near water.

Diet Mostly rodents (80–90% in KwaZulu-Natal, 97% in Zimbabwe), especially vlei rats, striped mice and multimammate mice; also insectivores (14% in KwaZulu-Natal), birds, reptiles, amphibians and insects. Occasionally raids poultry but does not kill small farm stock.

Life history Male and female stay together for several days during oestrus. Gestation 65–75 days. Litters of up to three are born in September–April in Zimbabwe, November–March in KwaZulu-Natal, in dens amongst long dense grass or under bushes.

Behaviour Active from late afternoon into the evening, during the night, and until late morning. Prey is located by sight or hearing and caught with a slap of one forepaw, or a high, arching pounce; 40–60% of pounces are successful. Birds may be snatched from the air. Playing with prey seems to be common. Servals readily enter water in pursuit of prey.

Solitary or in pairs, in overlapping home ranges of 15–30 km². Both males and females scent mark with urine, and rub their faces on grass or soil, probably depositing saliva. Faeces are left exposed, and the ground nearby is raked with the hind feet.

Field sign Faeces light grey, up to 2 cm in diameter, containing a great deal of rodent hair. Scratch marks on the ground near faeces.

Conservation Displaced by habitat loss to agriculture and forestry. Secure inside protected areas. Red Data Book: Rare. CITES Appendix II.

WILD DOG, JACKALS AND FOXES

Five species in the subregion, in three subfamilies: OTOCYONINAE, the bat-eared fox; CANINAE, the black-backed and side-striped jackals and Cape fox, and SIMO-CYONINAE, the wild dog.

SUBFAMILY OTOCYONINAE

BAT-EARED FOX

Bakoorvos
Otocyon megalotis

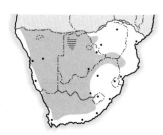

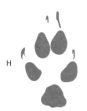

Description The overall impression is of a small, fluffy dog with huge ears. The neck and body are buffy brown, heavily grizzled with silvery grey. The muzzle is narrow, black on top and on the lower jaw. The top of the head is black, the sides of the muzzle and the forehead are white. The ears are enormous, up to 13 cm high, dark brown on the back. The legs are black and slim, with small feet. Each foot has five toes, of which four mark in the spoor; the front feet have long claws for digging. The tail is very bushy, black on top and at the tip. Females have two pairs of mammae on the belly. Total length 82 cm (70–92 cm); tail 28 cm (23–34 cm); shoulder height 30 cm;

weight 3,6 kg (3–5,4 kg). *See scale drawing on p. 246.*

Habitat Short grassland, grassland with bare ground, open woodland with sparse ground cover, Karoo, in areas with up to 600 mm of rain per year. The main habitat requirement is the presence of harvester termites, which make up a large part of the diet. Overgrazing improves the habitat for bat-eared foxes by increasing the number of termites, and their distribution is expanding.

Diet Termites, other insects, scorpions, sun spiders, small rodents, reptiles, small birds and fruit. Frequently eats small amounts of green grass, presumably to aid digestion. Does not kill farm stock. Quantities of food vary widely. Termites occur in up to 95% of scats, fruit in up to half. Mice and reptiles each occur in about 15% of stomachs, scorpions in about 20% of scats and stomachs. At least half of food intake is insects, of which up to 83% is beetles and their larvae and up to 41% locusts and grasshoppers. In the Free State bat-eared foxes eat 40 500 termites per hectare per year.

Life history Gestation 60 days. Litters of 4–6, with a sharp peak in births in October and November. Birth weight 1–1,5 kg. Weaned at four weeks; full-grown at four months. Killed by leopards, brown hyaenas, large raptors. One record of a bat-eared fox killed by a ratel. One pack of wild dogs in Hwange NP specialised in bat-eared foxes as prey.

Behaviour Active during the day in winter, at night in summer. Inactive during inclement weather, in the heat of the day in summer, and the cold of the night in winter. Shelters in disused aardvark or springhare holes, or digs its own burrows.

Prey is located by sound and smell. Underground prey is located precisely by holding the ears close to the ground, and is dug up with the front feet. Large insects are crushed with repeated quick snaps of the jaws, small rodents are bitten in the head, and swallowed in chunks, or nearly whole.

Lives in mated pairs which probably stay together for life. Family groups of a pair with up to four pups can be seen. In the Kalahari they forage individually for scattered prey, and in pairs or threes for concentrated prey. They may come together in large numbers at rich food sources: over 80 are reported feeding on crickets in a lucerne field in the Northern Cape. Both parents protect, groom and bring food for the pups.

Bat-eared foxes are exceptionally playful. They play with objects such as sticks and feathers, with each other, and there is even an observation of a bat-eared fox playing with a bontebok.

They defecate in middens; unfamiliar objects are marked with urine. The alarm signal is a soft growl. Cubs in distress call their parents with a loud, shrill chattering.

Field sign Narrow holes dug for buried larvae. Droppings are unsegmented sausages, 2 cm thick, tapered at the ends, nearly always containing insect fragments, sometimes with fruit pips or vertebrate remains. Deposited in middens.

Conservation Bat-eared foxes render a useful service to farmers by eating insect pests.

WILD DOG

Wildehond

Lycaon pictus

Description A lean, long-legged dog. The head is large, with a heavy muzzle and powerful jaws. The coat is blotched with black, white and yellow, every dog with a unique pattern. The ears are upright, large and rounded; the tail is bushy with a white tip. There are no dew claws on the front legs, and four toes on each foot. Females have six or seven pairs of mammae on the belly. Total length 127 cm (106–142 cm); tail 35 cm (32–42 cm); shoulder height 75 cm; weight 24–30 kg. Males are slightly bigger than females. *See scale drawing on p. 246.*

Habitat Open grasslands, open woodland and bushveld, and broken, hilly areas. Very wide ranging: only the largest of protected areas (e.g. Kruger NP, Hwange NP) have any chance of maintaining viable populations in the long term. In Kruger NP the

threat of predation by lions keeps wild dogs out of large areas of otherwise suitable habitat with plentiful prey.

Diet The most carnivorous of the canids: the main prey is antelope in the 15–50 kg range, such as impala; also larger species like kudu, smaller prey like hares, occasionally warthogs and bat-eared foxes. Southern African wild dogs do not hunt adult wildebeest and zebra, and these two species stand their ground to wild dogs. Very rarely scavenges (one observation in Kruger NP). Kills in Kruger NP: kudu 8%, impala 75%, small antelope 15%; in Hwange NP impala 54%, kudu 23%; in Hluhluwe-Umfolozi the main prey are nyala and impala.

Life history Typically one pair in a pack breeds, very rarely a second female gives birth, in one case three females in one pack. Litters may have more than one father. Gestation 70 days. Litters of 12–21 pups are born in May–June. First eats meat at 2–3 weeks, weaned at 5–10 weeks. When prey is abundant and vulnerable, dog populations can increase quickly: in the southern district of Kruger NP wild dogs increased from 67 in 1990 to 139 in 1993 while prey were weakened by drought in 1991–1992. Turnover of individuals is rapid; 80% of adults in Kruger NP are less than five years old. Causes of death of adults in Kruger NP, in order of importance, are lions, snares, and intraspecific fighting. Causes of death for pups are lions, other wild dogs, desertion, and disease.

Behaviour Packs hunt by day, occasionally in moonlight, moving along roads and game paths, and combing the bush for prey. Most active in the early morning and evening, resting in cover or lying in water during the midday heat. Prey is chased at speeds of up to 56 km/h over distances of up to 3–5 km (most chases are 1–3 km) and killed by disembowelling and dismembering, dying from shock and loss of blood. Some packs have specialist techniques: in Hwange NP large prey is gripped by the nose to immobilise it. They feed very quickly to avoid kills being stolen: 9 dogs can eat the 100 kg of meat from an adult kudu in 15 minutes. Adults feed pups on regurgitated meat, and share among themselves. A dog that wants meat begs by grinning, lowering its forequarters, raising its tail and giving a penetrating wail. Packs can drive off hyaenas who try to steal kills, because some dogs concentrate on guarding while the others feed. There is one record of warthogs putting wild dogs off a kill.

Packs vary from 2 adults with pups up to 50 dogs, usually 6–8 adults and up to 18 pups. Packs are bonded by intense social interactions, most involving mutual sniffing and muzzle licking. Adults as well as pups play. Wild dogs have a very strong body odour; dogs separated from their pack track their way back to it by smell. An alpha pair dominate the rest of a pack, and only they urine mark. Dogs disperse in single sex groups of up to five animals; new packs form when dispersing groups of opposite sexes meet. Packs have huge home ranges: 400–1 100 km^2 in Kruger NP, 750 km^2 in Hwange NP. Packs are anchored at dens for 13 weeks while pups mature.

A musical 'hooo', which is surprisingly quiet but carries 2–3 km is a long-range contact call. They twitter during intense social interactions such as pre-hunt rallies and greetings. The alarm call is a short, deep, growly bark. Puppies whine in distress.

A bitch on heat urinates more frequently; her mate urinates immediately on the same spot. The copulatory tie is brief. Pups are born and raised in an underground den. The mother stays on guard for the first 2–3 weeks. All pack members care for pups: adults regurgitate meat for puppies, or allow them to feed first at kills; subordinate adults may stay at the den as guards while the pack hunts. If a subordinate female gives birth the alpha female may kill the pups, adopt them and raise them with her own, or allow the mother to raise them herself. Pups start moving with the pack at 3 months, and join hunts at 14 months.

Conservation There are probably less than 5 000 wild dogs in the whole of Africa; only 6 countries have viable populations of more than 100. They are susceptible to infectious diseases such as canine distemper and rabies, which may be introduced to wild dog populations by free-roaming domestic dogs. In northwest Zimbabwe 12% of adults and 20% of pups are killed on roads annually. Red Data Book: Endangered. The status of the wild dog is less secure by far than that of the elephant.

SUBFAMILY CANINAE

CAPE FOX
Silwervos
Vulpes chama

S257 〔

Description A small and lightly built fox. Silvery grizzled grey on the back, flanks, upper limbs and tail; reddish brown on the head, lower legs and underparts. The muzzle is narrow and sharply tapered; the ears are large, with triangular points. There are five toes on the front feet, four on the hind feet; four on each foot mark in the spoor. The tail is very bushy (except during the moult) and has a black tip. Females have three pairs of mammae. Total length 92 cm (86–98 cm); tail 35 cm (29–40 cm); shoulder height 35 cm (32–43 cm); weight 2,8 kg (2,3–4,2 kg). In the Free State they are longer, but lighter, than in Botswana. Males are slightly bigger than females. *See scale drawing on p. 246.*

Habitat Semi-arid open grassland, light woodland and Karoo scrub, with up to 760 mm of rain per year; drier upland grassland in KwaZulu-Natal. Prospers on the wheat farms of the Western Cape.

Diet Rodents, hares, insects, carrion, birds; occasionally kills lambs under four days old. Frequently eats small quantities of grass, presumably to aid digestion. Mice occur in about 54% of stomachs, beetles in 48%, birds in 26%, crickets in 16–30%, reptiles in 12–30%, sun spiders in 26%, termites in 17%, scorpions in 13%, insectivores in 14%, hares 10%, farm stock 9%, carrion 14%.

Life history Gestation 50 days. Litters of up to six (usually three) are born in August–October. Cubs begin foraging with the mother at 16 weeks, and are independent at 21 weeks. In stock farming areas blanket predator control is probably the main cause of death.

Behaviour Nocturnal; can be seen at dens very early in the morning, and may be flushed from cover during the day. Shelters in dense cover, in rock crevices, or in disused springhare and aardvark holes, or may dig its own den. Forages alone, but several may congregate where food is abundant.

Lives in mated pairs. While the female has young cubs she stays at the den and the male brings food to her. Home ranges are 100–460 ha in the Free State, probably varying with locality and habitat. Living areas are marked with urine. A high-pitched howl, answered by the mate with a bark, is probably a long-range contact call, or an advertisement that an area is occupied. A bark is also used as an alarm call.

Field sign Punctures from the canine teeth are 14–16 mm apart (23–30 mm for black-backed jackal, 35–60 mm for domestic dogs border collie size and upwards). Droppings are long, thin sausages with tapered ends.

Conservation Can be a problem on sheep farms: losses of 4,5% of newborn lambs to Cape foxes have been reported. On crop farms renders a useful service by eating rodents and insects.

SIDE-STRIPED JACKAL

Witkwasjakkals
Canis adustus

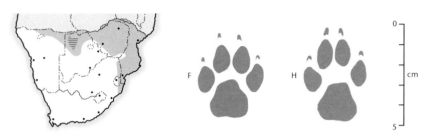

Description Somewhat like a medium-sized mongrel dog. Greyish or greyish buff; an indistinct pale stripe outlined with darker grey runs along the flanks and across the back just behind the shoulders. The lower parts of the legs are more buffy than the body. The ears are large, triangular with rounded tips, dark grey on the backs (reddish on the backs in black-backed jackal). The tail is bushy, black on top and nearly always with a white tip (tail tip black in black-backed jackal). There are five toes on the front feet, four on the hind feet; four toes on each foot mark in the spoor. Females have two pairs of mammae on the belly. Total length 1,1 m (0,96–1,2 m); tail 36 cm (30–41 cm); shoulder height 38 cm; weight males 9,4 kg (7,2–12,1 kg), females 8,3 kg (7,2–10 kg). *See scale drawing on p. 246.*

Habitat Generally a woodland species, but in northern KwaZulu-Natal it also occurs in grassland. Will move into city suburbs where there are parks and undeveloped areas.

Diet Mice and rats, hares, invertebrates, fruit and seeds, carrion, birds up to the size of guineafowl, reptiles. Sometimes raids crops; frequently eats small quantities of green grass, presumably as an aid to digestion. In Zimbabwe, wild fruit is found in

48% of stomachs, peanuts in 10%, mammals 35%, insects 31%, carrion 11%, birds 11%. In Botswana it eats more carrion (in 45% of stomachs).

Life history Gestation 57–70 days. Litters of 4–6 are born in August–October in Zimbabwe, and weaned at 8–10 weeks. Sexually mature at 10 months, disperse at 11 months. Lifespan 10 years.

Behaviour Nocturnal; occasionally seen at dusk and in the early morning. Shelters in heavy cover, in holes in the ground, or crevices among rocks.

Lives in mated pairs, but usually forages alone. Both parents bring food back for the pups, either carrying it in the mouth, or regurgitating it. Gives a series of yaps, probably as a contact or spacing call.

Field sign Droppings and spoor are very similar to those of the black-backed jackal; it may be possible to distinguish the spoor from the straighter back edge of the main pad in side-striped jackals.

BLACK-BACKED JACKAL
Rooijakkals
Canis mesomelas

S259 ☾ ☼

The same species is known as the silver-backed jackal in East Africa.

Description Somewhat like a medium-sized mongrel dog. The top of the back and neck are black, heavily mottled with silvery white patches. The flanks, legs and head are reddish buff to rich chestnut red, separated from the mottled back by a black line. The bushy tail is the same colour as the flanks at its base, and darkens towards the black tip (tip of tail is nearly always white in side-striped jackal). The ears are large, triangular with rounded tips, and reddish on the backs (dark grey on the backs in side-striped jackal). The muzzle is narrow and pointed. There are five toes on the forefeet, four on the hind; four toes on each foot mark in the spoor. Total length males 110 cm (96–130 cm), females 102 cm (89–125 cm); tail males 33 cm (28–37 cm), females 32 cm (25–40 cm); shoulder height 38 cm; weight males 8,3 kg (6–12 kg), females 7,2 kg (5,4–10 kg). *See scale drawing on p. 246.*

Habitat Occurs in almost any habitat except thick forest; in the wetter north and northeast it is replaced by the side-striped jackal. Independent of water, and more common towards the drier west. Persists in peri-urban areas.

Diet Omnivorous, taking rodents, hares and rabbits, small antelope and the young of larger species, farm stock, small carnivores, birds, reptiles and amphibians, carrion, fruit, garbage, insects and other invertebrates. Frequently eats small portions of grass, presumably to aid digestion. Depending on locality, insects occur in about half of stomachs, carrion in 25–37%, small mammals in 30–55%, vegetation in 10–25%, sun spiders 10%, and small antelope, hare-sized mammals and birds each about 10%. Even among jackals killed as pests, farm stock occurred in only 28% of stomachs, rodents in 31%, birds in 20% and carrion in 25%. On the Namib coast the diet is 86% seals and 12% birds, with some fish, nearly all taken as carrion. Intake equivalent to 500 vlei rats or 1 500 mice a year.

Life history Gestation 60 days. Litters of 2–8 (average 5), of which 1 or 2 survive to 14 weeks. In the KwaZulu-Natal Drakensberg most births are in June–September with a peak in July. In the former Cape Province mating from May–August, most births in July–October. Weans at 8–10 weeks; begins foraging at 14 weeks; permanent teeth erupt at 6 months. Sexually mature at 11 months but does not breed until paired up and established on a territory. Full grown at just over one year. Lifespan six years. Occasionally killed by larger carnivores; regularly eaten by leopards and brown hyaenas.

Behaviour Most active at dawn and dusk, but there is some activity throughout the day and night; becomes more strictly nocturnal in farming areas where it is hunted. Shelters at night in holes in the ground; rests during the day in shade, or sunbathes in cold weather.

Carrion is detected by smell: carcasses can be found from at least 1 km downwind. The sound of large carnivores at a kill also attracts jackals, and they may follow large carnivores in anticipation of a kill.

Rodents are captured with a typically canine high-arching pounce, pinned down with the forefeet and bitten across the back and neck. Tougher prey is shaken vigorously. Killing behaviour on lambs and sheep is not typical of canids: a sustained throat bite causing death by suffocation. Carcasses are opened at the flank, and usually the kidneys, liver, heart and tips of the ribs are eaten.

When large carnivores are on a kill jackals may wait their turn, or dash in and snatch scraps. They may pester hyaenas to such an extent that they abandon part of a carcass. They are fast and agile enough to evade lions and hyaenas, but do not take chances with cheetahs. Surplus food is cached. They eat wild melons for their water content, and in the Namib they lick settled fog.

Nearly always seen alone, but lives in mated pairs. Family groups of up to six are sometimes seen foraging together. Large numbers of jackals seen around carcasses are only temporary aggregations. Mating pairs form at about three years old, and stay together for life; if one partner dies the other finds a new mate. Pairs are territorial; males expel males and females expel females. Territories cover 1 800 ha in Giants Castle GR, KwaZulu-Natal; size probably varies with habitat. Both sexes scent mark with urine.

The long-range contact call is a distinctive wailing 'nyaa-a-a-a'. Each jackal has an individually recognisable call. Large predators such as leopards are mobbed with a persistent sharp yapping. A sharp bark or a rumbling growl is an alarm signal given by adults to pups.

Pups are born in underground dens. Both parents bring food for the pups: at first the food is carried in the stomach and regurgitated; as the pups mature it is carried in the mouth. Yearlings may stay in the parents' territory and 'help' to raise the next litter ('helping' may not always actually improve the survival of the pups).

Jackals very quickly become shy of traps and poisoned baits, and can learn from one another to avoid them.

Field sign Droppings are cylindrical with tapered ends, 1–2 cm thick, usually containing hair, insect fragments and bone chips, often deposited in a prominent position such as on top of a rock or a clump of grass.

On sheep and lamb kills: tooth marks either side of the windpipe, spacing between punctures 23–30 mm (35–60 mm for domestic dogs border collie size and upwards). Carcass opened on the flank, kidneys, liver, heart and tips of ribs eaten, no large bones broken. Domestic dogs often bite at the back, flanks and hind legs, and eat large bones. Caracals leave claw marks, and start feeding inside the back legs.

Conservation Black-backed jackals that kill sheep or lambs are a serious problem on some farms. Not all, probably not even most, black-backed jackals are sheep and lamb killers, and control needs to be targeted at the individuals that cause the problem, not at the whole species. In KwaZulu-Natal domestic dogs kill seven times as many sheep as jackals do. The most cost-effective means of limiting damage by jackals is better stock husbandry.

MUSTELIDS

Five species in the subregion, in three subfamilies: LUTRINAE, spotted-necked and Cape clawless otters; MUSTELINAE, the striped polecat and striped weasel, and MELLIVORINAE, the honey badger. Mustelids have well-developed anal glands whose strong-smelling secretions are used in defence or for scent marking.

SUBFAMILY LUTRINAE

OTTERS

Two species in the subregion.

CAPE CLAWLESS OTTER

Groototter

Aonyx capensis

S260

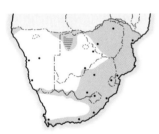  

Description The fur is short and very dense and varies in colour from light to very dark brown, appearing darker when wet. The sides of the muzzle and neck, and the chin, cheeks, and throat are white, off-white or buff (only limited pale patches in spotted-necked otter). The head is broad, with small eyes and ears. The legs are short, with five toes on each foot. The hind feet are webbed and have tiny nails, the front feet are only slightly webbed and have no nails or claws — hence the name. The tail is thick at the base, tapering sharply to a thin tip. The whiskers are long and white (short in spotted-necked otter). The chest is white (brown in spotted-necked otter). Females have two pairs of mammae on the belly. Larger than spotted-necked otter; total length 1,35 m, up to 2 m; head and body length 95 cm; tail 40 cm; weight 12–16 kg, up to 18 kg. Males are bigger than females. *See scale drawing on p. 285.*

Habitat Fresh water, estuaries, lagoons and the sea as long as fresh drinking water, food, and the cover of dense vegetation, holes or rocks is available. Prefers running water to dams and lakes, and cannot live in polluted water.

Diet Feeds mainly on crustaceans: in fresh water 50–70% crabs, 10–20% frogs, 15% dragonfly larvae, and 3–23% fish. Also very occasionally eats birds, rodents, reptiles, molluscs or herbivore dung. In sea water 13–40% crabs, 20–60% fish, 7–15% octopus, and a wide range of other items. May cause problems in fish farms or with captive wildfowl, but can be kept out with electric fencing.

Life history Gestation 60–64 days. Litters of up to three, usually two, are born at the end of the dry season: July–September in KwaZulu-Natal, December–February in Western and Eastern Cape. Weaned at about eight weeks.

Behaviour Active mainly during the late afternoon and early evening, and occasionally at dawn or in the early morning. Shelters in holts (dens) in dense vegetation, under rocks or in burrows it digs itself. More at home in the water than on land; swims by using its hind feet for propulsion and its tail as a rudder, cruises on the surface and dives for up to 30 seconds. Fish are hunted by sight; crabs and molluscs are felt for and captured with the dextrous forefeet, and bitten to death. The long whiskers detect vibrations from moving prey. Crabs are crushed and swallowed shell and all (water mongooses leave the carapace). Except for bony-headed barbel, fish are eaten from the head backwards (spotted-necked otters eat from the tail). After swimming, dries itself by rubbing on vegetation, the ground, or against rocks. Carries objects on land by holding them against its chest; a spotted-necked otter carries things in its mouth.

Usually seen singly, in twos, or in family groups of parents with up to three young. Home ranges of males in Tsitsikamma cover 9–13 km of coast; ranges along fresh

water are probably larger. Faeces, also called spraints, are deposited in small middens.

Field sign The faeces (spraints) are 22–29 mm in diameter (12–18 mm in spotted-necked otter, about 20 mm in water mongoose), and are found within 10 m (usually 2–4 m) of water. They contain fragments of crabs and have a fishy odour; dark brown when fresh, ageing to cream. The spoor is large (6–9 cm wide) and does not show claw marks. Patches of flattened vegetation or sand mark where an otter rubbed itself dry; smooth slides form where it enters and leaves the water.

Conservation Water pollution, clearing of vegetation near water, and development for industry, agriculture or housing all destroy otter habitat. The presence of otters is a sign of good water resource management. CITES Appendix II.

SPOTTED-NECKED OTTER

S261 R 🐾

Kleinotter

Lutra maculicollis

Description The fur is short and dense, varying in colour from chocolate to reddish brown. The throat and neck may show pale cream mottling, or be the same colour as the body (large area of white or buff in Cape clawless otter). The underparts are the same colour as the rest of the body (white in Cape clawless otter). The head is narrower than a Cape clawless otter's, the eyes and ears are small, and the whiskers are short (long in Cape clawless otter). The legs are short, the toes are webbed to their tips and have claws. The tail is flattened from top to bottom. Females have two pairs of mammae. Smaller than Cape clawless otter; total length about 1 m; head and body length 60 cm; weight 4–5 kg; males are bigger than females. *See scale drawing on p. 285.*

Habitat Fresh water only; dense vegetation or holes for shelter must be available. Cannot live in polluted water because its prey dies out. Favours deeper water than Cape clawless otters, and is more likely to be found in lakes and dams.

Diet Primarily a fish-eater: 40% fish, about 40% crabs, and 20% frogs; also insect larvae and occasionally birds. Fish makes up a bigger part of the diet when it is more available. Nearly all fish taken are less than 20 cm long, so spotted-necked otters are not a problem in fisheries.

Life history Gestation probably 60–63 days; 1 or 2 young per litter.

Behaviour Active in the early morning and late afternoon; shelters in holes or dense vegetation. Even more aquatic than the Cape clawless otter and spends more time underwater, surfacing briefly between dives. It covers about 5 m in each dive. Hunts by sight and catches prey with its teeth; carries things in its mouth rather than in the hands (Cape clawless otter carries with its hands). Fish are eaten from the tail forward (Cape clawless otter begins at the head). Crabs are crushed but spotted-necked otters are not strong enough to handle the larger ones. After a swim they dry themselves by rubbing on vegetation, the ground, or rocks.

Usually seen singly, or in family groups of up to five. Small groups of up to 10 adults may form in good habitat.

Field sign The faeces (spraints) are 12–18 mm in diameter (22–29 mm in Cape clawless otter, about 20 mm in water mongoose), and are found within 10 m (usually 2–4 m) of water. If the otter has been eating mainly crabs, its faeces contain their fragments and are dark brown when fresh, ageing to cream. A diet of mainly fish produces dark grey scats that fade to light grey. In either case the faeces smell of fish. The spoor is 4–4,5 cm wide; it shows claw marks and sometimes the web between the toes (no claws or web in Cape clawless otter, no web in water mongoose). Patches of flattened vegetation or sand mark where an otter rubbed itself dry, smooth slides form where it enters and leaves the water.

Conservation Spotted-necked otters are rare except in areas such as the Okavango where small fish are abundant. Water pollution, clearing of vegetation near water, and development for industry, agriculture or housing all destroy otter habitat. The presence of otters is a sign of good water resource management. CITES Appendix II.

SUBFAMILY MELLIVORINAE

One species in the subregion.

RATEL (HONEY BADGER)

Ratel
Mellivora capensis

Description Stockily built. White or pale grey on the back of the head, the back, and the top of the tail; black on the remainder, with a white line separating the two colours. The eyes and ears are small, the legs are short and powerful. The forefeet

are armed with long claws with sharp edges underneath, the hind feet have claws which are flat underneath. The tail is short. Females have two pairs of mammae. Total length 95 cm (90–102 cm); tail 22 cm (20–24 cm); shoulder height 25–28 cm; weight 12 kg (8–14,5 kg). *See scale drawing on p. 285.*

Habitat Occurs in a wide range of habitats except desert, moist montane areas and forest, but is uncommon throughout most of its range.

Diet Takes a very wide range of small animals, especially mice (30% of food intake), scorpions and spiders (14%), lizards (18%), and snakes (18%); also larger mammals (14%), grubs and bee larvae.

Life history Litters of two are born in summer.

Behaviour Active at any time except midday in the Kalahari national parks; outside protected areas it appears to be mainly nocturnal. Females cover about 10 km in a day's foraging and have home ranges of 54 km²; a male covered 27 km and had a home range of 174 km². A powerful digger: can dig itself into sandy ground in two

minutes. Most of its prey is dug out of burrows. Nomadic; digs a new den nearly every day.

Solitary, sometimes seen in small groups. Prey is detected by scent, and likely spots such as bushes are approached from downwind. Demolishes rotten logs to uncover insect larvae, raids beehives, and may break into poultry runs. Sometimes scavenges, stealing a springhare from an African wild cat, and a steenbok from a brown hyaena, and at Mana Pools NP and Hwange NP ratels scavenge garbage in the camp sites.

Its reputation for ferocity when disturbed is well founded; can kill pythons up to 3 m long. The black and white pattern is a warning to other animals to stay away. Under extreme duress it releases a foul-smelling secretion from the anal glands.

A hunting ratel may be shadowed by a pale chanting goshawk (*Melierax canorus*) or a black-backed jackal hoping to grab prey that escapes the ratel. The idea that ratels are led to beehives by honeyguides (*Indicator indicator*) is very likely a myth.

Field sign Droppings are cylindrical, up to 5 cm long, 1,5 cm thick, rounded at the ends (most other carnivore faeces have tapered ends), containing any of a wide range of animal remnants. Dug up rodent burrows, opened dung-beetle balls.

Conservation Because they are rare throughout most of their range, ratels are susceptible to local extinctions. Red Data Book: Vulnerable.

SUBFAMILY MUSTELINAE

Two species in the subregion.

STRIPED WEASEL / WHITE-NAPED WEASEL   S263 R (
Slangmuishond
Poecilogale albinucha

Description Africa's second smallest carnivore. Very sinuous build, with very short legs, as adaptations to hunting rodents in their burrows; shoulder height is only 5–6 cm. The forehead and top of the head are white and there are four white or pale cream stripes running down the back to the white, long-haired tail. The belly is black. This striking pattern of black and white gives warning of the weasel's foul-smelling anal gland secretion. The ears are very small. Females have two or three pairs of mammae. Total length about 48 cm; head and body length 30 cm (27–33 cm); tail 17,5 cm (16–20 cm); weight males 340 g (283–380 g), females 250 g (230–290 g). *See scale drawing opposite.*

Habitat Moist grassland or open woodland with more than 600 mm of rain annually and good numbers of small rodents is probably the optimum habitat, but striped weasels turn up occasionally in a variety of other habitats. They may need particular types of soil in which to dig burrows.

Diet A specialist predator of rodents up to its own weight; occasionally takes shrews and young ground birds.

Life history Mating September– February; gestation 32 days. Litters of 1–3 are born October–March. Eyes open at 52 days. Weaning begins at 5 weeks when the canine teeth erupt, and is complete by 11 weeks. First kills at about 13 weeks; full-grown by 20 weeks. Lifespan 4–6 years. Suffers both predation and competition for food from free-ranging and feral dogs.

Behaviour Most active at night; occasionally seen during the day. Solitary or in family groups of a female with up to three young. Males may be territorial. Shelters in burrows that it digs itself, or in other holes. Under threat it ejects foul-smelling secretions from its anal glands.

Striped weasels hunt in rodent burrows, locating prey by scent. Prey is tackled by biting at the back of the neck, pulling it off its feet by rolling sideways, clasping it with the front legs, twining around it and treading vigorously against it with the hind feet to break its spine.

Copulation lasts 60 to 80 minutes.

Field sign Faeces are up to 5 cm long, narrow and twisted, containing remains of small rodents.

Conservation The striped weasel is at risk from loss of its moist grassland habitat to tree plantations, crops, and overgrazing. Generally rare; heavily exploited for traditional medicine and magic. Red Data Book: Rare.

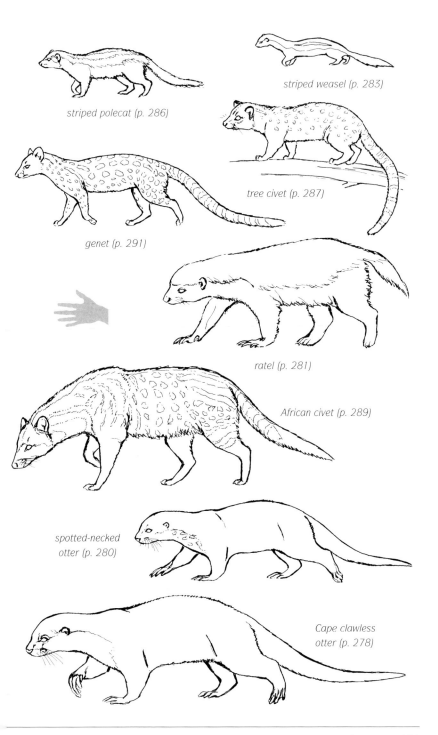

striped weasel (p. 283)

striped polecat (p. 286)

tree civet (p. 287)

genet (p. 291)

ratel (p. 281)

African civet (p. 289)

spotted-necked otter (p. 280)

Cape clawless otter (p. 278)

STRIPED POLECAT

Stinkmuishond

Ictonyx striatus

Description Strikingly patterned in black and white. There are white patches on the forehead and in front of the ears, and four white stripes down the back. The tail is white; the flanks, underparts and legs are black. The hair is long and silky (short fur in striped weasel). The legs are longer, the body much stockier, and the ears larger than in the striped weasel. The toes of the front feet carry long claws for digging. Females have two pairs of mammae. Total length males 60 cm (up to 67 cm), females 56 cm (up to 63 cm); head and body length males 37 cm, females 33 cm; tail 23 cm; weight males 982 g (681–1 460 g), females 675 g (420–880 g). Larger towards the north. *See scale drawing on p. 285.*

Habitat Occurs in almost any habitat; penetrates into desert along drainage lines. Most often seen as a road kill.

Diet Mostly insects (60%) and mice (20–30%); also spiders, scorpions and sun-spiders (10%), birds and their eggs, reptiles and amphibians. May raid poultry.

Life history Gestation 36 days. Litters of up to three are born October–March. Eyes

open by 6 weeks, weaned at 8 weeks, able to kill rats at 9 weeks, full-grown at 20 weeks. One litter per year unless the young die early, when the female may breed again. Lifespan 4–5 years. Thanks to their foul-smelling defence, striped polecats are rarely killed by any of the carnivores.

Behaviour Nocturnal, solitary, and possibly territorial; even family groups are rarely seen. Rests during the day in holes in the ground, rock crevices or dense vegetation.

Prey is detected by scent and sound; buried insects are dug up with the front claws, mice are bitten anywhere on the body until they are helpless and then killed with a bite to the neck. Striped polecats use the vile-smelling secretion of their anal glands as a defence against predators, but get killed on roads when they try the same tactic against oncoming traffic.

Copulation lasts for 60–100 minutes.

Field sign Droppings are 4–5 cm long, 1 cm thick, containing insect fragments and rodent remains.

Conservation Although striped polecats are very widely distributed, they are not common anywhere. Agricultural development and overgrazing reduce the availability of their prey, and domestic dogs kill them.

FAMILY VIVERRIDAE

CIVETS, GENETS AND MONGOOSES

Three subfamilies: VIVERRINAE, the civet and genets; HERPESTINAE, the mongooses and suricate, and NANDINIINAE, the tree civet. The HERPESTINAE can be separated from the others on external features: they have less compact feet with long, only slightly curved claws, and have no spots on their coats.

SUBFAMILY NANDINIINAE

One species in the subregion.

TREE CIVET   S265 ☾
Boomsiwet
Nandinia binotata

Description Somewhat similar in appearance to a genet. Brown with irregular, indistinct dark brown or black spots, and a characteristic white or yellow spot on each side just behind the top of the shoulder. The tail is long, ringed with dark brown or black except towards the tip, which is plain dark brown. There are no white facial markings (white on faces of genets). Ears low and rounded (higher and more pointed

in genets). Each foot has five sharp, curved, protractile claws. Total length 94 cm (87–98 cm); tail 48 cm (46–51 cm); weight 1,95 kg (1,4–3,1 kg). *See scale drawing on p. 285.*

Habitat Occurs in mountain and subtropical rainforest with rainfall between 1 000 and 1 400 mm annually.

Diet Fruit, berries, birds, mice and termites. May raid poultry.

Life history Gestation 64 days. Probably breeds throughout the year. Up to four young per litter.

Behaviour Strictly nocturnal. Shelters during the day in tree holes and dense tangles of creepers and foliage. A very agile climber and leaper, foraging in tall trees 30–50 m above ground; less at home on the ground. Solitary and territorial; male territories overlap those of females. Fruit trees may attract small aggregations.

Gives a loud hoot as a long-range spacing call; 'meows' in threat.

Conservation Like all forest dwellers, tree civets suffer from loss and fragmentation of their habitat when forest is cleared for agriculture.

CIVET AND GENETS

Three species in the subregion.

AFRICAN CIVET
Afrikaanse siwet
Civettictis civetta

S266   R   ☾

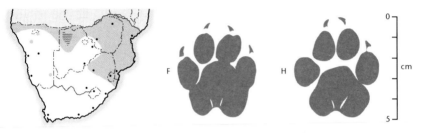

Description Stockily built. Greyish or grey-brown, heavily marked with black stripes, blotches and spots. The markings do not show clearly by spotlight. The head is dog-like, with black nostrils outlined by white patches on the sides of the muzzle, and black patches around and in front of the eyes, separated by a lighter stripe up the middle of the muzzle to the light coloured forehead. There are broad black bands on the sides of the neck, running down onto the chest and throat. The ears are small with rounded tips. The lower limbs are usually black, lightly built, with small feet carrying five sharp, curved claws. The tail is slightly bushy, banded with black, and with a black tip. Total length 1,3 m (1,2–1,4 m); tail 47 cm (42–50 cm); weight 11,25 kg (9,5–13,2 kg). *See scale drawing on p. 285.*

Habitat Forest and dense woodland, usually where there is surface water, but this may be because that is where the vegetation is thicker and more productive, not because civets are dependent on drinking.

Diet Omnivorous: insects, small rodents, fruit, birds, reptiles, amphibians, fish, invertebrates and carrion are all taken according to availability. In some areas, civets eat large quantities of millipedes, which most animals avoid. They frequently eat grass, probably to help digestion, and take rumen contents from antelope carcasses.

Life history Gestation 60–65 days. Litters of up to four young are born August–January. Weaning 1–5 months.

Behaviour Nocturnal; most active from 1–2 hours after sunset until midnight. Shelters during the day in holes, rock crevices, caves and dense cover.

Clambers on to low branches to reach fruit, but is a poor climber and does nearly all its foraging on the ground, making extensive use of pathways. Food is probably detected by scent and sound. Prey is killed by multiple bites, often with fierce shaking, and may be thrown to the side and grabbed again. The teeth are adapted to crushing rather than cutting, and vertebrate prey is held down by the forepaws and torn apart with the incisors and canines.

Solitary, or in family groups of mother with young. Lives in overlapping home ranges, or may be territorial.

Scent marks frequently by wiping the everted anal gland onto smooth objects. The marks have a rank odour which lasts for up to three months. The anal gland secretion used to be used as a fixative in perfumes. Defecates in middens near paths, which have the same odour as scent marks and may be used by more than one civet. If millipedes are an important part of the diet their remains accumulate in the civets' middens. Adult males spray urine.

If disturbed a civet either slinks quietly away or freezes and dashes away suddenly if approached too closely. In defensive threat it stands sideways-on, and makes itself look bigger by erecting a crest of long hair along the back.

Field sign Dark-coloured scent marks with a rank smell, on smooth objects. Middens near pathways; droppings are roughly cylindrical, containing a wide assortment of animal and plant remnants, including millipede rings.

Conservation Where coyote getters are used in attempts to control black-backed jackals they kill six times as many civets as jackals. Red Data Book: Rare.

SMALL-SPOTTED GENET

Kleinkolmuskejaatkat
Genetta genetta

Description Long, lithe and somewhat cat-like. Ground colour white or light buffy, with small black or rusty spots (large-spotted genet has larger spots), and black bars on the top of the shoulders. Along the mid-back is a strip of long, black hair that can be erected into a crest. The tail is ringed with black and the tip is white (black in large-spotted genet). The muzzle is long and pointed, black on the sides, and with white patches near the tip; the chin is usually dark (white in large-spotted genet). There are white patches below the eyes, and white stripes running up onto the forehead from the inner corners of the eyes. The ears are large, with rounded tips. The legs are usually black (light in large-spotted genet), and the feet have curved, sharp, protractile claws. Females have two pairs of mammae on the belly. Total length males 94 cm (86–105 cm); tail 45 cm (41–52 cm); weight males 1,9 kg (1,5–2,6 kg), females 1,8 kg (1,4–2,3 kg). *See scale drawing on p. 285.*

Habitat Woodland, scrub, fynbos. Occurs in arid areas and penetrates desert along rivers. Sometimes nests in roofs of buildings.

Diet Invertebrates, small rodents, lesser bushbabies, birds, eggs, reptiles, fruit, crabs. Sometimes raids poultry; occasionally scavenges. Prey remains in scats from northern Namib: small mammals 97%, insects 60%. Rodent remains occur in 50–60% of stomachs, insects in 40–70%, spiders and scorpions in about 35%, rep-

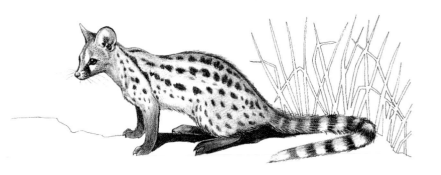

tiles in 10–20%, birds in 6–24%, fruit and vegetation in 5–24%, carrion in 8%, and millipedes in 5%.

Life history Gestation 70 days. Litters of 1–4 are born in August–March, apparently with two peaks in births. Eyes open at eight days; weaned at nine weeks. A minor item in the diet of larger carnivores.

Behaviour Strictly nocturnal; active from about two hours after sunset. Shelters in holes, rock crevices or dense cover during the day. Forages mainly on the ground, but is a very agile climber; usually flees into trees.

Solitary or in family groups. Scent marks with anal gland secretion; marks retain their musky scent for up to nine weeks. Defecates in middens near its den.

Hunts by stalking, rushing and pouncing like a cat, but kills with several bites. Eats small birds with their feathers.

Field sign Scent marks, middens near nest holes. Droppings are variable, typically cylindrical, up to 5 cm long and 1 cm thick, nearly always containing insect fragments. They have a musky odour. Feathers of small birds are not plucked (cats pluck at least some feathers).

LARGE-SPOTTED GENET (RUSTY-SPOTTED GENET) S268 ⟨

Rooikolmuskejaatkat
Genetta tigrina

Description Long, lithe and somewhat cat-like. Ground colour white or light buffy, with large black or rusty spots on the back (small-spotted genet has small spots), smaller spots on the legs and flanks, and black or rusty bars on the top of the shoulders. The crest on the back, if present at all, is smaller than in the small-spotted genet, and rises only from the lower part of the back. The tail is ringed with black or rust colour; the tip is black (white in small-spotted genet). The muzzle is long and pointed, dark brown on the sides with white patches near the tip, white on the chin (dark in small-spotted genet). There are white patches below the eyes, and white stripes running onto the forehead from the inner corners of the eyes. The ears are large, with rounded tips. The legs are white or pale buff (black in small-spotted genet) and the feet have curved, sharp, protractile claws. Females have two pairs of mam-

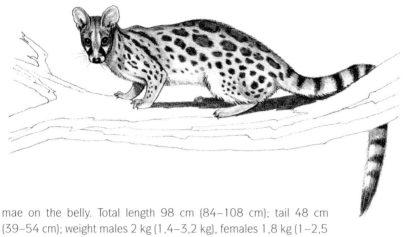

mae on the belly. Total length 98 cm (84–108 cm); tail 48 cm (39–54 cm); weight males 2 kg (1,4–3,2 kg), females 1,8 kg (1–2,5 kg). *See scale drawing on p. 285.*

Habitat Prefers forest and forest fringes and depends on the availability of drinking water; therefore occurs towards the wetter east and extreme south. Occurs in plantations and other stands of exotic trees. Commonly lives near human dwellings, especially if there is thick vegetation; sometimes shelters in buildings.

Diet Mostly insects and small mammals, including golden moles and bats; also other invertebrates, birds, frogs, and fruit. Sometimes raids poultry. Depending on locality, small mammal remains occur in 25–70% of stomachs, insects in 20–90%, spiders and scorpions in 10–30%, plant material in 10–25%, birds in 5–15%, millipedes in up to 10% and reptiles in up to 10%.

Life history Gestation 70 days. Litters of up to 5 (usually 1–3) are born August–March. Eyes open at 10 days. Full-grown and with adult teeth at 11 months.

Behaviour Strictly nocturnal; most active from just after sunset to 01h00. Shelters during the day in rock crevices, holes, fallen trees and similar cover. Forages mainly on the ground, but is a very agile climber; usually flees into trees. Hunts by stalking, rushing and pouncing like a cat, but kills with several bites.

Solitary, living in home ranges of 50–100 ha. Scent marks with urine and anal gland secretion, which has a musky odour.

The white markings on the face are social signals. Seven vocal signals are used.

Field sign Musky odour of scent marks, faeces and urine. Droppings are cylindrical, up to 5 cm long and 1 cm thick, nearly always containing insect fragments.

MONGOOSES

With 14 species, this is the largest subfamily of carnivores in the subregion.

SURICATE

Stokstertmeerkat
Suricata suricatta

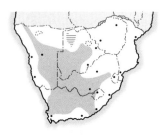  

Description   Silvery brown, paler in the northwest than in the south, with broad, irregular dark bands across the back (banded mongooses have narrow stripes). The underparts have sparse, short hair, and the dark skin shows through. The black roots of the hair show when it is fluffed up during sunbathing. The muzzle is long and pointed, there are black patches around the eyes, and the ears are small and set low on the head. The legs are long, and there are four toes on each foot, with long, slightly curved claws. The tail is long, thin and short-haired (bushy in banded mongoose) and has a distinct black tip. Females have three pairs of mammae on the belly. Total length 50 cm (45–55 cm); tail 22 cm (19–24 cm); weight 730 g (616–800 g in males; up to 960 g in breeding females). Breeding females have prominent nipples, males have prominent scrotums. *See scale drawing on p. 299.*

Habitat   Arid southwestern parts of the subregion in scrub, open woodland, and grassland, extending into fynbos in the Western Cape Province and savanna towards the east. Does not occur in true desert, in forest, or on mountains.

Diet   A very wide range of insects (especially larvae) and other arthropods, reptiles, amphibians, and occasionally small birds. Eats mammals very rarely, if at all. Opportunistic, taking what is most

readily available: in the southern Kalahari insects are 70% of the volume eaten, reptiles 20%, scorpions 5%, grasshoppers and crickets 3%. In Botswana beetle larvae occur in 91% of stomachs, scorpions in 35%, grasshoppers and crickets 17%, beetles in 17%, reptiles in 13%, centipedes and millipedes in 13%, and termites 9%. In the Free State beetles occur in 58% of stomachs, caterpillars and pupae in 43%, termites in 40%, grasshoppers and crickets 34%, spiders 21%.

Life history In small bands only one female breeds, in larger bands two or three. Breeding subordinates are usually at least three years old. Dominant females produce 1–3 (average 2) litters per year. Gestation 70 days. Litters of 4–5 are born October–June, with a birth peak in January–April. They emerge from the den at 2–3 weeks; forage independently at 3 months, and are sexually mature at 1 year. Killed by raptors, snakes, small carnivores: infants and juveniles are the most vulnerable.

Behaviour Active only during the day, emerging from dens around sunrise, and retiring before sunset. Spends 20–30 minutes sunbathing first thing in the morning; during summer takes a siesta in the shade or in a den. Dens are usually in old termite mounds or ground squirrel warrens, but groups may dig their own.

Lives in bands of 6–15 (average 10) of which 5–9 are adults and yearlings. Group composition is unstable, and there is a rapid turnover of members, with both males and females dispersing to other groups, usually to the neighbours of their home group. Males may take over groups by driving out the resident dominant males, or be integrated as subordinates. Prospective immigrants are threatened with 'churring' calls, approached with a rocking gait, attacked and chased. Aggression is most serious from adults of the same sex as the immigrant. Subordinate immigrants do extra babysitting duties.

There is a dominance hierarchy: subordinates creep towards dominants to greet them; dominant males scent mark the most. Older animals are higher ranking. Fighting within a group is rare except during the breeding season, when both males and females attack others of the same sex. Fights may lead to serious injuries and even death. Fights during group take-overs are also savage.

Bands are bonded by frequent mutual grooming, play even among adults, and huddling together. They forage as a group, but each finds and catches its own food. Prey is detected by smell and dug up with the forepaws. Holes may be so deep that the whole body disappears into them.

Bands are territorial. Meetings between neighbours involve chasing and fighting. Territories are marked with anal gland and cheek gland secretions. Marking is particularly frequent after disputes. Dominant males also rip grass tufts apart.

If more than one female in a group breeds they give birth at nearly the same time. Dominant females attack pregnant subordinates, and may kill their offspring.

Babies less than three weeks old are confined to the den, and all band members take turns to babysit while the group forages, huddling with the babies to keep them warm and guarding them from predators. Babysitters go hungry while on duty, but may babysit for three successive days. Between three weeks and three months, youngsters accompanying the adults on foraging trips are fed by caretakers of either sex. Immigrants care for youngsters as carefully as group members.

Very vulnerable to predators while foraging. Sentinels perch on vantage points and keep a look-out, giving a continuous peeping all-clear call. The alarm call for raptors is a rasping bark, and for ground predators a hoot. Sessions of sentinel duty are up to an hour or more long. Snakes, small carnivores, and raptors on the ground are mobbed and harassed. Jackals are chased off by the whole group advancing in a tight bunch with an exaggerated bouncy gait, looking like one big furry animal. Attacks on predators are led by the dominant male.

Field sign Foraging holes up to 30 cm deep. Droppings are up to 5 cm long, 1–1,5 cm thick, containing insect fragments, and are deposited in middens near warrens.

SELOUS' MONGOOSE
Klein witstertmuishond
Paracynictis selousi

S270 R (

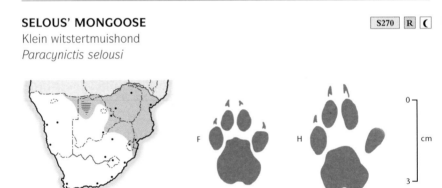

Description Tawny or greyish, with fine white banding on the hairs giving a grizzled appearance. The lower parts of the legs are black or dark brown, and the feet have four toes (only in this species, suricate and bushy-tailed mongoose), each with a heavy claw. The tail has a broad white tip (in white-tailed mongoose two thirds of the

tail is white). The muzzle is narrow and pointed; the ears are small, but bigger in relation to the head than in other mongooses. Females have three pairs of mammae on the belly. Total length 76 cm (63–89 cm); tail 35 cm (29–44 cm); weight 1,75 kg (1,2–2,2 kg). *See scale drawing on p. 304.*

Habitat Open scrub and woodland with sandy soils. Independent of water.

Diet Mainly insects but also takes reptiles, mice, frogs and birds. In Zimbabwe insects occur in 82% of stomachs, other invertebrates in 56%, small rodents 16%, reptiles 14%, amphibians 10%, birds 4%.

Life history Litters of up to four are born in summer.

Behaviour Nocturnal. Shelters in burrows that it digs itself, with several entrances and going down to 1,5 m, or uses holes dug by other animals. If chased, goes to ground in any convenient hole. Food and prey are located by smell and sound. Solitary or females with young.

Conservation Red Data Book: Rare

BUSHY-TAILED MONGOOSE
Borselstertmuishond
Bdeogale crassicauda

S271 C

Description Very dark brown, appearing black, grizzled with white flecks. Long haired; the tail is bushy throughout its length. There are four toes on each foot (only this species, suricate and Selous' mongoose), with long, heavy, curved claws. Females have one pair of mammae on the belly. Total length 70 cm (65–74 cm); shoulder height 15 cm; tail 26 cm (23–29 cm); weight males 1,9 kg (1,8–2,1 kg), females 1,6 kg (1,3–1,8 kg). *See scale drawing on p. 304.*

Habitat Rocky outcrops in river valleys. Often associated with dassies.

Diet Insects, reptiles, mice, scorpions and other invertebrates.

Behaviour Active in the early morning, evening and at night. Solitary.

Conservation Uncommon and with a limited habitat.

YELLOW MONGOOSE

Witkwasmuishond
Cynictis penicillata

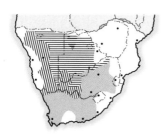

 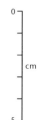

▓ *C. p. penicillata*   ≀≀≀ *C. p. bradfieldi*   ≡ *C. p. coombsii*

Description Appearance differs slightly between subspecies: *C. p. penicillata* (Western and Eastern Cape Provinces, Free State, KwaZulu-Natal, Northwest Province and Gauteng) is rich tawny-yellow or reddish yellow; *C. p. coombsii* (northern South Africa and Botswana) is faded, grizzled yellowish; *C. p. bradfieldi* (Namibia and the Northern Cape) is intermediate in colour. The tail is long-haired and has a white tip in *C. p. penicillata* and *C. p. bradfieldi* (black tip in slender mongoose). The tip of the nose is black (red or light brown in slender mongoose). There is no groove down the middle of the top lip (grooved in slender and small grey mongooses). The front feet have five toes with long claws on the second to fifth (claws shorter in slender and small grey mongooses), the hind feet have four toes, all with claws. Females have three pairs of mammae on the belly. *C. p. penicillata* is the biggest, total length 57 cm (43–75 cm); weight 830 g; *C. p. bradfieldi* total length 55 cm (46–65 cm); *C. p. coombsii* total length 51 cm (42–68 cm); weight 589 g. *See scale drawing opposite.*

Habitat Open scrub, grassland, Karoo, open woodland. Prefers more open areas than the small grey mongoose.

Diet Varies widely according to food availability: mainly insects, also other invertebrates, mice, bats, birds and carrion; accused of raiding poultry. Termites, especially harvester termites, are the single most important part of the diet. Eats fruit in winter when insects are less abundant. Insects occur in 52–91% of stomachs, beetles and their larvae in 33–60%, termites in 20–74%, butterflies and moths in 22%, spiders in 12%, plant material in 15–21%, mammals in up to 15%, birds in about 10%, and reptiles and amphibians in 10%.

dwarf mongoose (p. 312)

suricate (p. 294)

yellow mongoose (p. 298)

slender mongoose (p. 302)

banded mongoose (p. 310)

small grey mongoose
(p. 305)

Life history Females have two litters per year unless conditions are poor. In the former Transvaal, first matings in August, births in October, second matings in October, births in December. In Etosha NP, first matings in August, births in October, second matings in December, births in February. Gestation 60–62 days; 2–5 per litter (usually 2 or 3). Usually 1 or 2 emerge from burrow. First eats solid food at 4–5 weeks, weaned at 6–8 weeks (exceptionally at 5–6 months), forages independently at 16–18 weeks. Females mature at 1 year, males at 9–12 months. Potential lifespan 15 years. Snakes and monitor lizards take youngsters from warrens. Large raptors take adults.

Behaviour Active during the day, and at night in summer. Shelters in burrows that it digs itself, takes over from ground squirrels or shares with ground squirrels or suricates. Burrows may be small, with a single entrance, or form large warrens with up to 66 entrances, going down 1,5 m. Sunbathes to warm up after emerging from the burrow, even after a midday siesta in summer. Forages singly, up to 1,3 km from the warren. Food is detected mainly by scent and sound, and is scratched out of leaf litter and dung, or dug up from the soil.

Warrens are inhabited by colonies of up to 13, usually 2–3 adults and their young. Colonies may have 3–5 warrens and move between them every 6–8 weeks. Colonies are bonded by mutual grooming between members. Each colony has an alpha pair, which can be recognised by subordinates' lying on their sides when challenged by them. Juveniles outrank all adults.

Individual males have home ranges of up to 100 ha. Colonies hold territories of 2–6 ha, possibly up to 3 km². All colony members scent mark with anal gland secretion and cheek gland secretion. Subordinates, especially males, mark more than dominants and are more active in territorial defence. Male intruders are chased away, while females may be tolerated, especially during the mating season. There are middens outside warrens and secondary burrows, where all colony members defecate and urinate first thing in the morning. The faeces have a strong, distinctive odour.

Subordinate males cannot mate within the colony that there were born in, and they move to neighbouring groups; immigrant subordinate males mate when the dominant male is absent. Oestrous subordinate females move temporarily to neighbouring territories for mating, or disperse to other colonies.

Males court females by following them giving purring, 'cawing' and screaming calls. Initially females respond aggressively. Copulation lasts 3–4 minutes and is repeated for up to 45 minutes. High-ranking males also mount subordinate males.

A colony's females give birth within a few days of each other. They suckle one another's young, but each female prefers to suckle her own. This is the only species of mongoose in which colony members bring food to the den for the young. They also babysit while the mothers forage. Adults call youngsters at the den with a soft 'cawing'.

Mild alarm is signalled by a repeated short growl, an uncertain danger by a sharp 'tschak', and a sudden serious alarm by a bark. They flee with the tail arched upwards (slender mongoose keeps tail low and flicks it upwards as it reaches cover).

Field sign Scats are roughly cylindrical, up to 6 cm long, tapered at one end, and nearly always containing insect fragments (similar to those of suricates). Middens near warrens. Shallow holes where food was dug up.

Conservation Yellow mongooses are important rabies carriers. One symptom of infection is that they lose their fear of humans. Stay away from 'tame' mongooses!

LARGE GREY MONGOOSE (EGYPTIAN MONGOOSE / ICHNEUMON)

S273 ☼

Groot grysmuishond

Herpestes ichneumon

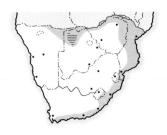

Description Substantially larger than any of the other mongooses that are active during the day (white-tailed mongoose is similar in size but is nocturnal and has a white tail). The body and head are proportionately longer, and the legs proportionately shorter than in most other mongooses. Dark grey, black on the lower limbs. The hair is long and coarse, the tail is long-haired at the base, but tapers in thickness towards the black brush on the tip. Each foot has five toes, all with long claws. Four toes mark in the spoor. Females have three pairs of mammae. Total length 1,1 m (1–1,2 m); tail 52 cm (45–58 cm); weight males 3,4 kg (2,6–4,1 kg), females 3,1 kg (2,4–4,1 kg). *See scale drawing on p. 304.*

Habitat Fringes of rivers, dams, lakes and swamps, and in humid and sub-humid grassland and sugar cane fields. Needs dense cover.

Diet Small rodents (40%), other mammals, birds, frogs, reptiles (especially puff-adders, *Bitis arietans*), insects, other invertebrates, and fruit. Grass is frequently eaten, probably as a purgative. Sometimes raids poultry but accusations of lamb killing are unsubstantiated. One report of an attack on a Cape grysbok lamb.

Life history Gestation 60 days. Litters of 1–4 are born in early summer and weaned at 4–8 weeks. Forages with the mother from 72 days, starts foraging alone at 4 months. Stays in the family group for a year.

Behaviour Most active in the late morning and again in the mid-afternoon; occasionally active at other times.

Usually solitary. Females have overlapping home ranges of 300–450 ha. Ranges of males overlap those of a few females. Groups of two or three females with their young may form in the summer breeding season. The anal glands are well developed; their secretions are probably used to mark home ranges. There is a repertoire of seven different calls. If threatened, makes itself look bigger by erecting its long hair.

Field sign Dropping are up to 10 cm long, 1,5 cm thick, tapered at one end.

Conservation Grassland habitat in KwaZulu-Natal is being planted with trees.

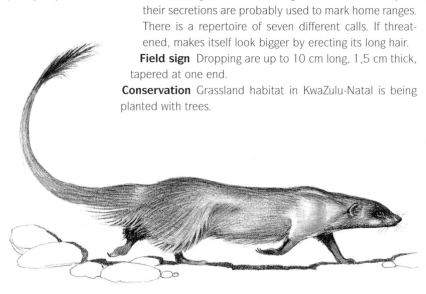

SLENDER MONGOOSE
S274

Swartkwasmuishond
Galerella sanguinea
Galerella swalius
Galerella nigrata

Note The classification and taxonomy of slender mongooses are complex and not yet entirely clear. On the basis of features that can be used for identification in the field, I have included the three species with distinct black tail tips under slender mongoose, and the species without a distinct black tail tip under small grey mongoose.

Description Small, with short legs and a long, low-slung, sinuous body. In *Galerella sanguinea* the colour is very variable, in general ranging from grizzled greyish to red-brown but with some individuals very dark red brown, almost black, and others, from the southern Kalahari, a striking flame orange. There is a reddish tinge to all the colours. The underparts are a paler or brighter version of the colour of the back and flanks. *G. swalius* is grizzled, greyish yellow on the back and flanks, dull yellow on the underparts, with no reddish tinge. *G. nigrata* is bright reddish brown or dark brown. The ears are small and set low on the sides of the head. The tail is long, with short

hair except at the tip which is characteristically black (white in yellow mongoose, same colour as rest of tail in small grey mongoose). The tip of the nose is red or light brown (black in yellow mongoose and small grey mongoose). The top lip has a groove down the middle (no groove in yellow mongoose). Five toes on each foot, with short curved claws; four toes mark in the spoor. Females have 1–3 pairs of mammae on the belly. Total length males 60 cm (56–65 cm), females 55 cm (51–60 cm); tail males 28 cm (24–30 cm), females 26 cm (23–27 m); weight males 637 g (523–789 g), females 460 g (373–565 g). Lighter in KwaZulu-Natal: males 553 g, females 430 g. *G. swalius* has a slightly longer tail than *G. sanguinea*. *See scale drawing on p. 299.*

Habitat   Occurs from arid areas in the west to wet ones in the east, in woodland, scrub, forest fringes and grassland, as long as there is some cover. Not found in true desert, forest, or the high Drakensberg. South of about 30° south and the Orange River it is replaced by the small grey mongoose.

Diet   Mostly insectivorous; also takes reptiles, small rodents and birds, a variety of invertebrates, and fruit. In winter it eats fewer insects and more vertebrates. Will scavenge road kills. Insects occur in 59–73% of stomachs, mammals in 17–25%, lizards in 27%, birds 8%, and fruit 7%.

Life history   Gestation 58–62 days. Litters of one or usually two are born October–March. Killed by raptors.

Behaviour   Active during the day; comes out at night to catch flying termites. Shelters in burrows which it might dig itself, hollow logs, holes in the ground, tunnels in termite nests and similar refuges. Sometimes sunbathes outside its burrow in the morning or late afternoon.

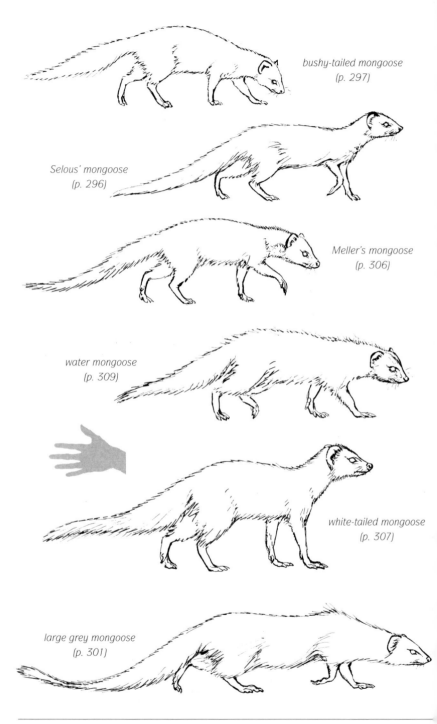

bushy-tailed mongoose
(p. 297)

Selous' mongoose
(p. 296)

Meller's mongoose
(p. 306)

water mongoose
(p. 309)

white-tailed mongoose
(p. 307)

large grey mongoose
(p. 301)

Nearly all foraging is on the ground, but it is an agile climber and readily takes to trees if pursued. Typically moves along roads and pathways, foraging into the margins of the vegetation. If alarmed it dives for cover. As it flees it keeps its tail low (tail lifted in yellow mongoose) and characteristically flicks it upwards as it reaches cover.

Solitary, living in home ranges of 50–100 ha. Scent marks with anal gland secretion, by cheek rubbing, and with urine and faeces which are deposited in middens, or scattered singly along pathways.

Field sign Middens of faeces, up to 3 cm long, 0,5 cm thick, very often containing insect fragments.

SMALL GREY MONGOOSE

S275 ☼

Klein grysmuishond endemic
Galerella pulverulenta

Note The classification and taxonomy of small grey mongooses are not yet entirely clear. On the basis of features that can be used for identification in the field, I have considered the small grey mongoose to be the species that lacks a distinct black tail tip, and slender mongooses to be the three species that have distinct black tail tips.

Description Grizzled dark grey all over. The tail may have an indistinct black tip (white in yellow mongoose, distinct black in slender mongoose). The tip of the nose is dark brown or black (red or light brown in slender mongoose, black in yellow mongoose). The top lip has a groove down the middle (no groove in yellow mongoose). The ears are small and set low on the head. There are five toes on each foot, with short, curved claws (claws long in yellow mongoose); four toes mark in the spoor. In the Free State: total length males 64 cm (54–76 cm); tail 30 cm (20–34 cm); weight males 911 g (680–1 250 g), females 683 g (491–900 g). In the former Cape Province: weight males 825 g (550–1 100 g), females 712 g (520–940 g). *See scale drawing on p. 299.*

Habitat A wide range from fynbos and forest to open Karoo. Not in high forest of Tsitsikamma. Prefers more bushy areas than yellow mongoose.

Diet Mainly insects and small rodents; also takes birds, reptiles, amphibians, an

assortment of invertebrates, and fruit. Will take carrion and garbage. Insects occur in 66% of stomachs, small rodents in 52%, carrion in 14%, birds, reptiles and sun spiders 9% each, and fruit 7%.

Life history Gestation 50 days. Litters of up to three are born August–December. Independent at four months. Potential lifespan eight years. Provides up to 25% of martial eagle (*Polemaetus bellicosus*) prey.

Behaviour Active during the day. Scratches in leaf litter but is not as enthusiastic a digger as slender and yellow mongooses.

Mostly solitary (89% of sightings) or in pairs (10%). Family groups containing more than one adult have been recorded. Lives in overlapping home ranges of 5–68 ha; males probably have larger ranges than females. Faeces are deposited in small middens near dens, or singly along paths.

Field sign Small middens of faeces, up to 6 cm long and 1 cm thick, tapered at one end, usually containing insect fragments and rodent hair and bones.

MELLER'S MONGOOSE

Meller se muishond
Rhynchogale melleri

Description Light brown or greyish brown all over except for the end half of the tail, which is black, brown or white. (Selous' and white-tailed mongooses also have white on the tail but their legs are darker in colour than the body). Five toes on each foot, four marking in the spoor. The upper lip is not grooved down the middle (grooved in

Selous' and white-tailed mongooses). Females have two pairs of mammae on the belly. Total length 83 cm (57–89 cm); tail 36 cm (31–39 cm); weight males 2,3 kg (1,75–2,7 kg), females 2,5 kg (2,4–2,9 kg). *See scale drawing on p. 304.*

Habitat Open woodland and grassland where there are termites.

Diet Almost exclusively termites, which were found in all stomachs and were the sole content in nearly half. Also takes other insects, reptiles and frogs.

Life history Litters of up to four are born in summer.

Behaviour Nocturnal and solitary.

WHITE-TAILED MONGOOSE $S277$ $\mathbb{C}$
Witstertmuishond
Ichneumia albicauda

Description Largest mongoose in the subregion, and has distinctively long legs (large grey mongoose is similar in size but has short legs). Dark grey to black, paler on the underparts. The legs are long and black (black or dark brown in Selous' mongoose). The first fifth of the tail is the same colour as the body, the rest is white and bushy (in Selous' and Meller's mongooses the tail is white only on the tip; black tip in large grey mongoose). The hair along the back and on the rump and tail is long and coarse and can be erected to make the animal look strikingly larger. The upper lip has a groove down the middle (not grooved in Meller's, grooved in Selous'). Five toes on each foot, all with claws; four toes mark in the spoor. Females have three pairs of mammae on the belly. Total length males 1,1 m (0,9–1,5 m), females 1 m

(0,9–1,1 m); tail males 42 cm (35–47 cm), females 44 cm (39–49 cm); weight males 4,5 kg (3,6–5,2 kg), females 4,1 kg (3,2–5,5 kg). *See scale drawing on p. 304.*

Habitat Savanna woodland in the better-watered east and north of the subregion.

Diet Mainly insectivorous; also takes a range of other invertebrates and small vertebrates. Takes carrion freely. Despite its large size, predation on dassies, rabbits and canerats has not been confirmed. In common with other predators it is accused on no evidence of killing lambs. In Zimbabwe insects occur in 86% of stomachs or scats, amphibians in 31%, small rodents in 18%, reptiles in 15%, fruit, earthworms and birds in 6% each. In KwaZulu-Natal insects and plants occur in 26% each, and mammals and amphibians in 11% each.

Life history Litters of up to four are born September–January and are independent at nine months.

Behaviour Strictly nocturnal; shelters during the day in disused springhare and aardvark holes, holes under rocks and fallen trees, and the larger tunnels in termite mounds. Modifies existing holes.

Usually solitary, or mothers with offspring. Food is detected mainly by smell while foraging on a zig-zag path with nose close to the ground. Grubs for insects in leaf litter and dung.

Field sign Disturbed dung pats. Middens near dens.

Conservation Killed by coyote getters set for jackals.

WATER MONGOOSE / MARSH MONGOOSE

Kommetjiegatmuishond
Atilax paludinosus

Description Stocky build for a mongoose. Reddish brown to black, darker on the limbs than on the body. The hair is long and coarse. The tail is long-haired at the base, short-haired at the tip, giving a sharply tapered profile. Each foot has five long, narrow toes, more like fingers, all with heavy claws, and with no webs between (all other mongooses and the spotted-necked otter have webs, Cape clawless otter has no claws or web). Four toes mark in the spoor. The head is large, with a short, broad muzzle. The tip of the nose is pink and black, or black. The top lip is grooved down the middle. Females from KwaZulu-Natal have two pairs of mammae on the belly, those from Zimbabwe have three pairs. Total length males 88 cm (82–97 cm), females 85 cm (79–90 cm); tail 35–36 cm (31–41 cm); weight 3,2 kg (2–5 kg). *See scale drawing on p. 304.*

Habitat Occurs near water, including estuaries and the sea. Occasionally seen away from water, possibly moving from one water body to the next.

Diet Frogs, crabs, mice, insects, fish, bird's eggs. Will take carrion. May raid poultry and domestic waterfowl. Generally, amphibians are found in up to 45% of stomachs or scats, crabs in up to 43%, mice in 14–26%, insects in up to 21%, birds in up to 14% and carrion in up to 14%. In the West Coast NP crab remains are found in 86% of scats, birds in 46%, fish in 25% and mice in 21%.

Life history Gestation 69–80 days. Litters of 2–4 are born August–February. Can

breed twice a year. Weans from 30 to 56 days, solid food is provided by the mother until 11 weeks. Families may stay together for the whole breeding season. Full-grown and sexually mature at 10–11 months. Potential lifespan 17 years.

Behaviour Active early in the morning and in the evening; shelters in nests in dense vegetation. Forages for submerged prey by feeling with its long front toes. Hard-shelled food is cracked open by throwing it to the ground or onto something hard such as a rock. Crabs, snakes and large rodents are bitten and immediately thrown sideways before they can bite back. Crabs are eaten piecemeal, leaving the carapace of large ones (Cape clawless otters eat the whole crab). Rarely swims, but readily paddles in shallow water. Dries itself by grooming with its teeth, leading to the presence of its own hair in scats.

Solitary. Lives in overlapping home ranges of 150–200 ha; males have smaller ranges than females. Faeces are deposited in middens, which may be used by more than one mongoose. Scent marks with anal gland and cheek gland secretions, which are individually identifiable.

Deters attackers by erecting its long hair to make itself look bigger, and giving a series of loud, sharp calls. Under severe stress it can squirt the smelly contents of its anal glands.

Field sign Discarded crab carapaces (Cape clawless otters eat the whole crab). Scats are cylindrical with tapered ends, about 20 mm diameter (Cape clawless otter 22–29 mm, spotted-necked otter 12–18 mm), and contain water mongoose hair. The spoor is variable in the degree to which the toes spread, depending on how soft the ground is.

Conservation Degradation of wetlands destroys water mongoose habitat.

BANDED MONGOOSE S279 ☼

Gebande muishond
Mungos mungo

Description Grizzled grey, in KwaZulu-Natal dark grizzled grey with a wash of reddish brown on the lower back. From just behind the shoulders to the base of the tail a series of narrow darker stripes run across the back (suricate has wider, less clear, bands). Each foot has five toes, all with claws; those on the front feet are long for digging. Four toes on each foot mark in the spoor. The tail is long-haired at the base, tapering to a thin darker tip (suricate has thin tail with dark tip). Females have three pairs of mammae on the belly. Total length 59 cm (54–67 cm); tail 24 cm (19–25 cm); weight 1,3–1,4 kg (1–1,6 kg), females are slightly larger than males. Smaller in Zimbabwe and Botswana: total length 54 cm. *See scale drawing on p. 299.*

Habitat Woodland. At least seasonally independent of water.

Diet Mostly insects, especially beetles and their grubs. Also eats fruit and a variety of invertebrates and small vertebrates; sometimes takes carrion, and in rest camps it searches through garbage for food scraps.

Life history Several females in a pack breed at the same time. Gestation 60 days. Litters of up to eight are born October–January; females can have two litters per year. First eats solid food at 3–4 weeks, accompanies adults at 5 weeks. Full-grown at 13 months; sexually mature at 10 months. All pack members care for young. Killed by large raptors.

Behaviour Active during the day, emerging from its den after sunrise and returning before sunset. Shelters in termite mounds, under fallen trees, etc. Uses springhare and aardvark holes and similar refuges as bolt holes when pursued.

Food is detected mainly by smell and sight, and obtained by digging in soil and litter and rooting in dung. Prey with distasteful secretions, such as toads and millipedes, is rolled and rubbed in the soil to clean it.

Highly social, living in packs of about a dozen, typically up to about 30. The largest pack recorded for the subregion is 75 in Kruger NP. Packs sleep together and forage in loose groups, each mongoose obtaining its own food. Foraging groups keep in contact by a continual high-pitched twitter. The alarm call is a sudden sharp chittering which causes pack members to freeze, stand up and scan the surroundings, and slip quietly away. Sudden alarms send them diving into nearby cover. If there are young in the group the adults bunch around them and the group moves off together. Small predators such as jackals are driven off by group attacks.

Groups live in home ranges which may be territories, as meetings between groups are aggressive. Each home range contains several dens which are used in rotation for

a few days at a time. Scent marks with anal gland secretion and urine. Pack members groom and anal mark each other.

Courtship is lively, with much chasing and rubbing. Male and female anal mark each other; the male's anal glands are enlarged in the breeding season. Females suckle each other's offspring indiscriminately, and until the young are five weeks old babysitters, usually adult males, stay at the den while the rest of the pack forages. Adults catch prey and give it to juveniles.

Field sign Scratched-over dung. Droppings are up to 5 cm long, 1–1,5 cm thick, tapered at the end, nearly always containing insect fragments, in middens near dens.

DWARF MONGOOSE
Dwergmuishond
Helogale parvula

S280

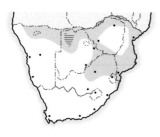

F   H   cm

Description Smallest of the mongooses and the smallest African carnivore. Very dark brown to black all over, with white or grey grizzling visible only at close quarters. Five toes on each foot, all with claws; four toes mark in the spoor. Females have two pairs of mammae on the belly. Total length 38 cm (34–41 cm); tail 16,5 cm (15–19 cm); weight 267 g (213–341 g). *See scale drawing on p. 299.*

Habitat Savanna woodland. Requires termite mounds or rock crevices for den sites. Independent of water.

Diet Mainly insects, also other invertebrates up to the size of large scorpions, reptiles, and occasionally mice and small birds.

Life history Only the dominant pair breeds successfully. If a subordinate female gives birth the dominant female kills the babies. Gestation 40 days. Litters of 2–5 are born at the start of the rainy season, and are mobile enough to follow the group at 4 weeks. Weaned at 6–7 weeks; competent foragers at four months. Lifespan 18 years. They are preyed on mostly by large grey mongooses; also taken by

raptors, especially small ones such as pale chanting goshawks (*Melierax canorus*), snakes, marabou storks (*Leptoptilos crumeniferus*), slender mongooses, black-backed jackals, and monitor lizards (*Varanus* sp.). Predation falls most heavily on mongooses less than four months old.

Behaviour   Studied in detail only in East Africa. Strictly diurnal, sleeping in secure refuges (usually the ventilation shafts of large termite mounds, which are warm as well as safe). Forages in a group, but each individual catches its own food. Prey is killed by a bite to the head. Adults do not share food with each other; babysitters give food to juveniles.

Highly social; living in groups of up to 32 (average 12). Groups are a breeding pair with successive litters of their offspring, and an occasional immigrant. The breeding pair are socially dominant, and retain their status for life. If the female dies a replacement from the subordinate adults is decided by a grooming contest. For a subordinate male to replace a lost dominant male he has to establish close social ties with the dominant female. Older animals dominate younger ones, except that juveniles have priority of access to food. Within each age group females dominate males. Foraging routes and sleeping sites are determined by the dominant female. Subordinate males attempting to mate are attacked by the dominant male. Young subordinate females' hormone levels are depressed by their low social status. Prospective immigrants to a group spend over a month following it around.

Groups defend territories of up to 1 km², foraging through the area on an 18–26 day cycle and moving to a new refuge every day. Territories are passed down through the generations of the group. Anal gland and cheek gland secretions are used to mark upright objects near termite mounds used as overnight refuges. Anal gland marks have a lifetime of 20–25 days. Marking is especially heavy after border disputes with neighbours. Fights between groups are led by the dominant male, followed by the juveniles, then the rest of the group, with the dominant female bringing up the rear. Fights rarely lead to serious injury, and are hardly ever fatal.

Until babies are 3–4 weeks old, babysitters remain at the den for half-day spells to guard them. Young are carried to new dens by their babysitters. From four weeks youngsters accompany the foraging adults. Each has a caretaker who catches food for it: the dominant male and subordinate adult females are usually the caretakers. Attempts to catch their own prey begin at six weeks; at four months they are skilled enough to forage independently.

Sick and injured adults are cared for by huddling, grooming and feeding until they recover or die.

While foraging they are very vulnerable to predators. Sentinels perch on vantage points and keep a look-out while the rest of the group forages. Subordinate males do nearly all the sentinel duty, spending up to 30% of their potential foraging time on watch, and are more likely to fall prey to raptors. They usually watch away from the group to detect predators stalking from behind, giving a continual all-clear call, and alarm calls when a predator is detected. Alarm calls signal type of predator (ground or bird), distance and degree of danger, and height of predatory birds, and cause different responses in the foragers, from bunching and looking around in mild alarms for ground predators, to scattering into cover for serious danger from raptors. Juveniles learn their sentinel duties from their older brothers. Groups with less than five adults are not viable because they have gaps in their sentinel schedules and lose all their offspring to predators.

Gives a continual nasal 'peep' call while foraging to keep the group together and maintain contact with the sentinels. A high pitched 'tsiii' is a signal that another group, or a snake, has been spotted. Perched raptors are screeched at from hiding. Predators on the ground are mobbed and attacked. Attacks are led by adult subordinates, followed by juveniles, then subadults, with the dominant male in the rear and joining in only occasionally. The dominant female only joins in if the group has three or fewer members. Attacks are usually successful in driving the predator away, and sometimes successful in making a predator that has already caught a mongoose release it again.

Field sign Middens near dens; droppings are up to 3 cm long, less than 1 cm thick, always containing insect fragments.

PRIMATES

BUSHBABIES

Three species in the subregion. The classification of the Lorisidae is changing as biologists begin to unravel the calls that the animals themselves use to signal and recognise which species they belong to.

THICK-TAILED BUSHBABY (LARGE-EARED GREATER GALAGO)

| S114 | C

Bosnagaap
Otolemur crassicaudatus

Description Uniform silver grey to dark brown, darker around the eyes but without any distinct markings on the face. The head is small and rounded, with a longer, broader muzzle than in the lesser bushbabies. Enormous, forward-facing eyes and huge, rounded ears. The eyes shine very brightly when caught with a light. The tail is longer than the head and body, and fluffy throughout its length, sometimes with a dark tip. The limbs are long; each foot has five toes, with nails instead of claws except on the second toes of the hind feet, which have long, curved grooming claws. Distinctly larger than either species of lesser bushbaby; head and body length 31 cm (25,5–40 cm); tail 41 cm (30–55 cm); weight 1,13 kg (0,567–1,81 kg). Males are slightly bigger than females. *See scale drawing on p. 318.*

Habitat Forest, thickets and savanna woodland.

Diet Fruit and acacia gum. Insects and occasional small vertebrates are eaten in some areas but not in others. Gum is especially important in winter. May lick moisture from leaves.

Life history Mating in June–July. Gestation 135 days. Litters of 1–3, usually (80% of litters) twins, are born in August–September in eastern Zimbabwe, and in

November in South Africa. Sex ratio at birth 1,3–1,7 males to 1 female. Newborn young are furred and their eyes are open; they can crawl within 30 minutes. They stay in the nest for three weeks and are then carried around by their mother when she forages, either in her mouth or on her back. Weaning begins at 3 weeks and is complete at 10 weeks. Genets probably kill juveniles, but not adults.

Behaviour Nocturnal and arboreal. An agile climber, and can leap 2 m horizontally and 5 m downwards. It does not land on its hind feet when leaping. On the ground, walks on all fours and only rarely hops on the hind feet; may move as much as 100 m on the ground and forage there for up to 15 minutes at a time. Shelters during the day in nests of fresh leaves in the densest foliage. Lives in communities of several adults of both sexes, and their young. Females sleep with one or more generations of their offspring, and sometimes with an adult male. Males avoid one another.

Individuals have fixed overlapping home ranges marked with chest gland secretions, lip and chin gland secretions, ano-genital secretions, and urine which is dribbled onto the feet and then transferred to branches as the bushbaby climbs, giving a firmer grip at the same time. Forages singly or in small groups; mothers forage with their young up to an age of 10 months. Groups are attracted to rich food sources such as trees of ripe fruit.

Gives a wide range of calls; the advertisement call is a sequence of 3–17 loud, drawn-out cries repeated at regular intervals, the last call fading away. Sequences usually last more than four seconds. They sound uncannily like crying human babies, hence the common name. Also makes a rasping sound by scraping a rough pad on the feet along branches.

Conservation Suffers from habitat destruction. CITES Appendix II.

LESSER BUSHBABY
(LESSER GALAGO) (MOHOL GALAGO)
Nagapie
Galago moholi

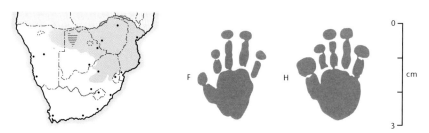

Description Light grey, or light grey washed with buff or brown, tinged yellow on the upper limbs and the underparts. The head is broad and rounded, with a short muzzle. There are dark markings between and around the eyes, and a small white stripe on the nose (Grant's lesser bushbaby has a large white stripe). The eyes are very large, and shine very brightly when caught with a light. The ears are large, rounded and very mobile. The limbs are long; there are five toes on each foot, with nails rather than claws, except for the second toes of the hind feet which carry a long, curved grooming claw. The tail is long, and bushy towards the tip. Females have one pair of nipples on the chest and one pair on the belly. Total length 37 cm; head and body 15 cm (9–20,5 cm); tail 23 cm (11–28 cm); weight 158 g (95–244 g). In South Africa males are heavier than females. *See scale drawing on p. 318.*

Habitat Woodland, savanna, riverine bush and forest fringes with acacia trees as a source of gum.

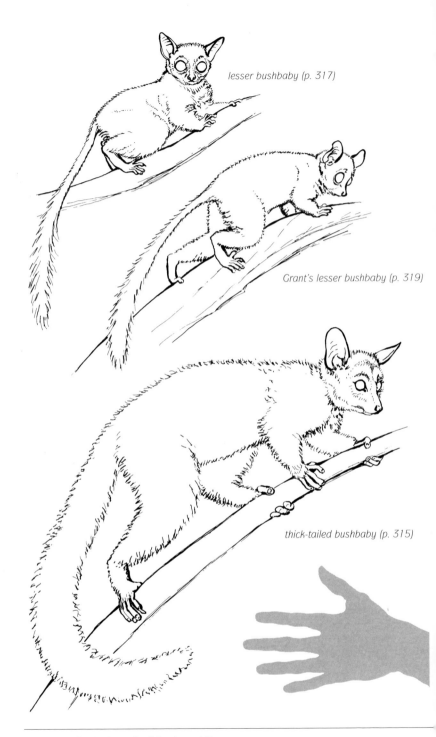

lesser bushbaby (p. 317)

Grant's lesser bushbaby (p. 319)

thick-tailed bushbaby (p. 315)

Diet Invertebrates and acacia gum. Gum is especially important in winter when insects are scarce. Lesser bushbabies are not known to eat fruit or vertebrates in the wild.

Life history Gestation 125 days. One or usually (80% of litters) two young are born in summer. May have two litters per year, one in October–November and one in January–February. Weaned at six weeks, independent at two months. Taken by genets, snakes, large owls, diurnal raptors and ground carnivores.

Behaviour Nocturnal and arboreal. An exceptionally agile climber and leaper; can jump 2,22 m upwards, and 5 m between thorn-covered branches. Usually lands on its hind feet. On the ground it takes long hops on its hind legs. During the day it shelters in tree holes, platform nests built in thick foliage, or occasionally in empty birds' nests.

Lives in communities with male ranges overlapping the territories of several females with their young. Territories are scent marked with chest gland secretion and urine, which is dribbled onto the feet and then deposited as the bushbaby climbs around. Males and females usually sleep separately. Young males disperse to other communities, females typically stay in their groups.

Females carry their young with them when foraging, and park them on a nearby twig. Insect prey is located by sight and sound and captured with the hands.

Gives a wide range of calls; grunts, clicks, cackles and moans and a series of high-pitched *tchak-tchaks* which rise to a noisy chattering when highly alarmed. The advertisement call is a long series of barks, lasting up to an hour. Predators are mobbed with series of alarm calls.

Conservation Not threatened. CITES Appendix II.

GRANT'S LESSER BUSHBABY

S116 ⟨

Grant se nagapie
Galagoides granti

Confirmed
Unconfirmed

Description Cinnamon-brown (distinctly browner than lesser bushbaby) with bright yellow underparts. The head is rounded, but more pointed than in the lesser bushbaby; the muzzle is long, pointed and concave on top. The eyes and ears are large, there are dark rings around the eyes, and a large white stripe on the nose (the lesser bushbaby has a small white stripe). The limbs are long; there are five toes on each foot, with nails rather than claws, except for the second toes of the hind feet which carry a long, curved grooming claw. The tail is long and moderately bushy (more bushy than lesser bushbaby) and has a dark tip of variable size (no dark tip in lesser bushbaby). Head and body length 15 cm (12–19 cm); tail 22 cm (17–27 cm); weight 145 g (104–203 g). Males are heavier than females. *See scale drawing on p. 318.*

Habitat Coastal and evergreen forests.

Diet Fruit, insects, gum and small vertebrates. Eats more insects than the lesser bushbaby.

Life history Gestation 120 days. One, rarely two, babies in a litter. Taken by genets, snakes, large owls, diurnal raptors and ground carnivores.

Behaviour Nocturnal and arboreal. Runs and climbs on all four limbs; when it jumps it lands on all fours, or on its forefeet (lesser bushbaby lands on the hind feet). Communities of up to six share territories and sleep together. The advertisement call is a sequence of up to 18 double or triple calls lasting 3–6 seconds, reaching a crescendo over the first few calls and frequently trailing into a series of deeper, rapid staccato notes. Also loud, drawn-out screeches, often preceded by an explosive buzz.

Conservation Locally abundant but may suffer loss of habitat when forests are cleared. CITES Appendix II.

MONKEYS AND BABOONS

In contrast to the wide diversity of species further north in Africa, there are only three species in the subregion.

CHACMA BABOON

S117 ☼

Kaapse bobbejaan / bobbejaan
Papio cynocephalus ursinus

The baboons in southern Africa are one of several subspecies of *Papio cynocephalus,* a species which is widespread in southern and eastern Africa.

Description Colour varies from brownish grey to dark brown or nearly black, usually grey-brown. Adult males have a dark mane on the neck and shoulders. The hair is long and coarse. The backs of the hands and feet are dark brown or black. Babies have black hair and pink skin. The ears have pointed tips, and the muzzle is long and broad. The limbs are long, the arms longer than the legs; the fingers and toes are long and dextrous. The first third of the tail is held stiffly upwards, with the end two thirds hanging down. There are callosities of thickened skin on the rump. Females have a pair of mammae on the chest. Total length males 1,3–1,8 m, females 1,1–1,15 m; tail males 60–84 cm, females 55–61 cm; weight males 27–43 kg, females 14–17 kg. *See scale drawing on p. 326.*

If the penis and scrotum are not visible males can be distinguished from females by their larger size, longer muzzles, larger canine teeth, and callosities which meet in the middle below the anus instead of being widely separated as in females.

Habitat As long as food, water and suitable sleeping places are available, baboons can live almost anywhere.

Diet Omnivorous; their staple food is grass, corms, bulbs, fruit and other vegetation, but they also eat invertebrates, including shellfish, eggs, small vertebrates, fish, birds, and mammals. A troop in the Namib survived for up to 11 days without water by eating succulent vegetation and fruit.

Life history Females have reproductive cycles of 29–42 days, average 36 days. When a female is sexually receptive the sexual skin on her rump swells and turns bright pink. Maximum swelling is reached 5–6 days before she ovulates, and males compete for access to females in this condition because matings then have a higher chance of leading to conception. The most dominant male has privileged access. Gestation six months. Single young, rarely twins, are born at any time of the year. Weaned at 6–8 months. Females reach sexual maturity at 6–7 years, and give birth every 2 years, increasing to 4 years in poor habitats such as the Drakensberg. Lifespan 20–30 years. Due to their inaccessible roosts, sentinels and guards, baboons suffer only occasional losses to large carnivores; leopards are the most likely predator.

Behaviour Active during the day, sleeping at night in large trees or on cliff ledges. Baboons are intensely social, living in female-bonded troops of between 4 and about 100 individuals with an average troop size of about 40. Troops are smaller in poorer habitats, e.g. the Drakensberg, and larger in richer areas like the Okavango. There is usually more than one male in a troop.

Troops have home ranges, but are not territorial and tend to avoid other troops. If troops do meet, the males herd their females away, often biting, striking and dragging those who stray. This teaches the females to avoid other troops, and they move away when they sight one.

Females stay in the troop that they were born in; males emigrate and may move from troop to troop. There are separate dominance hierarchies among the males and females; males outrank females. Daughters inherit their mother's rank. Male domi-

nance depends on physical condition, and high rank is held for only 6–12 months, depending on sex ratios in the population. Females can rise in rank by forming alliances with close female relatives, or with male 'friends'.

Young babies ride under their mother's belly; as they grow they change to riding sideways on her back, and then astride, using her tail as a backrest. Males are protective towards infants that are probably their offspring, and act as babysitters while the mother forages, probably to protect the youngsters from infanticide by immigrant males.

Although disputes are accompanied by loud screams and squeals, baboons are usually quiet, and social vocalisations are mainly soft grunts. The very loud, two-syllable 'wa-hoo' bark is an alarm call and threat to other troops, and is given mainly by adult males.

Field sign Droppings are irregular and roughly rounded; they are often deposited on top of rocks and when fresh have a strong, distinctive odour. Stones and rocks turned over in search of food.

Conservation CITES Appendix II.

VERVET MONKEY S119 ☼

Blouaap

Cercopithecus aethiops

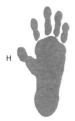

Description Lightly built, with long arms and legs. The body is pale grizzled grey (much lighter than samango monkey), tinged yellow down the middle of the back in monkeys from northern Namibia, tinged reddish in those from the northeast of the subregion. The underparts and inner sides of the limbs are white, the hair around the anus and base of the tail is reddish brown. The face is black, outlined by a white band across the forehead and down the cheeks. Long canine teeth, especially in adult males, up to 3,2 cm above the gum. Adult males have a bright blue scrotum and a scarlet penis. Babies are dark with pink faces. Females have one pair of mammae on the chest. Total length males 1–1,3 m, females 1–1,1 m; tail 50–65 cm; weight males 5,5 kg (3,8–8 kg), females 4,1 kg (3,4–5,2 kg). *See scale drawing on p. 326.*

Habitat Occurs in a wide variety of woodland and tree savanna, including exotic

wattles and city suburbs. Dependent on water.

Diet Mainly a wide range of vegetable foods but also some insects, birds' eggs and small vertebrates. Can be a serious pest in fruit orchards, crops and gardens.

Life history Females do not give visible indications of when they are sexually receptive; males may recognise their readiness to mate by their behaviour and odour. Gestation 210 days. Single young, rarely twins, are born mostly in September–December. Wean at four months. Killed by crowned and martial eagles, leopards and pythons.

Behaviour Active during the day, sleeping at night in trees or on cliffs. Highly social, living in female-bonded troops including more than one male, typically with 20–30 members, but larger or smaller depending on circumstances. Females stay in the troop that they were born in; males emigrate at puberty and move from troop to troop, spending about three years in each. Males and females have separate dominance hierarchies. Only high-ranking males have access to receptive females. A female's rank depends on alliances with her female relatives. Social bonds are cemented by allogrooming. Troops have territories with well-defined boundaries.

Vervets have a wide range of calls, including three distinct warning calls for terrestrial predators, snakes and predatory birds. Adult males give a loud 'nkau' bark, which gives vervets their Zulu name.

Field sign Droppings are roughly rounded and lumpy, usually containing fragments of vegetable foods. Discarded fragments of food and inedible pods, rinds, etc.

Conservation Vervet monkeys are adaptable and resilient and can be serious pests. The species is in no danger. CITES Appendix II.

SAMANGO MONKEY

S120 R ☀

Samango-aap
Cercopithecus mitis

Description Slightly larger and stockier in build than a vervet monkey, and much darker in colour. The shoulders, limbs and tail are black or charcoal grey; the back from the shoulders to the base of the tail is suffused with reddish brown, the reddish

colour intensifying towards the base of the tail. The throat is white, the underparts and inner sides of the limbs off-white or buffy, the face dark brown. Newborns are dark grey or nearly black. Females have one pair of mammae on the chest. Total length males 1,4 m, females 1,1 m; tail 50–70 cm; weight males 9,3 kg (8,2–11 kg), females 4,9 kg (4,5–7 kg). *See scale drawing on p. 326.*

Habitat Confined to forest, including plantations.

Diet Fruit (50–90%), flowers (13%), leaves (26%) and insects (6%), especially caterpillars. Samangos sometimes strip bark, and are considered to be a pest in pine plantations.

Life history Single young, rarely twins, are born in September–April. Weaning age unknown; independent at two months.

Behaviour Active during the day, sleeping in tall trees. Highly social; lives in troops with up to about 35 (usually 13–21) members. Smaller troops include a single adult male and 6–8 adult females and their young; larger troops include 3 or more mature males. Troops have exclusive home ranges of up to 18 ha. Males which are not attached to a troop live singly or in small bachelor groups. Unattached males take over female groups by defeating the resident male. In dense populations 'gangs' of males may move into a group, mate and leave again.

A loud, repeated 'nyah' is an alarm call given only by adult males. Adult males also give a loud booming call during encounters between troops. Females and infants squeal, chatter and scream when threatened. Adult males act as guards and sentinels for their troops.

Field sign Fruit, pips, peels, etc. dropped from trees.

Conservation The samango monkey's dependence on forest makes it susceptible to habitat destruction. Red Data Book: Rare. CITES Appendix II.

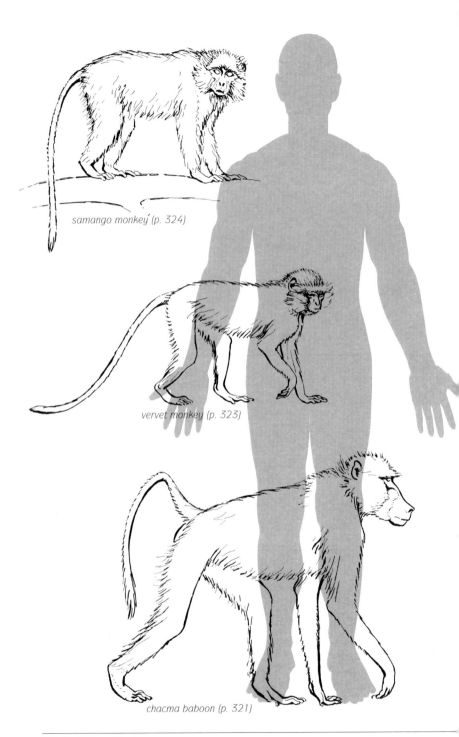

samango monkey (p. 324)

vervet monkey (p. 323)

chacma baboon (p. 321)

TUBILIDENTATA

Only one species in the world.

AARDVARK (ANTBEAR)

`S288` `V` `(`

Aardvark
Orycteropus afer

Description Unique and unmistakable. Covered by a sparse coat of coarse, white or buffy hair with the pinkish or yellowish-grey skin showing through. Looks pale pink by spotlight. Females have a lighter coloured head, and the end of the tail is white. The snout is long and like a pig's, with slit-shaped nostrils that can be closed while digging. The ears are long with pointed tips. The hindquarters are much heavier than the forequarters, and the back slopes upwards to the rump. The tail is long and thick, especially at the base. The legs are sturdy and exceptionally strong. There are four toes on the front feet with long claws that are concave underneath and have sharp edges, and five toes on the hind feet with shorter, more curved claws. The only teeth are a row of cylindrical molars and premolars. Females have one pair of mammae on the belly and one pair between the hind legs. Total length 1,6 m (1,4–1,75 m); tail 54 cm (44–63 cm); shoulder height 60–65 cm; weight 53 kg (40–65 kg, exceptionally 100 kg). *See scale drawing on p. 329.*

Habitat Widely distributed from the arid west to the wetter east. The main habitat requirement is a supply of ants and termites for food.

Diet Ants (70%), termites (30%) and occasionally other insects. More ants are eaten in the winter, more termites in summer. Also eats the underground fruit of aardvark pumpkins (*Cucumis humifructus*). Pips pass through the digestive system intact and germinate in aardvark droppings. Other items recorded are fungi and fat mice; the mice might have been taken from their refuge in a termite mound.

Life history Gestation seven months. Single (occasionally two) young are born in

May–August. Babies accompany the mother as early as two weeks old. First eats solid food at 14 weeks, weaned at 16 weeks, and starts digging for its own food at 6 months. Full-grown at 12 months, sexually mature at 2 years. Potential lifespan 24 years. A minor item in the diets of large carnivores. Pythons take young. The meat is tasty and very popular for human food. Also used for traditional charms and medicines.

Behaviour Nocturnal. Two sorts of burrows are dug for shelter. Tunnels penetrating a few metres into the soil with one or a few entrances are used for a few days at a time and possibly returned to later. Very large tunnel systems with several entrances and extending 6 m down into the soil are used regularly, and are where females give birth. A metre of tunnel can be dug in 5 minutes. Once inside, the aardvark blocks it up with soil. Aardvark holes provide shelter for at least 17 mammal species.

Solitary except for mating pairs and mothers with young. Home range size probably depends on food availability. Marks with anal gland secretion and buries its faeces, but how this relates to home range use is unknown.

Covers up to 15 km (possibly as much as 30 km) in a night's foraging. Underground ant and termite nests are detected by smell and scraped open with the front claws, typically to a depth of 20–40 cm. The long, sticky tongue, which can be protruded 25–30 cm, is inserted into the tunnels of the nest and withdrawn with the insects sticking to it. Termite nests on the surface are torn open, and the hole may be big enough for the aardvark to disappear into. In some areas, but not necessarily all, termite mounds are opened on the west side, where termites congregate as the setting sun warms that side of the nest. An aardvark's sense of hearing is acute, and probably serves mainly to detect predators. Its eyesight is poor.

Field sign Droppings are oval, 4 cm long, and consist mainly of sand, buried in a scrape about 10 cm deep. Large tunnels, 40–50 cm diameter. Occupied holes have swarms of small flies near the entrance. Shallow scrapes and diggings into underground ant and termite nests. Large holes in termite mounds.

Conservation Aardvarks are not common anywhere, and so are susceptible to local extinctions. If anything they do good by eating termites, but they are unpopular on farms because their tunnels undermine roads and dams, and are a danger to farm machinery. Red Data Book: Vulnerable. CITES Appendix II.

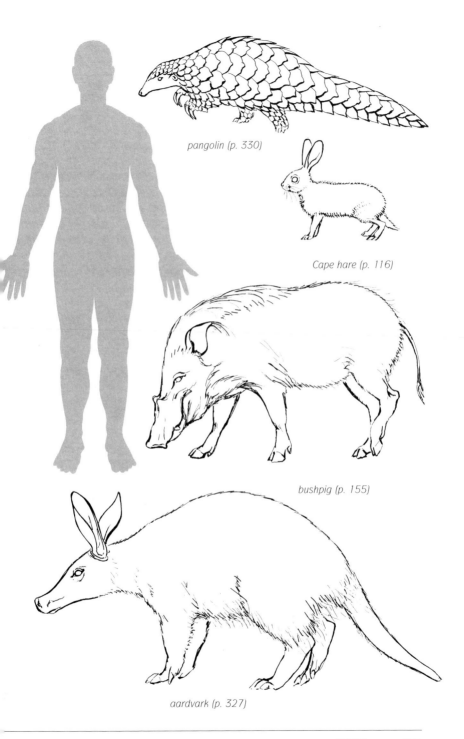

pangolin (p. 330)

Cape hare (p. 116)

bushpig (p. 155)

aardvark (p. 327)

ORDER

PHOLIDOTA

PANGOLINS

FAMILY MANIDAE

Distinguished from other mammals by their covering of overlapping horny plates.
One species in southern Africa.

PANGOLIN
letermagô
Manis temminckii

S310 | V | (

F

H

0
cm
5

Description Unmistakable. The upper surface of the neck, body and tail and the sides of the legs are covered by triangular, overlapping horny plates made of fused hair. The eyes are small and the ears are just slits in the side of the head. The legs are short and heavily built; the forefeet have a nail on the first toe, curved claws up to 5 cm long on the second, third and fourth toes, and a short claw on the fifth. All five toes of each hind foot have a small nail-like claw. The tail is long and heavy. A well-developed anal gland produces a stinking secretion. Females have one pair of mammae on the chest. Total length males 81 cm (93–129 cm), females 77–104 cm; the tail is slightly less than half the total length; weight males 10,7–15,9 kg, females 4,6–10,1 kg. *See scale drawing on p. 329.*

Habitat Occurs in a wide range of habitats except swamp, forest, open grassland and desert.

Diet Mainly ants, also some termites.

Life history Gestation 139 days. Single young are born in June–July. First takes solid food at 4 weeks.

Behaviour Solitary and mainly nocturnal, with occasional daytime activity. Hides during the day in aardvark or springhare burrows, holes, or piles of vegetation. Walks on its hind legs; the front feet rarely touch the ground. It locates ants' nests by smell,

---

scratches them open with its claws and licks up the ants with its long (25–40 cm), sticky tongue. Pangolins have no teeth; they grind their food in a muscular gizzard.

When threatened a pangolin rolls up with its head protected by its tail. Its scales have sharp edges which can inflict severe cuts as the pangolin slides its tail sideways across its body. Young ride crossways at the base of their mother's tail; when they are older they ride lengthways on her back. If threatened the mother rolls up around her offspring, enclosing its head and most of its body.

The long thick tail gets in the way of mating in the usual mammal position and a male pangolin mounts from the side with his tail wrapped round the female's.

Field sign Opened ants' nests.

Conservation Although they are widespread, pangolins are uncommon. They are exceptionally sensitive to insecticides. Their habit of rolling up when threatened leads to their getting tangled in, and killed by, electrified game fences. Pangolin scales are sought after for traditional medicine, and poaching is a major cause of death. Red Data Book: Vulnerable, CITES: Appendix II.

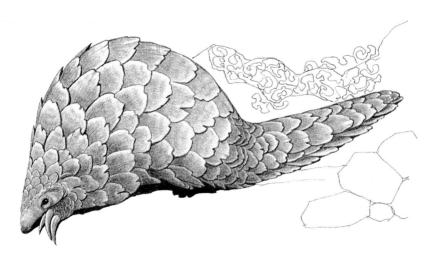

PINNIPEDIA

S E A L S

FAMILY OTARIIDAE

FUR SEALS

Only one species, the Cape fur seal, breeds in southern Africa. Other fur seal species and elephant seals (*Mirounga leonina*, family PHOCIDAE), S284, occasionally turn up as vagrants from the sub-Antarctic.

CAPE FUR SEAL
Kaapse pelsrob
Arctocephalus pusillus

S281

Description Dark to light brown, looks black when wet, slightly darker on the back than on the underside (front of the chest is light yellow to orange in vagrant sub-Antarctic fur seals, *Arctocephalus tropicalis*; neck and chest silvery grey in vagrant Antarctic fur seals, *A. gazella*). Small pups are black. The whiskers are very long, thick and stiff. Total length males up to 2,1 m, females up to 1,6 m; weight males up to 190 kg, females up to 75 kg. *See scale drawing on p. 337.*

Habitat Occurs in coastal waters up to 160 km from the coast from southern Angola to Algoa Bay. Hauls out onto land at 26 breeding colonies, of which 6 are on the mainland, the rest on islands and rocks, and at 8 non-breeding colonies. Colonies contain a few dozen to several thousand seals.

Diet Mostly small, schooling fish; also some squid, octopuses, crayfish and other crustaceans. Individual seals cause serious problems for commercial fishermen by tearing nets and stealing fish from lines.

Life history Gestation one year. Single pups at a birth, 90% in late November–December. Birth weight 5–7 kg. Females mate five days after giving birth. Pups first take solid food at 3–4 months, wean at up to 12 months. Lifespan: 6% live to 20 years, 1% to 30 years. Seals are an important prey item for great white sharks (*Carcharodon carcharias*); brown hyaenas and black-backed jackals kill pups at west coast mainland colonies.

Behaviour Dives down to 200 m, and can stay underwater for 6–7 minutes. On land the eyes run continually because there are no ducts to drain tears into the nose.

Breeding bulls haul out onto land at breeding colonies in late October, establish small territories by fierce fighting, and defend them for six weeks, living off their blubber. The largest bulls get the best territories, closest to the water. Females haul out in November and bulls herd them into their territories. After giving birth and mating again, the females are allowed to leave the territories.

A female alternates trips to sea to feed with visits to the colony to suckle her pup. When she returns she bellows to call her pup, which responds by bleating. The two recognise each other's voices, and confirm identity by sniffing. Females suckle only their own pups.

Pups start swimming at 5–6 months, and start moving offshore and feeding seriously at 7 months.

ORDER
CETACEA
WHALES AND DOLPHINS

Whales and dolphins are the most structurally specialised of mammals. They have no hind limbs, and their front limbs are modified into flippers. A pair of horizontal flukes at the end of the tail provide propulsion. The head and body form a single stream-lined unit with no visible neck. They have almost no hair, at most a few bristles on the chin and snout. Like all mammals they breathe air, and the females feed their young with milk. The nostrils open as a blowhole on top of the head, and exhaled breath forms a 'blow' whose shape can help to identify species. Dolphin groups hunt cooperatively by herding fish shoals against the water surface. When swimming fast near the surface they jump clear of the water in shallow arcs to save energy; this behaviour is known as porpoising. They communicate, navigate and detect prey by echolocation with a variety of clicks, pops, whistles and squeaks, which can some-times be heard above the surface.

In South African waters it is against the law to approach within 300 m of whales and dolphins in boats or aircraft without a permit.

COMMON DOLPHIN
S224

Gewone dolfyn
Delphinus delphis

Description Black or dark grey on the back, yellow-brown on the front half of the flanks, dark grey on the back half of the flanks, white on the belly. There is a narrow black stripe running low on each flank from below the eye. The flippers and flukes are dark grey. The dorsal fin is broad and slightly hooked. Length up to 2,5 m; weight up to 75 kg, some males larger.

Habitat One form occurs inshore around the coast from Lamberts Bay in the west to Algoa Bay in the east and follows the sardine run into southern KwaZulu-Natal waters in winter. A second form is found offshore.

Diet Squid and fish, especially pelagic schooling fish such as pilchards (*Sardinops sagax*) and anchovies (*Engraulis japonicus*).

Life history Gestation 10–11 months. Length of calves at birth 70–85 cm; weaned at 14–19 months. Interval between births 1,3–2,6 years.

Behaviour Forms schools of between 50 and several thousand. Often seen travelling rapidly in tight schools, and often rides the bow waves of boats or ships.
Conservation The status of the southern African population is uncertain. They are caught in shark nets. CITES Appendix II.

HUMPBACK DOLPHIN

S228

Boggelrugdolfyn
Sousa plumbea

Description Grey on the back, slightly lighter on the belly. Stockily built, with a long rostrum ('beak'). There is a distinct hump on the back, with the small, broad, slightly hooked dorsal fin growing out of the middle of it. Length up to 2,8 m; weight up to 280 kg.

Habitat Inshore water less than 50 m deep along the Indian Ocean coast as far west as Gansbaai.

Diet Mainly fish; two thirds of the diet is coastal or estuarine species, one third reef species.

Life history Little known; calving appears to be in summer.

Behaviour Characteristically when surfacing the rostrum breaks the surface of the water before the body arches or pitches and submerges again. May associate with bottlenose dolphins.

Conservation CITES Appendix I.

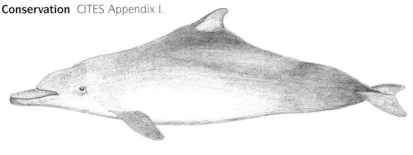

BOTTLENOSE DOLPHIN
Stompneusdolfyn
Tursiops truncatus

Tursiops truncatus now includes both the Atlantic bottlenosed dolphin, S229, and the Indian Ocean bottlenosed dolphin (formerly *Tursiops aduncus*), S230.

Description The body is robust and stocky, dark on the back, becoming lighter down the flanks towards the belly. The dorsal fin is broad and slightly hooked. There are two size forms: *Tursiops truncatus truncatus*, total length up to 4 m; weight up to 430 kg; and *T. t. aduncus*, total length up to 2,5 m; weight 115–220 kg.

Habitat *T. t. aduncus* occurs in inshore waters as far west as False Bay; *T. t. truncatus* is found offshore from the east and west coasts, and close inshore off the Namibian coast from Walvis Bay northwards.

Diet Fish and squid.

Life history Gestation one year. Calves are 0,9–1,3 m long at birth; weaned at up to 18 months. Interval between births 2–3 years. Sexually mature at 5–12 years, at a length of 2,2–2,6 m. Approximately 10% of bottlenose dolphins caught in shark nets have scars from shark attacks.

Behaviour Forms schools of up to 50 in inshore waters; up to several hundred offshore. Most performing dolphins are bottlenose dolphins.

Conservation Status uncertain. CITES Appendix II.

HEAVISIDE'S DOLPHIN

Heaviside se dolfyn

Cephalorynchus heavisidii

Description Black down the middle of the head and back from the blowhole to the dorsal fin, spreading down onto the flanks about half way along the body. Grey on the sides of the head and chest and the lower flanks to about two thirds of the way back along the body. White on the underside of the chest between the flippers, in a stripe along the midline back to the genitals, and in a stripe running obliquely upwards on the rear of each flank. There is a dark patch around each eye. The head is blunt, with no definite rostrum ('beak'). The dorsal fin is a broad triangle (sickle-shaped in most other dolphins). Total length up to 1,7 m, weight 70 kg. *See scale drawing on p. 337.*

Habitat In water less than 200 m deep off the west coast between Cape Point and northern Namibia (17° S).

Diet Mainly fish and squid.

Life history Gestation unknown. Limited data suggest that calves are born in summer. Large sharks are potential predators.

Behaviour Forms groups of less than 10 with home ranges of 55 km². Often approaches boats.

Conservation Status uncertain. They are accidentally caught in fishing nets. CITES Appendix II.

SOUTHERN RIGHT WHALE

Suidelike noordkaper
Eubalaena australis

Description Huge. Black all over (humpback whale has white underside) except for some white patches on the belly and occasionally on the back. There are pale, roughened areas on the head called callosities, where whale lice attach to patches of thickened skin. Individuals can be recognised by their unique pattern of callosities. There is no dorsal fin (small fin in humpback whale). The flippers are short (long in humpback whale) and blunt at the ends. The blow has a V shape. The mouth is huge and contains plates of baleen through which the food is filtered. The eyes are tiny in relation to the rest of the body, and set only about a quarter of the way up the side of the head. Total length 12,5–15,5 m; flukes 5 m wide; weight 30–60 tons.

Habitat Most likely to be seen between June and October in the inshore waters of the southern Cape from Lamberts Bay to Algoa Bay, which offer some of the best shore-based whale watching in the world. Migrates to 50° S in the southern oceans in summer and autumn.

Diet Planktonic copepods (tiny crustaceans). While on the breeding grounds it feeds little or not at all, and lives off blubber accumulated while feeding in the southern oceans.

Life history Mating peaks in July–August. Gestation just over a year. Single calves are born in July–October, with a peak in August, in inshore waters of the southern Cape. Calves average 6,1 m long. Weaning age unknown; calves are still suckling when the southward migration begins in November. Average 3 years between births; cows first calve at 10 years, exceptionally at 6 years.

Behaviour Arrives off the southern Cape coast in July and leaves in November,

migrating to 40–45° S by January and to 50° S by March.

Splashes with its flippers, and smashes its tail flukes down on the surface, possibly to signal to other whales. Breaches by rearing above the surface and falling back. Bellows given while at the surface can be heard from hundreds of metres away.

Groups of 7–8 males compete for matings with each female, and she will mate with more than one of them. The male producing the most sperm has the best chance of fathering a calf, so males have 500 kg testes, the largest of any animal.

Conservation By 1935, southern right whales had been exploited almost to extinction. International protection was granted in 1935, but not enacted in South Africa until 1940. Since then the population has begun to recover: the South African stock is now 1 500–2 000 individuals of which 460 are known adult females. Numbers are growing at 7% per year. CITES Appendix I.

HUMPBACK WHALE

Boggelwalvis

Megaptera novaeangliae

Description Black on top, white underneath (white on southern right whale in patches only). The small dorsal fin is set far back (no dorsal fin in southern right whale). The flippers are long, one third of body length (short in southern right whale), black on top and white underneath, with serrated leading edges. The underside of the head and belly for about half the body length has grooves running along it. The blow is broad, and 2,5–3 m high. Total length 11,5–16 m; weight 40 tons.

Habitat Most likely to be seen in coastal waters while migrating. Feeds off Antarctica.

Diet Krill (*Euphausia superba*), a species of planktonic shrimp. Feeds only while in the far southern oceans; while migrating and breeding it lives off stored blubber.

Life history Breeds off Mozambique and possibly Madagascar, and off Namibia, Angola and possibly Gabon. Mating peaks in August–September. Gestation 11,5 months. Births peak in August–September. Length at birth 4,5–5 m. Weaned at 11 months.

Behaviour Feeds in the southern oceans, and migrates north, using coastal waters as corridors, to mate and give birth.

Males sing complex songs to attract females. Songs change during the breeding season, but all the males in each population sing the same song. Males fight over females.

Conservation Humpback whales have been protected in South African waters since 1963, and the population has shown a good recovery from very low levels; in 1990 over 1 700 individuals migrated along the KwaZulu-Natal coast. CITES Appendix I.

BRYDE'S WHALE
Bryde se walvis
Balaenoptera edeni

S241

Description Grey on top, sometimes mottled due to parasites; pale on the underside of the rear half of the body. A small sickle-shaped dorsal fin is set about two thirds of the way back along the body (no dorsal fin in southern right whale). The distinguishing characteristic is a series of three ridges running backwards on top of the head from the mouth to the blowhole. The flippers are short. The blow is tall (3–4 m) and narrow (V-shaped in southern right whale). Total length 13,5–14,5 m, sometimes larger; weight 16–25 tons.

Habitat Most likely to be seen inshore in water less than 200 m deep between Port Elizabeth and 32° S on the west coast.

Diet The bulk of the diet is pelagic fish such as maasbankers (*Trachurus trachurus*),

pilchards (*Sardinops sagax*) and anchovies (*Engraulis japonicus*). Recorded as accidentally swallowing penguins (*Spheniscus demersus*) and gannets (*Sula capensis*) feeding in the same fish shoals.

Life history Little is known. Gestation one year. Births throughout the year. Length at birth 4 m.

Behaviour May migrate between the south coast in summer and the west coast in winter, probably to take advantage of spawning fish. Cows with calves are more common west of Cape Agulhas.

Conservation CITES Appendix I.

VISIBLE WHALE SIGNS

Southern right whale	Bryde's whale	Humpback whale	
No dorsal fin			Dorsal fin
	Not usually seen		Tail
	Not usually seen		Flipper
			Blow

GLOSSARY

adpressed	lying close to a surface.
aggregation	a group of animals with no social structure.
alpha-	a prefix denoting that an animal is the highest ranking in a group.
ambient	surrounding.
anterior	to the front.
antitragus	a lobe of skin near the base of the outer edge of the ear in bats.
arboreal	living, or adapted to living, in trees.
biotic zone	a continuous geographic area that contains ecological associations distinguishable from those of neighbouring zones, especially at the species and subspecies level.
bulla	a globular bony capsule housing the structures of the middle and inner ear, situated on the underside of the skull.
callosity	a hardened, thickened area of skin.
cheekteeth	the teeth that lie behind the canine teeth.
commensal	an organism living with another and sharing the same food, one or both benefiting from the association.
crepuscular	active at dusk and dawn.
digit	a finger or toe in vertebrates.
dispersal	movement away from the place of birth.
diurnal	active during the day.
dominance	social status that allows privileged access to resources because subordinate animals defer to dominant ones.
dorsal	on or pertaining to the back.
echolocation	a means of locating objects from the way that they reflect sounds.
endemic	occurring only within a certain area.
feral	wild, escaped from domestication or introduced and reverted to the wild state.
flehmen	an act performed by some mammals in which the upper lip is retracted, the nostrils wrinkled, the head perhaps raised and the tongue sometimes moved rhythmically. This opens ducts into the Jacobsen's organ and pumps chemicals into it for sensory detection. Flehmen is often used by adult males to test a female's reproductive condition by detecting chemicals from her vulva or urine.
form	a shallow, unlined depression in the ground used by hares and rabbits as a nest.
foxing	a fading of the colour of hair, which gives it a reddish tinge.

gregarious	living together in colonies or other types of groups.
habitat	the kind of place, with respect to climate, vegetation and other factors, in which animals of a given species live.
harem	a group of females guarded by a male who maintains mating rights over them by driving off other males.
hierarchy	a social structure in which the animals in a group can be arranged as on the steps of a ladder (linear hierarchy) or of a pyramid (branching hierarchy).
home range	the area in which an animal goes about its routine activities.
infrasound	sound with a frequency too low for humans to hear.
inguinal	situated in the groin, between the side of the abdomen and the thigh.
interfemoral	situated between the legs. Applies in particular to the membrane between the hind legs of bats.
Jacobsen's	chemical sense organ lying between the mouth and nasal passages and connected to one or both of them. Brought into use during flehmen.
mammae	the milk-producing mammary glands, visible externally as nipples, breasts and udders.
mandible	the lower jaw.
metatarsal glands	glands on the ankles of the hind legs.
muzzle	the part of the face that lies in front of the eyes.
nipple clinging	the behaviour of some young murids, which remain semi-permanently attached to their mother's nipples.
nocturnal	active at night.
nuchal patch	a patch of hair on the nape of the neck of hares and some rabbits which differs in colour from the rest of the upper parts of the body.
oestrus	period during which a female is sexually receptive, and mating can lead to conception.
pedal	of or on the feet.
pelage	the coat of hair.
pinna	the external part of the ear.
posterior	towards the back, behind.
preorbital	in front of the eyes.
prehensile	capable of grasping.
preputial glands	glands next to the penis or vaginal opening.
proximal	closer to a given point.
rhinarium	the area of naked skin around the nostrils on the tip of the muzzle.
rostrum	the part of the skull in front of the eye sockets, the upper part of the muzzle.

scat	a carnivore's faeces.
species	potentially or actually interbreeding populations of animals.
thermoregulation	an ability to regulate body temperature when the temperature of the surroundings changes.
torpor	a state of reduced metabolic activity, lowered body temperature and reduced oxygen consumption.
tragus	a small cartilaginous process in the opening of the ears of bats.
ultrasound	sound with a frequency too high for humans to hear.
vomeronasal organ	alternative name for Jacobsen's organ.

FURTHER READING
AND REFERENCE SOURCES

ACOCKS, J.P.H. 1988. *Veld Types of South Africa*. Third edition. Memoirs of the Botanical Survey of South Africa.

APPS, P.J. 1992. *Wild Ways. A Field Guide to the Behaviour of Southern African Mammals*. Southern Book Publishers, Halfway House.

CARO, T.M. 1994. *Cheetahs of the Serengeti Plains*. University of Chicago Press, Chicago.

DE GRAAF, G. 1981. *The Rodents of Southern Africa*. Butterworths Press, Pretoria.

ESTES, R.D. 1991. *The Behavior Guide to African Mammals*. University of California Press.

MEESTER, J.A.J., RAUTENBACH, I.L., DIPPENAAR, N.J. and BAKER, C. 1986. 'Classification of Southern African mammals.' *Transvaal Museum Monograph*, 5: 1– 359.

MILLS, M.G.L. 1990. *Kalahari Hyaenas*. Unwin Hyman, London.

OWEN-SMITH, N. 1988. *The Megaherbivores*. Cambridge University Press, Cambridge.

RAUTENBACH, I.L. 1983. *Mammals of the Transvaal*. Ecoplan, Pretoria.

ROWE-ROWE, D.T. 1991. *The Ungulates of Natal*. Natal Parks Board, Pietermaritzburg.

ROWE-ROWE, D.T. 1992. *The Carnivores of Natal*. Natal Parks Board, Pietermaritzburg.

SKINNER, J.D. and SMITHERS, R.H.N. 1990. *The Mammals of the Southern African Subregion*. Second edition. University of Pretoria, Pretoria

SMITHERS, R.H.N. 1983. *The Mammals of the Southern African Subregion*. University of Pretoria, Pretoria.

SMITHERS, R.H.N. 1986. *South African Red Data Book – Terrestrial Mammals*. South African National Scientific Programmes Report 125.

SPINAGE, C. 1994. *Elephants*. T. and A.D. Poyser Ltd, London.

STUART, C. and STUART, T. 1994. *A Field Guide to the Tracks and Signs of Southern and East African Wildlife*. Southern Book Publishers, Halfway House.

INDEX OF SCIENTIFIC NAMES

INDEX OF AFRIKAANS NAMES

INDEX OF ENGLISH NAMES